T

Saul of

by David Dryden

A layman's journey through the epistles of Paul and the book of Hebrews comparing the teachings with those of the Jewish Bible

The Apostle Paul

Saul of Tarsus: The Bitter Root

Published by David Dryden

Copyright 2017 David Dryden

All rights reserved.

Cover picture: By Fubar Obfusco - Foto taken himself, upload to English wikipedia by Fubar Obfusco, Public Domain, https://commons.wikimedia.org/w/index.php?curid=177247

Important note: This book contains Hebrew. I don't know if the text will be printed properly by the publisher. For easy access and portability, you can still use this book. Understanding is still very accessible without the Hebrew. In addition, the Hebrew Bible is available on many resources such as webpages and bible software available for Windows, Linux and Android if you want to go any deeper and check the passages I refer to.

Thanks to …

First, I thank the one true God and I hope that this book can help someone get closer to truth, closer to him.

I'm also thankful to my wife (the driving force of my life, my queen and purpose) and my children who are great at helping me see the fun in life.

My parents, my father for his example of dedication and my mother who, despite her educational shortcomings, overcame them and wrote a book of her own.

My siblings, my sister for always giving a wise word, encouragement and her eye for detail, and my brother for steadfast friendship and support.

James Woods, author of "Leaving Jesus," who lent me the space I needed to work on this and keep it safe. He also let me work with him when he made his book and has always been a role model.

Who wrote this book?

David Dryden, passionate about God and His truth and has been writing articles about the topic of the relationship between the Jewish Bible and the christian new testament for over a decade.

Having an advanced layman's knowledge of Biblical Hebrew and new testament Greek strengthened his command of English. His twenty year experience with playing a variety of musical instruments and writing songs, as well as teaching adults and children about biblical concepts, has granted him a unique approach to conveying complex ideas in simpler terms.

Further equipped with knowledge of the power of computers and the internet, and having access to biblical resources online and offline, David seeks to share his desire for truth with others to help uplift and build up.

Contents

Introduction

It was their last visit to my house and they had left me some of their publications to "explain" some things to me. Yes, some Jehovah's Witnesses has spent a number of weeks doing bible studies with me, attempting to convince me of the claim that Jesus was the Messiah. Although I did like their friendliness, the substance of what they taught was distasteful when compared to the plain word of scripture, specifically the Jewish Bible, erroneously known as "the old testament". And although I had been frustrated before at their inability to debate using scripture, I hadn't seen anything yet with regards to what would frustrate and annoy the living daylights out of me.

Having pointed out that Ezekiel 37 and Isaiah 11, when read according to their plain meaning, didn't match their view of Messiah, the Jehovah's Witness (JW) that was most friendly left me some booklets and pages to describe their understanding of these passages. What I saw turned frustration into rage. I normally read through what they have to give me to see where they were coming from, with a pen to note down my thoughts in their book or on their print-outs. And turning page after page, I was compelled to write down one word in particular to describe what the substance of their belief was: THEFT! They had stolen the name of Israel and the blessings entitled to that nation, and claimed their fulness for their own, leaving real national Israel with the empty husks of a purely limited and physical gift that never fully fulfilled the words of the Scripture! I was mad! Now is not the time to get fully into what they taught, but what they did teach only left a stink up my nose, a fury in my heart that wouldn't go away.

But I had met this before in different forms. Whether it was in the lesson books in the sabbath "keeping" church I used to be a part of, or in the lectures and sermons of mainstream christian teachers in universities or churches I would visit with university friends there, or in a one-to-one discussion with a JW, this "replacement theology" teaching was stained all over the christian church, and it was all the more plain to me after I had rejected the christian faith. And this doctrine wasn't the only one to contradict the words of the Jewish Bible. There were others like the incessant need to link the role of the Messiah with Jesus' death; or the continual claim that "the dispensation of the Mosaic law" is over and we're now in a dispensation (time-span) of grace where we don't have to worry about the condemnation that the law is supposed to bring; doctrines such as these that would ease themselves from the mouths of a multitude of christians. But these doctrines would have no basis in the Jewish Bible, only in the mindset of the christian who would impose such beliefs on the Hebrew Scriptures.

My first instinct was to go after the JWs and their teachings and, using the plain words of scripture, to rip them to shreds! But then I stopped and realised something. This teaching existed in most or all forms of christianity, not just the JWs. In essence, by going after them, I would be trying to whip the disciples who had learned their doctrine from someone else, and it was this someone else who would then simply go on to teach his doctrine to some other vulnerable and impressionable person who would then continue to spread his poison. What is the point in going after the pupils when the teacher is left free to promulgate his views? What is the point of attacking the branches of a weed infestation when it would be much more effective to go after the roots?

So who or what is the source of the venomous teachings of these people?

Here I introduce the unrepentant culprit: Paul of Tarsus, writer of almost half the books of the christian scripture, the "new testament", and whose influence can be seen in other books in those same writings! If the new testament consisted only of the writings of the disciples of the "flesh and blood" Jesus, many of the current doctrines of modern christianity would never have come to pass, or at least it would not be likely. But Paul and the epistles (letters) ascribed to him does so much to spread his brand of doctrine, doctrines that would forever alienate christianity from Torah-faithful Judaism. He is the primary teacher of mainstream christianity - in which I include the JWs - and the main source for their anti-Israel, anti-law doctrines (some christians like to say that they are not anti-Israel or anti-law, but actions speak louder than words).

In this book, I will be going through the epistles in the christian scriptures that are commonly said to be written by Paul, paying careful attention to how he uses, misuses, and abuses the words of scripture. I also will look at those parts of his writings that confront and conflict with the plain understanding of the Jewish Bible, and I will critique them as best I can. I find out things that surprise me and teach me a bit more about the sort of person this man was and about what the true intent of the Jewish Bible is. Here I look the main teacher of christianity in the "eye," and confront him to his "face" (figuratively speaking - he's dead now) and question him and his doctrines. I do not pretend to perfectly destroy his efforts, or to totally refute his teachings. But, at the very least, I have tested his letters against the Hebrew Bible, the so-called "old testament," and have written my findings and conclusions.

I don't pretend that this is a scholarly work made by someone with years of school-learning in ancient Hebrew, ancient Greek, comparative religion and ancient history. Rather, this is a personal work. This is the result of me doing the best with the resources and knowledge in order to not just be a blind follower of something or something. If I were to accept or reject Paul and his writings, it would be because I took the time to read his words and compare them to the source material he used and judge for myself, with as humble and God-ward an attitude as I could have, whether this man was one led by God's spirit or led by his own ego.

As usual, I pray that my opinion will at least challenge you, the reader, no matter what point of view you have. I hope I challenge you in the way that you strive to draw closer to the Almighty and to his truth, because that is the greatest thing in this whole universe.

Let's proceed.

Romans

Chapter 1

verse 3

... concerning his son, who came into being, out of the seed of David according to [the] flesh ...

According to Paul, Jesus was descended from David. Unfortunately there is only conflicting evidence for this claim. The plain reading of Luke and Matthew give different lists of ancestors for Jesus, both supposedly coming from Joseph. I'll show you a few of the conflicting differences.

(15) And Eliud begat Eleazar; and Eleazar begat Matthan; and Matthan begat Jacob; (16) And Jacob begat Joseph the husband of Mary, of whom was born Jesus, who is called Christ. (Matthew 1:15-16)

(23) And Jesus himself began to be about thirty years of age, being (as was supposed) the son of Joseph, which was the son of Heli, (24) which was the son of Matthat, which was the son of Levi, which was the son of Melchi, which was the son of Janna, which was the son of Joseph,... (Luke 3:23-24)

I ask you to just read what it says. According to Matthew, the father of Joseph, Mary's husband, is Jacob. And Jacob's father is Matthan, and Matthan's father is Eleazar. Yet according to Luke, the father of

Joseph is Heli, whose father is Matthat, whose father is Levi. This list of different names carries on for some time.

Now one christian response is that the men could have two different names, and thus Jacob (from Matthew) is another name for Heli (from Luke), and Matthan is Matthat, and so on. But this doesn't work. If this logic were true, then the amount of names between King David and Joseph, the husband of Mary, would be about the same, e.g., in Matthew there would be about 28 names between David and Joseph, and in Luke there would be about 28 names between David and Joseph. But this is not the case: Matthew has 25 names between Joseph and David (not including Joseph and David); and Luke has 40 names between Joseph and David. Therefore it cannot be the case that there are two different names for the same guy.

Another argument that christians like to use is that Luke's genealogy is really the lineage list of Mary and not Joseph. Therefore, in Luke 3, the name "Joseph", as Jesus' father is just there for show, as an empty gesture, or to fulfil some made-up legality or law that the father must be mentioned and not the mother. Thus Heli is the father of Mary and not Joseph. But there is a significant problem with this: it's not what the text of Luke says! The christians who use this argument make much of the words "as was supposed" and make up arguments that say that Jews would never allow the names of women to be in the genealogy records. But what does the text clearly say? Jesus was supposed to be the son of Joseph, but Joseph was the son (not son-in-law) of Heli. No mention is made whatsoever of Mary in the context of the genealogy. No link is made in the whole "new testament" between Mary and Heli. This argument is made not based on the text of the new testament, but on the belief that the gospels must agree. The texts of Luke and Matthew clearly disagree on the genealogy list.

But the fact is that two things essentially destroy the notion that Jesus is the seed of David based on the gospels.

1.The genealogy of Luke goes through the wrong son of David. Luke's genealogy goes through Nathan, the son of David. But the promise of kingship only goes through Solomon according to the words of the Jewish Bible (1 Chronicles 22:5-10; 1 Kings 8:17-20; 2 Chronicles 6:7-10). With Solomon and his descendants being heirs to the messianic promise, all the other sons of David, such as Nathan, don't have the messianic right. So Luke's genealogy is worthless.

2.Joseph was not the father of Jesus. In the Hebrew Scriptures, the only way to become a seed of David is for your biological father to be a seed of David. This can be seen by looking at all the genealogical lists in the Jewish Bible (erroneously called the "old testament"). The kings of Judah had wives of different nationalities, but the child always became king because of the father, not the wife. It is the man that determines whether the child gets the kingly right. Because Joseph, who was supposed to be of the seed of David, was not the biological father of Jesus, then Jesus is not the seed of David, regardless of any ancestry Mary may have.

This isn't meant to be a total refutation of Matthew and Luke, so I'll leave that to articles such as Genealogical Scams and Flimflams at http://www.thejewishhome.org/counter-index.html or http://www.outreachjudaism.org/articles/marys-geneology.html or the plethora of books and articles out there that focus more on this issue.

To conclude all this, all that needs to be said is that Paul makes the claim that Jesus is the seed of David. There is no good evidence of that, so it's just a baseless claim.

verse 17

(16) For I am not ashamed of the good news of christ for it is the power of Deity [leading] to salvation for all the believers; to the Jews first, and to the Greek; (17) for in it, righteousness of Deity is revealed from faith to faith, even as it has been written, "But the righteous [person] shall live by faith." (Romans 1:16,17)

So what is Paul saying here? He is saying that the Lord's righteousness is shown through a person's "faith" - the Greek word πιστις pistis. And he uses Habakkuk 2:4 as some form of support for his claim. Now what does Paul mean by pistis or "faith"? As you read further in Romans, Paul is preaching to the reader that righteousness, being in a right standing before the Almighty, doesn't come from obedience and actions ("deeds of law", keeping the Laws given by the Lord to Moses). Through this we can conclude that Paul isn't talking about "faithfulness or reliability in actions and deeds". He is talking more about a faith, a mental conviction, in Jesus and his death and "good message" or "gospel." So, to summarize, to Paul, the Creator's righteousness is seen in a mental conviction about Jesus as the "christ". What does he use to support his claim? Habakkuk 2:4!

Now is Habakkuk 2:4 speaking simply of a mental conviction? Does it have anything to do with Jesus? To answer this, I'm only going to focus on the Hebrew version of Habakkuk and the words used in Habakkuk 2:4. Even if I do say a passing statement on the context, I'll leave more of a treatment of that for my critique of Hebrews 10:35-39. But until then, here is a translation of Habakkuk 2:4.

Look here: his soul is swollen [in pride], not upright in him; but the righteous [person] shall live in his 'emunah.

The question is this: what is 'emunah? Now people put a lot of importance on the way a word is first used in scripture. Here it is:

And Moses' hands [were] heavy, and they took a stone, and set it under him, and he sat upon it; then Aaron and Hur held up his hands, with this [one] at one [hand] and the other at one [hand], and his hands were 'emunah until the going down of the sun. (Exodus 17:12)

Here, the word 'emunah refers to being steady and firm and faithful. We are talking about an action here, where arms are actively steady.

The context shows no sign of belief. The only two references to 'emunah in the books of Moses also have nothing to do with belief: the one already mentioned, Exodus 17:12; and Deuteronomy 32:4 which says that the Almighty is a Deity of 'emunah and without iniquity. This last references means that the Deity of Israel is faithful, firm, and reliable in his dealings with humanity. This is also seen in the following phrase "without iniquity", doing no wrong. So at least in the Torah (another name for the five books of Moses), the word 'emunah refers to a reliability, a faithfulness in action, not necessarily "belief" or a mental conviction. In fact, generally in the Hebrew Scriptures, the main meaning of 'emunah is more "faithfulness", or "fidelity, reliability, steadiness, or firmness", rather than simply "faith". And faithfulness speaks more of action than a mental conviction. I'll give you an example to show why the natural and biblical meaning of 'emunah doesn't agree with Paul's usage of a mental conviction devoid of actions.

We know that these days marriages are more likely to last when the spouses are faithful in their actions to one another which are in agreement to the marriage covenant, rather than simply having a belief or a mental conviction. Faithfulness speaks of a reliability that is only evident, really seen, in a person's actions and words, not simply a mental conviction.

And just to confirm the fact that we are talking about an externally active reliability in a person's action, the Hebrew Scriptures say that all the commandments of the Almighty are 'emunah (Psalm 119:86). Yet it is the obedience to these commands that Paul is speaking against!

So we have Paul and Habakkuk speaking of two different things: Paul is speaking of a mental conviction, particularly about Jesus as the "christ"; and Habakkuk is speaking of faithfulness, a consistency in action, not simply a mental conviction.

Now some may argue that Paul is quoting from or referring to an ancient Greek translation of the Hebrew Scriptures called the

Septuagint, or the "LXX". For a discussion of this, see <u>my critique of Hebrews 10:35-39</u>. To at least give you a short conclusion here, the LXX does not support Paul's interpretation and, in fact, goes in an interesting different direction. Others may say that modern Jews translate the word as "belief" or "faith". But it must be understood that the more modern Jewish conception of faith and the Pauline conception of faith are two different things. And with this in mind, I'll tackle this from a different angle.

Let's imagine that the word 'emunah could be translated as "faith". Would we still come up with the same conclusions as Paul? What is Paul's conclusion? Looking at Romans 1:16-17, Paul's "faith" means accepting the "good news of Jesus", i.e., believing that Jesus is the christ who bore the sins of humanity and who "God" resurrected from the dead (Romans 10:6-11). What is the more modern Jewish conception of "faith"? Here, we can kill two birds with one stone. Let's look at what it means when it says that Abraham believed in, had faith in, Deity, and it was considered to be "righteousness" (which simply means a righteous deed or thing).

Remember, Paul's faith is a conviction - even a constant, persisting conviction - that says Jesus is the christ. Essentially, it is a conviction that something is, that a fact exists: the fact being that Jesus is the christ. But what was Abraham's faith in Genesis 15:6? If we use the same sort of faith that Paul was talking about, then Abraham's faith would be that the Being that had led him all these years was Deity. But that is not the sort of faith Abraham had. He already knew that the person who he was talking to was the Creator/Possessor of heaven and earth (Genesis 14:22) and the Deity of the universe. The "faith" that Abraham had was that he trusted IN the Person who he already knew to be who he said he was. His trust had nothing to do with some belief that the Almighty was who he said he was, but that the Person who Abraham already knew to be the Almighty would do as he promised. The trust of Abraham was in the promise because he already knew the person from whom it came. This is not the same as a belief that Jesus is who he said he is.

Applying this understanding to Habakkuk 2:4, one Jewish way of understanding it would be that a righteous man would live because of his trust in the promises and faithfulness of the Deity he already knew to be who He said He was. This is different to Paul's notion of believing that "Jesus is Lord". Christians will try to argue with this, saying that the gospel of Jesus is believing in Deity's promise, but, if you think about it, their essential claim is really that Jesus is who he says he was, which is something totally different to the Jewish understanding of faith or trust.

To give an analogy to show the difference between Paul's faith and Abraham's trust, it's like the difference between saying that "I believe that the man who raised me is my father", and saying that "I believe that my father will do what he promised me". In the first one, I'm affirming my father's very identity; in the other I already know my father's identity, and in that already-existing relationship, I trust in my father's word. Two different things.

So no matter how you flip it, Paul's idea of faith is both contrary to the biblical view of 'emunah-faithfulness, which destroys the very notion that Paul is trying to expound from scripture, and the Jewish understanding of faith/trust. It will be seen later that he also takes the verse out of context and twists it to agree with his own agenda.

Chapter 2

verse 6

Paul either quotes Psalm 62:12 or Proverbs 24:12 to say that the Almighty deals with people according to their deeds. This is one of the rare times that Paul actually gives the real meaning of a verse.

verse 24

For the name of the Deity is being blasphemed among the nations because of you [Jews], even as it has been written. (Romans 2:24, NB, I add the word "Jews" to give the understanding given by the context, which agrees with christian commentators)

Paul here is saying that, somewhere in the Jewish Scriptures, it is written that the name of the Almighty is being blasphemed amongst the nations, implying that it is done by Gentiles, non-Jews, because of the Jews' hypocrisy in claiming to hold to the standard of God's law whilst breaking that same law (see Romans 2:17-23). We have to ask where in scripture it says this, since Paul claims that it has been written there.

The commentators amongst christianity normally give two possible biblical sources which are supposed to back up Paul's claim.

One place that christians think Paul is referring to is Isaiah 52:5, which says the following:

(3) For GOD has said this: You were sold for nothing, and without silver you shall be redeemed. (4) For my Lord GOD has said this: My people went down to Egypt firstly to sojourn there, and the Assyrian oppressed him [i.e., my people] without cause. (5) And now what do I have here - declares GOD - since my people has been taken away for nothing? its rulers howl - declares GOD - and continually, all the day, is my name blasphemed. (Isaiah 52:3-5)

Now this passage is talking about Israel being taken captive by another country, whose rulers howl in pride over taking and capturing the people of Israel/Judah (the "rulers" should apply to those who are oppressing Israel whilst in captivity since Israel would have no real rulers for itself in captivity). So the context is talking about Israel's mistreatment in a foreign land, the blasphemy that results, and the Lord's promise of redemption.

Is this the same message of Paul who says that the name of the Lord is blasphemed amongst the Gentiles because of Israel's hypocrisy as he states in Romans 2:17-23???? No such thing is in this context. In fact, the whole context speaks of different times and different situations, things that were not happening to Israel in Paul's time. So, if he's using this verse, then he's taking it out of context - it says nothing about Paul's point.

Other christians say that Paul is referring to Ezekiel 36:22, which states the following:

(16) Moreover the word of GOD came to me, saying: (17) Son of man, when the house of Israel dwelt in their own land, they defiled it by their conduct and by their doings; their conduct before Me was as the uncleanness of a woman in her impurity. (18) Therefore I poured out My fury upon them for the blood which they had shed upon the land, and because they had defiled it with their idols; (19) and I scattered them among the nations, and they were dispersed throughout the countries; according to their conduct and according to their doings I judged them. (20) And when they came to the nations to which they came, they profaned My holy name; in that men said of them: These are the people of GOD, and have come out of His land. (21) But I had pity for My holy name, which the house of Israel had profaned among the nations, to which they had come.

(22) Therefore say to the house of Israel: My Lord GOD has said this: I don't do this for your sake, O house of Israel, but for My holy name, which you have profaned among the nations, to which ye came. (23) And I will sanctify My great name, which has been profaned among the nations, which you have profaned in the midst of them; and the nations shall know that I am GOD - declares my Lord GOD - when I shall be sanctified in you before their eyes. (24) For I will take you from among the nations, and gather you out of all the countries, and will bring you into your own land. (25) And I will sprinkle clean water upon you, and you shall be clean; from all your impurities, and from all your idols will I cleanse you. (Ezekiel 36:16-25)

You know, I learn a whole lot by firstly quoting these passages, and then going through the passage to check its translation and how understandable it is. I see what is said and in what way it is said, and that, in itself, equips me to answer Paul.

Remember what the charge of Paul is: Jews are hypocrites for preaching the law and yet not keeping it, and for that reason, the name of Deity is blasphemed amongst the nations. Now let's compare this to what Ezekiel is saying IN CONTEXT!!!

What is the crime of Israel according to this passage in Ezekiel 36? Look at verse 18: they had shed blood, which points to murder, and had committed idolatry-proper. Now I use the words "idolatry-proper" because christians have a tendency to say that any sin is idolatry in a way because it is the act of making your own human will or desire, or that of some other human, superior to the Lord's. But the idolatry that the Israelites were committing was literal idolatry, where you make figures and graven images or an aspect of creation, and you actively worship them. In verse 18, the Hebrew word translated as "their idols" refers to images literally carved or formed out of materials (see strongs number 1544 and Deuteronomy 29:17 and 2 Kings 23:24). This is not the hypocrisy that Paul speaks of.

In what way was the Lord's name blasphemed, according to Ezekiel 36? See verse 20: in that the Gentiles would say that this is supposed to be GOD's people yet they aren't even in their land. This is not what Paul is saying. Paul said the nations blasphemed because of the Jews' hypocrisy, whereas Ezekiel is saying that the blasphemy resides in the fact that the Lord's people are not in the land that the Lord had given.

[ASIDE: The way that the notion of blasphemy is used in scripture is not as simple as some say. One form of blasphemy can be to directly insult the Creator with one's words (see Leviticus 24:10-16). But here, in Ezekiel, we can see that blasphemy can also refer to an act that diminishes the Lord's holiness or sanctity. That means an action that disrespects ("disses") the Most High.]

It should be apparent that Ezekiel makes it clear that it is not the nations who are profaning or blaspheming the Creator: it is the Jews that are doing it. Whenever Ezekiel speaks of profaning the holy name, he says "YOU [the Israelites] profane the name". And as I have shown before, it is the fact that the Israelites are not in their land that causes the profanation.

This fact is also made plain in the way the Lord gets his respect back, or sanctifies his name: he brings the Israelites back to the land of Israel! And take note: it is after the people are in their land that the Almighty cleans up their ways and conduct, which includes getting rid of their idols. Look at the order of Ezekiel 36:24-25. He doesn't say "I'll clean you up and then put you back in your land". He says "I'll bring my respect back by bringing you back to the land of Israel, and then I will make you clean".

Now what does all this have to do with the message of Paul? To be blunt, nothing! Paul's complaint against Israel has nothing to do with the murder and idolatry spoken of Ezekiel 36. The claim of the Jews' sacrilege spoken of in Romans 2:22 is not the idolatry of Ezekiel 36. And there is no point trying to link the shedding of blood in Ezekiel to Jesus' saying that being angry with someone is equivalent to murder, which makes it figurative. Paul's claim has nothing to do with the Jews being in exile outside of their land, which is the main subject of Ezekiel 36.

So what has Paul done? If he was referring to Ezekiel 36, this is what he's basically done: he has taken a phrase - not even a whole verse, but rather a simple phrase - out of context, ripped it from its natural surroundings, and formed it into his own heart's desire. Again, he doesn't expound or explain or use the true meaning inside the words of scripture, which is exegesis; instead, he puts his own message into a phrase of scripture. This is called eisegesis.

verses 17-29

I'll let you read this passage. I'm not going to quote the whole of it. But to summarize, Paul tries to build the argument that if the religious Jews, who are circumcised according to the law, sin and break that law like the non-Jews, who are uncircumcised according to the law, then the Jews, circumcised people, are regarded as non-Jews, uncircumcised people. Therefore, according to Paul's logic, if non-Jews, the uncircumcised people, then do the things that are right and good according to the law of the Jews, the circumcised people - Paul calls it keeping the righteousness of the law - then they should be considered as Jews. Therefore, Paul concludes, it is not a physical circumcision that makes one a real Jew. Rather, what makes a person a real Jew is what's on the inside, the "spiritual" heart circumcision.

If you found that all confusing, I'll simplify it even more. To Paul, it's what's inside that counts, not what's on the outside. A real Jew is not necessarily one who is circumcised but a person who has a "spiritual" circumcision. If a Jew doesn't keep the law, he isn't a Jew. If a Gentile, a non-Jew, does the things that are right and good according to the law, then he is a real Jew. If you think I'm mistaken, let me just quote the relevant bit of what Paul says.

(28) For the Jew is not one who is openly apparent; neither is the circumcision that which is openly apparent in the flesh: (29) But the Jew is the one who is concealed; and the circumcision is that of the heart, in the spirit, and not in the letter; whose praise is not of men, but of God. (Romans 2:28-29)

So all you need is the circumcision of the heart to be a concealed, secret, but real Jew.

The question that I would have is where Paul gets this idea. Does it agree with what the Hebrew Scriptures has to say? And if it doesn't agree with the Hebrew Scripture, can it have any truth? Well, to answer that last question first, since the five books of Moses and the rest of the "old testament" is the basis of truth, if Paul contradicts it -

meaning that he contradicts truth - then he must be teaching error. If he makes a claim that has no basis from it, then nothing much can be said or trusted about his conclusion. So let's take a look.

From start to finish, the Hebrew Scriptures lets you know the purposes of literal, physical circumcision. Reading Genesis 17, circumcision is the sign of an agreement between the Almighty and Abraham's descendants, especially the descendants of Isaac and Jacob. It is a link between those descendants and the land of Israel. And, based on the context of this chapter, even the hypocrisy of a circumcised Jew described by Paul wouldn't cut off that descendant from the covenant, the link between a people and the land. It takes something much more serious. The circumcision given to Abraham was not the spiritual circumcision that Paul is talking about. A non-Israelite male, a person who is not the descendant of Abraham that doesn't bear this physical mark has no part of this promise and covenant based on Genesis 17, regardless of whether they act the part or not.

That's the start of circumcision and it is physical.

In the prophecy of Ezekiel concerning the future Third Temple, he describes the state of the only men who would be allowed to minister in the Temple. This is what he says.

> *(6) And you shall say to the rebellious, to the house of Israel, Thus has said Lord GOD, You have done enough with all your abominations, O house of Israel! (7) In your having brought the sons of the foreigner, uncircumcised in heart, and uncircumcised in flesh, to be in my sanctuary, to pollute it, even my house ... (9) Thus has said Lord GOD, No son of the foreigner, uncircumcised in heart and uncircumcised in flesh, shall enter into my sanctuary, of all the sons of the foreigner that are in the midst of the children of Israel.*
> *(Ezekiel 44:6,7a,9)*

As you can see, even in the future, circumcision of the flesh, the outward circumcision is important. Please take careful note: nobody is ignoring the importance of having one's heart in the right condition, i.e., circumcision of the heart; but the physical circumcision is a necessity. Someone who tries to enter the temple having a supposedly circumcised heart but having no outwardly fleshy circumcision would be excluded.

So from end to beginning, and from beginning to end, the physical sign of circumcision is important and does make a great difference.

But christian commentators like to point to Jeremiah 9:25-26 to prove the point for Paul. It says as follows:

(24) Behold, the days come - GOD declares - that I shall deal with all them that are circumcised in their foreskin. (25) Egypt, and Judah, and Edom, and the children of Ammon, and Moab, and all that have the corners of their hair polled, that dwell in the wilderness; for all the nations are uncircumcised, but all the house of Israel are uncircumcised of heart.

Let's look at what we can plainly understand. The Almighty is punishing all who are supposed to be circumcised whilst having some form of foreskin. The next verse explains that the nations listed are to be punished as well as Israel because Israel acts just like the nations, i.e., they are uncircumcised of heart.

What can we derive here? Based on the text, as far as it comes to punishment, everyone gets punished for sins. No one would disagree with that. We can see here how the circumcised are like the uncircumcised. But remember that Paul asserts something else: that if a non-Jew keeps the "righteousness of the law", his status of being uncircumcised should then change to being circumcised and they become the real Jews/Israelites. Let's see if there is a basis for this in the Hebrew Scriptures. Errrr .... There's no sign of that anywhere. We see righteous Gentiles. But we see nowhere in scripture the concept of spiritual Jews who are uncircumcised in the flesh.

In essence, what we have is Paul making a baseless assertion. One side of his argument, as far as it impacts the Jews, has some basis; and that is only if we focus on one aspect of having the physical circumcision, namely, a symbol of faithfulness to their covenant. But if we look at the whole purpose of circumcision and the role the physical circumcision has to play in the future, then Paul's argument on this side gets weaker and weaker. You find that although the Jews are punished for their wrongs, they are punished as Jews and accepted again as Jews based on a special covenant. But the other side of his argument, with regards to righteous Gentiles somehow being "real" Jews, this has no textual foundation whatsoever in the Jewish Bible. The Gentiles are dealt with according to their own covenant, i.e., universal divine law.

And some may say, "well if it's true in one way, then it must be true in the other way". The question to ask here is: who says? And who makes the rules? Our logic? Even a christian would argue against that sort of thinking. But in this case, where it suits their agenda, then Paul's argument based on logic (and it is purely logical, not a word from the Almighty) makes the rules, even when the Almighty gives no basis for it at all. For the Jews who actually know the law and respect it as the word of the Almighty, Paul's logic has no foundation, no basis in divine authority.

An analogy of this would be someone who is part of a kingdom in which there are certain commandments from a king and a passport of citizenship. And there is an outsider who knows of the king and the laws, but has no such passport. The citizen of the country breaks some of the laws, and the outsider likes the laws and keeps them. The citizen of the country gets punished for his crimes based on the laws of the land. But the outsider, who is not a citizen, and thus is not entitled to the benefits that a citizen would get, is appreciated but that's more or less all the outsider gets. Without that passport, the outsider remains an outsider. And with the passport, the citizen remains a citizen. The passport makes all the difference. Marriage and the marriage agreement/certificate would be a similar analogy that shows the weaknesses of Paul's logic.

The same is true for circumcision. It is a sign of a special relationship. The sins that Paul lists do not literally make a Jew into a non-Jew because he is still part of that relationship and would be punished within that relationship. There is only a similarity between a rebellious Jew and an ignorant non-Jew. And a non-Jew doesn't become a Jew, a part of that special relationship, by just acting the part but not taking on the sign of that special relationship. The "spiritual" part of the relationship makes a real difference actually within that relationship.

This is shown even clearer in the fact that this "spiritual" circumcision, the circumcision of the heart, is only spoken of in the Mosaic Law, and - there and everywhere else in the Hebrew Scriptures - only in reference to those in that covenant relationship, between the nation of Israel and God (Deuteronomy 10:16; 30:6; Jeremiah 4:4; 9:26).

Now this is not to say that the righteous acts of us non-Jews mean nothing, since the Almighty praises all righteous people (e.g., Psalm 1:6). But circumcision is a passport that leads to much more responsibility and blessing within a specific relationship, a relationship which Paul has to belittle and view in a very narrow way in order to spiritualize it in a way that has no biblical basis.

People may say that Paul was actually speaking from inspiration and that his words were coming from Deity. But Paul gives no such claim. He seems rather to be arguing his case, his agenda. And such claimed inspiration has to agree with the Hebrew Scriptures, which it doesn't.

Chapter 3

verse 4

Paul quotes Psalm 51:4 to say that the faithlessness of some people makes the judgment of Deity more clear and decisive. It is a fair rendition and usage of the verse in Psalms.

Following this Paul begins his argument, supposedly based on numerous scriptures, that all are υφ' αμαρτιαν huph' hamartian, "under sin", meaning either under the power of or condemnation of sin. Let's see how he tries to do this and test each prooftext according to its context.

verses 10-12

Here, Paul apparently quotes Psalm 14:1-3 or Psalm 53:1-3. Let's compare his depiction of what the Bible has to say, with what the Bible actually says.

PAUL: (10) ... There is none righteous, no, not one. (11) There is none that understands, there is none that seeks after God. (12) They are all gone out of the way, they are together become unprofitable; there is none that does good, no, not one.

THE PSALMIST, DAVID: (1) ... The fool has said in his heart: 'There is no deity'; they have acted corruptly, they have abhorrently done deeds; there is none that does good. (2) GOD looked down from heaven upon the children of men, to see: is there anyone who understands, that seeks after Deity? (3) All have turned away, they are together spoiled; there is none that does good, no, not one. (Psalm 14:1-3, [Psalm 53:1-3 is similar enough])

Now, as you can see, Paul leaves out quite a bit, but his intent is clear: this is the first "quote" he uses to prove his point that no one at all is righteous (Romans 3:19,23). Now does this passage really say that there is no one at all that is righteous? Is such a concept even realistic in the so-called "old testament"???

Taking a general biblical approach first, it will be seen that there are righteous individuals throughout history. Noah was a righteous man (Genesis 6:9; 7:1). Job was a man of integrity and upright (Job 1:1,8). When Abraham debated with Deity about saving Sodom, his argument would have been pointless if there was no such thing as a righteous person on the earth (Genesis 18:23-33); his first statement - "would you sweep away the righteous with the wicked?" - would have been pointless, since according to Paul, there is none righteous! Yet according to Abraham's understanding, there were righteous people in the world who should not be judged as the wicked. Exodus 23:7 prohibits the execution of innocent and righteous people. But in order for a law to have any purpose, then the situation must exist for the law to have an application. For example, if there are no such thing as roads, there is no point in my commanding people to drive on the right side of the road. Why not? Because there are no roads for me to drive on! There's no point in me forbidding a person to draw a square circle because there is no such thing. So in order for Exodus 23:7 to have any validity, there must be such a thing as a righteous person. There is a well known psalm which says "if the foundations be removed, what can the righteous do?" But this question makes no sense if there are no righteous people. So again, there must be righteous people for this verse to make sense. According to Psalm 5:12, the Almighty blesses the righteous. A biblical proverb says that the name of GOD is a strong tower which the righteous can run to for protection. In Isaiah 57:1, righteous people are being killed. Ezekiel 18:5-9 gives the description of a righteous man showing that a man can be righteous.

Time and time and time again, the Jewish Bible speaks of righteous people, and the obvious assumption of the whole 24 books (or 39 books according to the christian canon of the "old testament") is that there are righteous people, righteous because of what they do, as opposed to what they believe (see Ezekiel 18:5-9 comparing it with Deuteronomy 6:24-25).

As will be shown later, the problem with Paul and his christian disciples throughout history is that they mistake righteousness for absolute moral perfection, a concept unknown to man in the Hebrew

Scriptures. The Scriptures relate the fact that only the Almighty is perfect and that creation is not. Ecclesiastes 7:20 makes it plain that there is not a righteous man on earth that always does good and never sins. But remember what it says in contrast to what it doesn't say. It does not say "there is no righteous man on the earth". It says that there is no righteous man who lives absolutely perfectly. So righteousness, in the human sense as far as the bible says, is not absolute perfection which is impossible. There were righteous people throughout history as the bible says, and each and every one of them contradicts Paul's conclusion. And if he and his christian disciples require more than what the bible demands, what the Creator himself says, then we can reject their human error and just lean on the word of the Lord which grants righteousness to all who would live a life committed to obedience.

So that was the general biblical approach, which shatters Paul's argument before we even get into the verses that he uses. And this biblical context already shows us that Paul is wrong, so there is no need to go further through each of the scriptures he "uses". But still, we can take a look at each one and see if they give any sort of different message.

So focusing on Psalm 14 and/or 53, what do we see? Do they say that all mankind is wicked and not righteous? The very first verse of Psalm 14 tells us who the Psalmist is talking about: "the fool says in his heart, there is no Deity". The next sentence can only then refer to that category of people, i.e., the fools who ignore divine authority. The second verse shows that the Lord looks down on man to look for a worthy person, but then it refers back to the category in the first verse, "they," the fools, and concludes that none of them is good. It isn't talking about every single person on the planet. This is made even more plain when verses 4 and 5 continues to speak of the fools and the wicked who eat up "My people", referring to the people of the Lord; and it then sets apart a group of people called "the righteous generation", which means a group of people living at the same time who are righteous. Now it is important to note that not every people or every individual in the world did, in those days up until our time, oppress Israel. So contextually, Psalm 14 is talking about a people or people group who have come and taken hold of Israel. That people which had done so are seen as wicked and foolish, whilst there is still a group of people, most likely Israelites, who are righteous. So the context of Psalm 14 contradicts Paul's message.

If we take a look at Psalm 53, we can see that there is a more overt statement that reinforces what has been said before about a people oppressing Israel.

> *(6) There, they were in great fear - there wasn't [such] a fear; for Deity has scattered the bones of him that encamps against you; You have put them to shame, because God has rejected them. (7) Oh that he would give, from Zion, the salvations of Israel! When God returns the captivity of His people, let Jacob rejoice, let Israel be glad.*
> *(Psalm 53:6,7)*

So the chapter isn't simply talking about every single individual person all around the world and saying that we are all evil: the passage is talking about an enemy nation or enemy nations that are besieging or holding captive Israel.

And just to make a point that I shall repeat, it must be realised here that Paul is using poetic texts to make a literal point. This means he is using something that could be either figurative and/or hyperbolic (exaggerated) as though it were literal. That is a potentially unbalanced approach. And it is also the opinion of the ancient Jews that the passage is prophetic, but does not refer to the whole world in opposition to the Jews, but rather it refers to certain nations that have oppressed and exiled the Israelites (see Rashi's commentary of Psalm 14). So if we take it as prophetic, there are righteous people. And if we take it poetically, there are righteous people. Whichever way you take it, it contradicts Paul's notion that there are no righteous people.

So what has Paul done here? He has taken verses out of context and has edited it so that you cannot see who the Psalm is really talking about, and then twisted its meaning to say something it never meant.

verse 13a

Let me give you Paul's little quote of Psalm 5:9.

PAUL: Their throat [is] an open sepulchre; they were deceiving with their tongues...

Remember that Paul is trying to make the point that both Jew and Gentile is under the power and condemnation of sin and that there is none that is righteous.

Now let me quote the actual verse from King David, Psalm 5:9, but this time with its preceding verse to give even a tiny bit of context.

(8) O GOD, lead me in Thy righteousness because of them that lie in wait for me; make Thy way straight before my face. (9) For there is no sincerity in their mouth; their inward part is a yawning gulf, their throat is an open sepulchre; they make smooth their tongue [with flattery]. (Psalm 5:8-9)

My simple question to any one who is reading is this: who does verse 9 refer to? Who has no sincerity in their mouth, whose insides are like a gaping hole, whose throats are like open tombs, and who flatters with their tongues? Do we have any clue? We do! The verse before tells us that David is talking of them that lie in wait for him. Again, this does not refer to every human being on the planet. It doesn't even refer to every single Israelite or Jew; just those who opposed David.

Any conclusion that tries to state that no man is righteous based on Psalm 5:9 is further ripped to shreds when we look at the final verses of Psalm 5.

(11) And all those that take refuge in You will rejoice. They shall always shout for joy, and You shall protect them; let them also that love Thy name exult in You. (12) For You shall bless the righteous; O GOD, You surround him with favour as with a shield. (Psalm 5:11-12)

So David ends up speaking of those who take refuge in GOD, showing their trust in him. He speaks of those who love the name of Deity. And his final verse speaks of the righteous person, who is blessed with the Lord's favour!

So once again we see the words of scripture countering Paul's words. Or we see Paul use a Psalm to say that there are no righteous people in the world, and yet in that same psalm, there are righteous people in the world. It seems that Paul has taken another verse out of context. [Get used to the phrase "out of context" throughout this series on Paul: this will not be the last time you see it!]

verse 13b

> *PAUL: ... the poison of asps is under their lips.*

Paul quotes a phrase from Psalm 140:3 which says as follows:

(1) ... Deliver me, O GOD, from an evil man: preserve me from a man of great violence; (2) [those] that devise evil [things] in [their] heart; every day they are gathered together for war. (3) They have sharpened their tongues like a serpent; adders' poison is under their lips. (Psalm 140:1-3)

Always keep in mind the aim of Paul in using these texts: he wishes to show that everyone is a sinner, condemned by sin.

But what is the writer of this Psalm, apparently David, saying? David is asking for protection from deceptive and destructive people.

Yet once again, the writer isn't talking about every single human being, neither does it seem to be his intent to speak about the sinful condition of humanity.

There is a similarity between this text and the previous one, where it seems to be talking about a group of people who oppose the writer. David has a specific group of people in mind and it is not mankind.

Again, a person who read the whole Psalm will see the error in using this to say that no one is righteous, as Paul would have us believe. Look to the end of the Psalm where it says,

> *Surely the righteous shall give thanks to Your name: the upright shall dwell before Your presence. (Psalm 140:13)*

In the very same psalm we have David talking of the righteous and the upright. We have people living before the presence of the Almighty. It seems like even He disagrees with Paul's conclusions. You can't say that there are no righteous people when the same chapter you quote from says that there are righteous and upright people.

There is only one way that Paul can come to his conclusion based on this verse: he takes the verse out of context.

verse 14

> *PAUL: Whose mouth is full of cursing and bitterness: ...*

Paul then quotes a section of Psalm 10:7. In order for you, the reader, to see what the psalm is actually talking about in context, I would have to quote the whole thing. So I ask that you please read the whole psalm yourself, that is Psalm 10. Here I shall just give some quick quotes to let you know who the subject of the song is.

The song starts with the question as to why the Lord is so far away whilst the wicked persecute the poor (vs. 1-2). So immediately we have two groups of people: the wicked; and those who the wicked oppress, who are therefore not the wicked. The psalm continues by focusing on the wicked person and his ways. This wicked person proudly says to himself that the Lord will not seek out anything that he does, since there is no deity anyway, no divine governance on earth (v.4). It is this wicked person whose mouth is full of cursing and bitterness (v.7). Look at some more descriptions of this person in the following verses.

(8) He sits in the ambush spots of villages; in secret places he slays the innocent; his eyes are on the watch for the helpless. (9) He lays in wait in the secret place as a lion in his lair, he lays in wait to catch the poor; he catches the poor, when he draws him up in his net. (Psalm 10:8-9)

So this person seeks to capture the innocent, a group of people that shouldn't exist in Paul's mind. I mean, who is innocent if no one is righteous?

Regardless of that point, the fact is that this psalm still doesn't aim to speak of all humankind. It is speaking of a certain despicable kind of person. It sets this wicked group apart from those who they prey upon, so it cannot be used to speak about all people. So Paul's use of the verse to prove his point actually does nothing to help him. He wishes to use his broad paint brush and smear everyone with condemnation, to say that no one at all is righteous and thus we are all guilty and helpless under sin's power. The chapter describes one set of people without condemning everyone as Paul does.

So once again, Paul takes a verse out of context.

verses 15-17

(15) Their feet are swift to shed blood. (16) Destruction and misery are in their ways. (17) And the way of peace have they not known: (Romans 3:15-17)

Paul here quotes Isaiah 59:7-8 which is one of the best verses he has used so far. Paul only quotes a few sentences but he didn't butcher the verses of Isaiah. The verses, on their own, do show a picture of evil acts. But the question we should ask is if the people and place that Isaiah speaks of is so devoid of good people, then why does it say this two chapters away?

(1) The righteous one perished, and no man set it to heart, and pious men are taken away, with none understanding that the righteous one is taken away from the evil to come. (Isaiah 57:1)

That is the niggling fact that has and will always hinder Paul's doctrine of universal sinfulness and that none is righteous. Wherever he stakes a claim in one place in scripture that there is no righteous person and that we are all evil devilish creatures turning away from Deity, full of deceit, laying in wait for blood, not knowing what the word "peace" means, the Hebrew Scriptures say, "some people are righteous", "not everyone is wicked", "there are those who obey the will of the Lord" and "you can choose the way of righteousness".

Rather than going deeper into this passage, which is needless, and concluding my thoughts too early, let's finish this one off by just stating the obvious: Paul takes a verse out of context and twists it to say what it doesn't say.

verse 18

Paul's final quote in his little prooftext frenzy is from Psalm 36:1 which, according to Paul, says:

PAUL: There is no fear of God before their eyes. (Romans 3:18)

Now Paul's rendition is slightly different to the verse in Psalms, which says,

The declaration of Transgression to the wicked, in the midst of my heart, [is that] there is no fear of Deity before his eyes. (Psalm 36:1)

So this is what transgression says to the wicked: there is no fear of Deity in the eyes of the wicked. He does what he likes! So again, the psalm is talking about a certain type of person. The psalm continues in the same vein as Psalm 10, which Paul quoted before, describing the ways of the wicked man: the words out of his mouth are iniquity; he plans his crimes while he's relaxing on his bed; and he doesn't reject evil.

But is there anything in this scripture that would make us think that the psalmist is trying to speak about the whole human race? Again, let me quote verse 11 of the same chapter of Psalms.

(11) O draw out Your lovingkindness to them that know You; and Your righteousness to the upright in heart. (Psalm 36:11)

I just want to alert you to the fact that if we compare the description of wicked people to this verse, then they don't match. A wicked person is not "upright in heart". A person who is described as "there is no fear of Deity before his eyes" cannot be called "one who knows Deity" as this verse says. So, again, this verse is talking about a group of people who are not wicked and thus are righteous. In life, and in Torah, there is no such thing as neutral.

So once again, the passage that Paul quotes refutes his conclusions. He has taken another verse out of context and twisted its meaning to include all mankind when it never did.

To Paul, all these out-of-context verses point to the fact that the whole world is guilty. But when all these verses are read in context it is apparent that the whole world is not guilty. There are righteous people and wicked people, so not everyone is to be condemned. Yet some naive or well-indoctrinated christian will say that if a person sins once then they will always be guilty of sin or be a sinner, they are no longer righteous. It has already been shown that this is a fallacy, and will be shown again and again throughout this book. According to scripture, righteousness is based on what you do. Ezekiel clearly tells us that if a person turns away from his sins and tries to live according to what is right in the eyes of Deity, his sin will not be remembered against him, and he will live according to his righteousness. That same prophet echoes what is said in the law (Deuteronomy 6:24-25), that a person who abstains from wrong things and lives according to the right ways, then he is righteous, including that person who sinned: once he aims to live the righteous lifestyle, his sins are forgotten and he is considered righteous. That is the word of the Almighty, not the logic of man, like Paul's words.

Also, Paul's reliance on poetic scriptures must be noted. He keeps on taking poetic scriptures and twisting them into a hyper-literal sense to apply to everyone, yet none of these passages in context are really a divine declaration or condemnation on all mankind in the midst of a narrative (more literal) portion of scripture. All we really see from these passages that Paul uses is that Paul has a powerful knack for ignoring what scriptures say for the sake of his own agenda.

verse 20a

According to Paul,

εξ εργων νομου ου δικαιωθησεται πασα σαρξ ενωπιον αυτου
By (lit. out of) deeds of law, all flesh shall not be declared righteous before him. (i.e., no flesh, no one at all shall be considered righteous before Deity) - Romans 3:20

For all those who don't know Ancient Greek, I hope it doesn't confuse you to see that Greek sentence there. I'm just trying to stay as true to the supposed language of Paul as possible so I don't get charged with twisting his words.

Let's first understand what Paul is saying in this verse. After going through all those mistreated proof-texts, he believes that he has shown that the whole world is guilty and thus he has built his platform for verse 20. He says that by deeds of law, that is by doing those things which the law commands, no one can be declared righteous before the Almighty. And what does it mean to be declared righteous? Basically, Paul is saying that according to the standards of the law of Deity, no one can be said to be righteous; no one can be said to be living according to all those laws.

But here we meet with one of the greatest contradictions between Paul's doctrine and the teaching of the whole Hebrew Bible. As we have seen previously, the Tanakh (another name for the Jewish Bible or "the old testament") is not afraid to call people righteous. One of the most obvious undercurrents of the Jewish Bible is that there ARE righteous people. Paul says that no one can be declared righteous, and the Jewish Bible calls people righteous. That is a contradiction.

Just consider this in a really plain way:

* Paul says that by the deeds of the Law, no one can be called righteous before the Almighty.
* Yet, the Law given to Moses is the word and will of the Almighty;
* Therefore, to keep the Law, to do the deeds of the Law, i.e., the word of the Lord, is to do what the Almighty says;
* So Paul is saying that you can't be called righteous by doing what the Almighty says, i.e., his Law.

Now can you see how unreasonable that is? Simple understanding shows this to be so wrong. When you do what your father says, then according to his standard, you are right. If you do what a national law commands, then according to that law, you are innocent and righteous. That makes sense. Even if you break a law, such as breaking the speed limit in your car, or dropping litter where it is forbidden to do so, as soon as you pay for your crime, according to the law, and then continue to try to keep the law, you are still generally regarded as a law keeper.

If that is the case using simple understanding and our own experience, then how much more is this true when a person takes the time to read the Hebrew Bible without the indoctrination of Paul?

Before I carry on, I just need to explain something for those who are hyper-literalists. There are people in this world who will only accept an argument if that argument contains a proof that says a specific word they are looking for. For example, think of the case of a mother who is devoted to her thieving son, so devoted that she always argues his innocence. After being caught stealing again, it is discovered that this time there is an eye-witness to the crime who has given a written statement. In that statement, the eye-witness uses phrases like "the boy took the man's property without asking" and "he snuck in, while the man wasn't there, and opened the cabinet and took the silver". The mother looks at the statement and then shouts out triumphantly that again her son is innocent of the crime. And why? Because not once in the statement did the eye-witness use the words "theft" or "steal". But anyone with just a little sense and no bias would recognise that although the words "theft" and "steal" aren't there, the son is still guilty. Why? Because the acts contained in the eye-witness statement fulfil the criteria and definition of stealing which is to take something without consent or permission. Once that definition is fulfilled, there is no need to say the word explicitly.

In the same way, there are some people who will look throughout scripture and see that the specific words "righteous" or "just" (synonymous to righteous) are only used on specific people a few times and would therefore say, "that shows that only a few people are righteous". But they trip themselves up by being so rigid (we'll, for now, overlook the fact that their premise has already be contradicted in the Jewish Bible by the very fact that Paul says no one at all is righteous and the scripture says that specific people were righteous), since there are many people who fulfil the definition or criteria for being righteous and thus don't need to have that specific word applied to them. And what is that definition? To be righteous is to continually and repeatedly do those things that agree with a standard of morality and justice. It is to do those moral and correct things generally throughout one's life in a repeated and reliable way. That is the definition of being righteous, and it is this definition that we will be looking for throughout scripture.

The Law itself shows us what brings righteousness and what makes a person good.

(24) And GOD commanded us to do all these statutes, to fear GOD our Deity for our good always, and that he might preserve us alive, as [it is] this day. (25) And it shall be righteousness for us, if we observe to do all this commandment before GOD our Deity, as he has commanded us. (Deuteronomy 6:24,25)

(15)See, I have set before you today life and the good, death and the evil, (16) because I command you this day to love GOD your Deity, to walk in his ways, and to keep his commandments and his statutes and his decrees; and then you shall live and multiply; and GOD your Deity shall bless you in the land to which you go to possess it. (17) But if your heart turns away, and you don't obey, and you get drawn away, and bow down to other gods, and serve them, (18) I make it explicit to you today that you shall surely perish; you shall not spend many days upon the land, to which you go over the Jordan to go there to possess it. (Deuteronomy 30:15-18)

As can be seen, according to the Almighty, the way of righteousness, good, and life is found in the keeping of his laws. This is confirmed in other places in the Hebrew Scripture.

(9) How shall a youth make/keep his conduct pure? by guarding it according to your word. (10) With all my heart I have sought you: don't let me stray from your commandments. (11) In my heart I have

treasured up your saying, in order that I may not sin against You.
(Psalm 119:9-11)

And it is by doing the law, keeping its commandments in your actions, that you obtain righteousness.

> *(5) And a man, when he be righteous, and do justice and righteousness - (6) He hasn't eaten upon the mountains, and he hasn't lifted up his eyes to the idols of the house of Israel, and he hasn't defiled the wife of his neighbour, and he hasn't come near to a menstrous woman; (7) And he hasn't mistreated anyone, he restores his pledge for a debt, he has seized nothing by robbery, his bread he gives to the hungry, and the naked he covers with a garment; (8) He hasn't given [lent out money] for interest, and he doesn't take the increase, he withdraws his hand from injustice, he executes true judgment between man and man; (9) He has walked in my statutes, and he has observed my decrees to act truthfully - he is righteous, he shall surely live, declares Lord GOD. (Ezekiel 18:5-9)*

Seeing that according to the Jewish Bible, "godly" acts and devotion to the Almighty are the basis of being declared righteous, we can see the following in that light.

> *(9) These are the generations of Noah: Noah was a righteous man and perfect in his generations, and Noah walked with Deity.... (1) And GOD said to Noah, Enter, you and all your household, into the ark; for I have seen you righteous before me in this generation.*
> *(Genesis 6:9; 7:1)*

Before I continue, I'm just wondering if you see what I see. Paul says that no one shall be declared righteous before Deity, and here we have Noah declared righteous before Deity. It looks like the scriptures have already refuted Paul. Some may say that this was before the law of Moses, but a little bit of study will show that there was a law, a standard of righteousness, before Moses. And righteousness, according to the Hebrew Bible, is based on what you do, not necessarily on what you believe. Anyway, I'll just carry on.

(1) There was a man in the land of 'Uz, Job was his name; And that man was perfect and upright, and fearing Deity, and eschewing evil. (8) Then GOD said to the Accuser, Have you set your heart upon my servant Job; for there is none like him on the earth, a man perfect and upright, who fears God, and eschews evil? (Job 1:1,8)

(4) And I will cause your seed to multiply as the stars of heaven, and I will give to your seed all these countries; and in your seed shall all the nations of the earth bless themselves. (5) Because Abraham obeyed my voice, and kept my charge, my commandments, my statutes, and my laws. (Genesis 26:4,5)

And also the mediums and the necromancers and the divining idols and the images and all the disgusting things that were seen in the land of Judah and Jerusalem Josiah destroyed in order to carry out all the words of the Law that were written in the scroll which Hilkiah the priest found in the house of GOD. And before him, there was not a king like him who returned to GOD with all his heart and all his soul and with all his resources according to all the Law of Moses, and after him there didn't arise one like him. (2 Kings 23:24-25)

What does all this show? That there were righteous people, people who kept the commandments of the Lord, throughout history.

Even consider David! People like to focus on his bad points, the grave error he made in his life, as though it left an unwashable stain on his life. But what was the Almighty's opinion of David?

(34) And I will not take the whole kingdom out of his hand: but I will make him leader all the days of his life for David my servant's sake, whom I chose, because he kept my commandments and my statutes... (38) And it shall be, if you obey all that I command you, and walk in my ways, and do that is upright in my sight, to keep my statutes and my commandments, as David my servant did; that I will be with you,

and build you a sure house, as I built for David, and will give Israel to you. (1 Kings 11:34,38)

And I tore the kingdom away from the house of David, and gave it to you: and yet you have not been as my servant David, who kept my commandments, and who followed me with all his heart, to do that only which was right in my eyes; (1 Kings 14:8)

What is amazing is that kings after David were compared to him with regards to devotion and obedience to the Almighty. All this goes to show the principle that a righteous man is not necessarily a perfect one, since it is written that "there is no righteous man in the land that does good and never sins" (Ecclesiastes 7:20). This verse doesn't say that there are no righteous men at all, but rather there are no righteous men who have never in all their days done something wrong, i.e., absolutely perfect humans; but yet, they are still called righteous, even if they are not perfect!!! This contradicts Paul's usage of the word "righteous" as "perfect". As with king David, being righteous is about striving to do the will of the Almighty, including truly repenting when one does wrong. That is a righteous person!

All this goes to show that scripture plainly says: that there are people who were declared righteous before Deity; righteousness is simply obeying what the Lord says; and that Paul's words are nonsensical and scripturally baseless to say that by doing deeds in accordance to the law, doing what the Lord says, no one can be called righteous.

Now some christians may say that Paul is not saying that there is no righteousness in doing what the Lord says and keeping his Law. They will continue that it is just wrong to keep the law in order to be righteous since only faith can bring righteousness because Jesus brought the end of keeping the law for righteousness. But this view is problematic in so many ways. Firstly, it is the most obvious sign that they follow Paul, a man who never spent any of his life with the living Jesus as the "new testament" describes him, but received revelation from some spirit being he claimed to receive revelation from, who he claimed to be the spiritual Jesus. According to the living Jesus there was much benefit in keeping the law, doing those deeds of law. He said that he didn't come to do away with law but to keep it.

[NOTE: "fulfilling the law" is not the same as "fulfilling prophecy", a horrible error that christians make. To fulfil prophecy is to cause the events foretold to happen, and thus there is no more need for fulfilment because it has happened. To fulfil a law is to comply with the standard set in that law, and there will always be a need to fulfil that law in future because the standard will remain for as long as the law is set. In the case of the commandments of the law, they are all set to last forever. To give a concrete example, Jeremiah prophesies that after 70 years from the destruction of the first Temple the Israelites will be released from Babylonian exile and return to their land of Israel. The fulfilment of this prophecy would be that 70 years after the destruction of the first Temple, the Israelites are set free from their exile in Babylon and come back to Israel. After that, there is no more need to fulfil the prophecy because it's done, finished and completed. But there is a law that says at the end of the 14th of the 1st Hebrew month, people who are circumcised according to the tradition of Abraham and Moses, i.e.,Israelites, should celebrate the Passover, and this should be done for all time. So if an Israelite celebrates the Passover at the end of the 14th of the 1st Hebrew month, he has fulfilled the law; but, unlike a prophecy which would then be over, the law would still have to be kept, fulfilled, the next year at the same time. Or the law that says that sabbath should be kept weekly, when a person keeps it as they should one week, then they still have to fulfil it the next week. So Jesus' fulfilling the law doesn't mean the typical christian understanding of "when Jesus fulfilled the law, that means he filled it to the brim so that it doesn't have to be kept anymore" which really twists the meaning of "fulfil the law". They swap the meaning of "fulfil a prophecy" with that of "fulfil law" even though the law never claims to be prophecy. Christians can really make their bible mean what they want it to.]

Anyway, back to the subject. Jesus said that he never came to abolish the law but to keep it. He said that whoever keeps all the law would be great in the kingdom of heaven (Matthew 5:17-19). In the Greek version of Matthew, Jesus even says that people should do what the rabbis teach, although not follow what they do (Matthew 23:2-3). When asked how a person should get eternal life, Jesus was told that in order to receive eternal life a person should essentially keep the law, to which Jesus agreed (Luke 10:25-28). The well-known story of a young rich ruler is told a lot amongst christians, although there is a lot of irony in that. Why? Jesus is asked how a person may obtain eternal life, and Jesus' first answer is, "keep the commandments"! Of course, the story goes on and the ruler's love of riches becomes apparent, but still the first answer of Jesus has not disappeared (Matthew 19:16-22)! [Pauline christians normally scoff and say that Jesus was only saying that because really it is impossible to keep the commandments (according to Paul); it's just strange that, of all people, Jesus never said that himself!!!] So at least according to the living Jesus, it is possible to obtain eternal life, and therefore also righteousness, by keeping the commandments of the law. In addition, the "new testament" itself has people being called righteous before Deity and blameless in commandment-keeping (Luke 1:5-6), which still contradicts Paul's point.

So that was the first point against some christian logic.

The other point is that, as I may have said before, the problem with Paul's conception with righteousness, which has been accepted apparently uncritically by his followers, christianity throughout the ages, is that he mistakes righteousness for absolute perfection. But that is not the definition of righteousness for human beings as has been shown in the Hebrew Bible. The Hebrew Bible shows that devotion to the Almighty by one's just actions is the means to being called righteous. The Almighty isn't some unreasonable tyrant who asks the impossible of his creatures and then punishes them for "falling short of his glory". I won't go into that argument any further since I'll go deeper into that point later.

The fact is that christians say that it is wrong to keep the law in order to be righteous. But we have the words of the law saying that that is the very purpose of keeping the law: to be righteous (Deuteronomy 6:24-25 cf 4:1-8). It is through the observance of this law that Israel would gain wisdom and understanding. So this claim of some christians which they derive from Paul ("Jesus is the end of law-keeping in order to be righteous for believers" Romans 10:4; to rely on the law is to have a curse upon you, Galatians 3) is basically against what the law says for itself; it's basically against what the Almighty said about the law, through his closest servant Moses.

Let's move to the next part of Paul's verse.

verse 20b

The whole of verse 20 is as follows,

*Because by deeds of law no flesh shall be declared righteous before Him, **for by law is knowledge of sin**. (Romans 3:20)*

The whole of this verse gives an eye-opening picture of Paul's doctrine. We already know that the first half means that keeping the law doesn't make anyone righteous before the Almighty. Paul isn't talking about legalism as some would have us think. There are two definitions of legalism, only one of which apply to this verse. One definition of legalism is the strict adherence to the letter of the law rather than its intent. But Paul isn't talking about strictness here, and reading through the writings of the Pharisees and their modern counterparts, Orthodox Judaism, and the Sadducees and their modern counterparts, the Karaites, it is difficult to prove the claim that they were legalists based on their own methods and ways. There's no point in trusting an accurate and full description of these groups to the "new testament", which seeks more to prove its own validity and the insufficiency of any other way of thinking.

The other definition of legalism is based firmly in christian theology. This definition says that legalism is where you keep the law in order to get "salvation", to be saved from the guilt and pollution of sin and from eternal damnation and death to get eternal life. This still isn't exactly what Paul is talking about since he is talking about righteousness, not salvation. Rather than go into a deep theological or philosophical debate as to what Paul is talking about, let's just use his words to get meaning.

So Paul is not talking about legalism per se. All he is saying is that the law can't make a person righteous, and the next sentence tells us why: because the law can only give knowledge of sin. That means that the law can only let you know how to identify sins, wrong actions and thoughts and the ins and outs of such wrong things. It can show a person how much they have sinned and how far they are away from righteousness ... and that's all! According to Paul, that is all the law can do: it can't make a person righteous because it can only show you your sin! Christian commentators of old time, especially the "respected" Martin Luther, compares the law to a mirror: it shows you that you are dirty (due to sin), but that is all; it doesn't clean you, it doesn't free you from filth; it just shows you your dirt (or it shows you that you're dirt).

The question we can ask is whether this is true. Rather than ask Paul, who has his own opinion, what does the scripture say about the Law of Moses? What does the Law say about its own capabilities? What does the Jewish Bible say about what the Law can do for people?

If you've read this book up to this point, then you would have already seen that the Law itself contradicts such a limited and decrepit view. It is true that by knowing the law you can know the sinful acts to avoid and you can find out if you have sinned. But is that all? I'll summarize what I have shown above and also add some more biblical facts to help us see the truth about Paul's way of viewing law. So I'll show you some of the things I've found that the Jewish Bible and the Law of Moses says about the power of the law.

If one simply reads through the Jewish Bible, it would be plain to see the importance of obedience to the Almighty and his Law. Through Abraham's obedience to the Creator's laws, he and his descendants would be blessed, have a special relationship with Deity, would get the land of Israel, and the whole world would be blessed through them (Genesis 26:3-5). Through Israel's obedience to the law, and the eternal covenant that came with it, they were and still are a people preserved and treasured by Deity above all nations (Exodus 19:5). Through the law, they were made and kept holy and pure (Leviticus 11:44; Numbers 15:40; Psalm 119:9). The law is key to Israel's chosen status (Deuteronomy 26:18-19). The law gives life, good, and righteousness (Deuteronomy 6:24-25; 30:15-20). The kindness/mercy/devotion of the Most High is attached to those who keep his commandments and their descendants (Exodus 20:6; Psalm 103:17,18). The commandments bring happiness and blessing (Psalm 119:1). The commandments bring light and direction (Psalm 119:105). Through obedience to the law, wisdom and understanding are obtained (Psalm 119:100). In fact, obedience to the law is much preferable to the Lord than blood sacrifices or other forms of sacrifices (1 Samuel 15:22; Jeremiah 7:21-23), which is why repentance, a return to obedience, is the essential ingredient to forgiveness, with or without any form of offering (Ezekiel 18). Thus through the obedience to the law, forgiveness can also be obtained, since the law gives the ways to draw close to Deity Essentially, the law teaches a person about the true Deity that should be served and the things he really wants (Deuteronomy 10:12-13).

You see, Paul and his followers help harbour such a lame and grossly inaccurate view of law, a pessimistic and vain view. To them, the law's only purpose is to see your shortcomings. That's it! Through the law is the knowledge of sin, how you can go wrong. But how can you read laws like "love the Lord your Deity with all your heart" and "love your neighbour as yourself" and "make sure that the orphan, foreign resident and widow are protected and their rights upheld" and "when you harvest your field, leave some of the harvest in your field for the poor" and "judges should pursue righteous justice" and "don't follow the majority to do wrong" and get the impression that obedience to the law only shows you your shortcomings and your sin??? Words like these give something to strive for as a goal that can be reached as is seen in Deuteronomy 30:11-14 which says:

(11) For this commandment which I am commanding you today, it is not too wonderful for you, and it is not far removed from you. (12) It [is] not in the heaven [for you] to say: "Who shall go up for us to the heaven and take it for us and make us hear it that we may do it?" (13) And it [is] not across the sea [for you] to say: "Who shall go across for us to the other side of the sea and take it for us and make us hear it that we may do it? (14) For the word is very near to you, in your mouth and in your heart [for you] to do it.

The law was given in a way that it could be kept and those who do it would be blessed and be happy in a good and righteous life. It's a righteous aim that can be reached; not one full of disappointment and sin, but rather one of opportunity and possibility. We'll come back to this scripture again soon in Paul's writings.

All this goes to show that the claim that "keeping the law makes no one righteous because it gives understanding of sin" is utter nonsense when one looks throughout the Hebrew Bible and sees that it gives so much more. It does make a person wise and righteous, and through it is much more than knowing what sin is, but also knowing one's Creator and the way that he has given to be righteous in his eyes, a way that can be followed.

verses 21-26

Paul speaks of a righteousness outside of, apart from, the Law which comes by believing in Jesus as messiah and sacrifice for sin. This righteousness is supposed to be spoken of in "the Law and the Prophets", namely the Jewish Bible. But Paul gives no evidence for this claim, and the Hebrew Bible speaks of no such righteousness, a righteousness which is not based on deeds of obedience to some law. So we just have his word for it, and without the basis of the truth of the Torah and the Jewish Bible, it is worth nothing.

A question that can be asked is the meaning of the following phrase of Paul:

For all have sinned and come short of the glory of the Deity.
(Romans 3:23)

The answers I have heard fall along the lines of "we have sinned and missed out on God's perfection". But with the help of christian commentators, a clearer picture can be obtained when looking at the words of each part. "all have sinned" is easy to understand: everyone has done something wrong. "and come short" means that everyone was lacking or deficient in some way. This means that in Paul's eyes everyone has failed in some way. "the glory of the Deity" is the difficult part. What does the "glory of Deity" mean? What is "glory"? The Greek word, δοξα, doxa, in the christian scriptures, can mean "a good opinion of someone, praise, honor, glory", or "splendour, brightness". Seeing these definitions gives us a few options as to the possible meanings:

* everyone has come short of a good opinion/praise/honour that comes from Deity: this means that because everyone has done at least something wrong, everyone has failed to get any praise or honour from Deity.
* everyone has come short of giving honour due to Deity: this means that because everyone has sinned, no one can really give him proper honour and praise because the sin puts such a condemnation upon them, and any sin is an insult against Deity that cuts us off from him.
* everyone has come short of seeing the glory of Deity: this means that because the holiness of Deity cannot ignore and tolerate sin, a man who has committed any sin will not be allowed, in the afterlife, to see the holiness and glorious splendour of Deity, and thus will be cast to the outer darkness, the "eternal" death.

So because the god of Paul demands absolute perfection, something impossible for humanity, in one way or another, humanity is cut off from a good relationship with Deity.

Again, a cursory glance through the Hebrew Scriptures shows that each one of these understandings is incorrect. The root idea of being cut off from a good relationship with Deity also is contradicted by the history of Israel and the world as recounted in the Jewish Bible. The Law shows that the Almighty loved the patriarchs of the Israelite nation (Deuteronomy 4:37; 10:15) and the nation Israel itself (Deuteronomy 7:7-9), which shows a relationship. He makes covenants with people like Phinehas and David who he delights in for different reasons, or maybe the very same reason. And what is that reason?

GOD takes pleasure in them that fear him, in those that hope in his mercy. (Psalm 147:11)

It even says about his special people, Israel, and the humble:

For GOD takes pleasure in his people: he will beautify the meek with salvation. (Psalm 149:4)

The scriptures also state a fact that was a reality back in the days of Solomon and even now:

For whom GOD loves he corrects; even as a father the son in whom he delights. (Proverbs 3:12)

Even David could say, according to the plain meaning of the psalm:

(10) For You shall not abandon my soul to the grave: You shall not allow your pious [servant] to see the pit. (11) You shall let me know the path of life: fulness of joy is with Your presence; pleasures are at your right hand for evermore. (Psalm 16:10-11)

According to the psalm, David is speaking of himself enjoying pleasures forever with the Almighty. Although ripped out of context by the apostles and their christian followers, applying it only to their "jesus", the simple reading shows that a pious servant of the Almighty can enjoy his presence, most likely, in the world to come, the hereafter.

The notion that because people have done something wrong in their lives and thus are forever cut off from Deity undermines the divine teaching about repentance and reconciliation spoken of in scripture (Deuteronomy 4:26-31; Jeremiah 3:22; Ezekiel 18 and 33; Zechariah 1:3), which says that when a person returns to the Almighty, he will return to them and their sins will be forgotten and the relationship will be restored. Read the whole of Psalm 103 and realise how silly the idea is that any one sin in a person's life forever cuts them off from a good relationship with Deity. Read the life of David and the good things the Almighty always says about him and realise how senseless is the notion that a sin in a person's life restricts them from ever having any praise, commendation, or good opinion from Deity. From the beginning of time, repentance has been the way to draw close to Deity after sin, and righteousness and obedience have always led back to a good standing before Deity. Such a teaching also makes a mockery of God's mercy and his cleansing sin even in the Hebrew Scriptures. With this sort of thinking, it's as if a person is never really truly forgiven by the Almighty, which flatly contradicts the Jewish Bible. Don't get me wrong! We do sin and it does negatively impact our standing with the Almighty. But by recognising the error and doing all we can, all we've been told by the Person we've wronged, to rectify our mistakes, the relationship can be healed and possibly made even stronger!

So even this seemingly innocuous verse by Paul that all have sinned and fallen short of the glory of Deity makes no sense in a contextual reading of the Hebrew Bible.

Chapter 4

verse 3

Paul makes the following claim:

> *(2) For if Abraham was declared righteous due to deeds, he has grounds to boast, but not before Deity. (3) Because what does the scripture say? "But Abraham believed in the Deity and it was reckoned to him as righteousness." (Romans 4:2-3)*

So what is Paul's message? If Abraham was called righteous because of what he did, then it only gives him the right to boast about himself and his own deeds; the Almighty has nothing to do with it because it is man's deeds that bring righteousness. So in Paul's eyes, if man does good, the Almighty gets no glory out of the deeds of man. So what is Paul's solution? Well, scripture really tells us that Abraham simply believed, had a mental conviction or a conviction of the heart or both, and then the Almighty saw that conviction as "righteousness". There were no deeds involved. Abraham only had to believe and he was declared righteous.

But does this really show us in what way Abraham was righteous? Is this what set him apart in the eyes of Deity?

If one would just take a look at what the Torah actually says about Abraham's life (and it's important to see what it says about his life rather than just pick on one verse and get an opinion based on one verse), there was a feature, a character trait, that really marked this man as special. From Genesis 12:1 to Genesis 25, what really sticks out about Abraham was not his faith, but rather his obedience. From the beginning where the Almighty tells Abraham to leave his father and family, his land of birth, and go to a land that he didn't know, to his being asked to sacrifice his only beloved son, Abraham shows the amazing strength of character to obey the Almighty. If there is anything that marked his life, something that showed up more than once, in fact a good number of times, it was Abraham's obedience.

Think about it: being asked to leave his family, everything he knew, and his land of birth, to go to a land that he didn't know, to his being asked to sacrifice his only beloved son, Abraham shows the amazing strength of character to obey the Almighty. If there is anything that marked his life, something that showed up more than once, in fact a good number of times, it was Abraham's obedience. And as I have shown before, when the Almighty tells Isaac why he was given the promise and blessing of Abraham, He says the following:

(3) Sojourn in this land, and I will be with you, and will bless you; for to you, and to your seed, I will give all these countries, and I will perform the oath which I swore to Abraham your father; (4) And I will make your seed to multiply as the stars of heaven, and will give to your seed all these countries; and in your seed shall all the nations of the earth be blessed; (5) Because that Abraham obeyed my voice, and kept my charge, my commandments, my statutes, and my laws. (Genesis 26:3-5)

So when the Almighty himself summarises the reason why the land, blessing and promise would be given to Isaac and his descendants, he never spoke of faith or belief. He only spoke of obedience.

Now compare this whole life of obedience to the one statement, the one verse, which states that Abraham believed and it was seen by the Almighty as a righteous thing to do. The verse doesn't even clearly say that Abraham believing made him righteous. It says that Abraham believed and his believing was regarded as a righteous thing. Plus, just taking this verse on its own robs it of its contextual meaning. It's not as if Abraham believed in just anything. It wasn't that Abraham was just introduced to God and he therefore believed that God existed and that he was master of the universe. The Lord had said to Abraham that his own offspring would be numerous when, at that time, Abraham had no children and his wife was barren. Abraham trusted the Lord in what he had promised, and that was seen as righteous. There is little to say that faith, in and of itself, directed to anything, is a righteous thing, or that it makes a person righteous. Paul's usage of this verse is superficial and cut off from context; he neglects the whole lifestyle of Abraham.

Even a plain reading of the "new testament" book of James kicks out Paul's idea of deeds having nothing to do with a person being declared righteous. It must be understood that this is what Paul is saying: if Abraham was declared righteous due to deeds, because of Abraham's actions, then he, Abraham, would have cause to boast of himself, so therefore justification (being declared righteous) must be something apart from, having nothing to do with, deeds! This is confirmed when Paul says:

... therefore we reckon a man to be declared righteous by faith, apart from works of law. (Romans 3:28)

And yet we have James saying, in agreement with the general tenor of the Hebrew Scriptures:

(19) You believe that there is one Deity; you do well: the devils also believe, and tremble. (20) But do you want to know, O vain man, that faith apart from deeds is dead? (21) Wasn't Abraham our father declared righteous by deeds, when he had offered Isaac his son upon the altar? (22) Do you see that faith worked with his deeds, and faith was completed by deeds? (23) And the scripture was fulfilled which says, Abraham believed the Deity, and it was reckoned to him as righteousness: and he was called the Friend of God. (24) You see then that a man is declared righteous by deeds, and not by faith only. (James 2:19-24)

Because of the christian necessity to make all their scriptures, the new testament, agree, they try to paint a different picture of this, as though James is really trying to say the same thing as Paul. But it is easy to see how James' statement, "do you want to know ... that faith apart from deeds is dead?" and "a man is declared righteous by deeds" contradicts Paul's statement "we reckon a man to be declared righteous by faith apart from deeds of law". We have seen that "deeds of law" is simply obedience to what the Creator says in one way or another.

The point of all this is to say that Paul tries to make out that if righteousness comes from our deeds then the Almighty gets no praise or honour; we can be proud of ourselves alone since it is our deeds. Simple logic shows this thinking to be erroneous when we just think what the source of our deeds are: if it is obedience to the Lord, then he is the source of such obedience and thus our righteousness. He gave the righteous law and/or command, and thus keeping it and doing its deeds glorifies the One who gave such a law. He also tries to say that righteousness can only come apart from deeds, yet he ignores the common theme of Abraham's whole life, what the Almighty had to say about him, and even what a man who seems to have more right to be called Jesus' follower (i.e., James) says about the subject. We've already seen that the recorded words of the living Jesus contradict Paul's. And regardless of the words of Jesus and his followers, the Hebrew Scriptures contradicts the fundamental ideas of Paul. All these other sources show that righteousness comes from deeds, especially deeds of the law of the Lord.

All in all, Paul doesn't really have a leg to stand on.

verse 5

Paul continues,

(4) Now to one who works is the reward not accounted according to grace, but according to what is owed. (5) But to one who doesn't work, but believes on him who justifies the ungodly, his faith is counted as righteousness. (Romans 4:4-5)

Paul here is talking about Deity as one who declares righteous the ungodly, the wicked. In his attempt to show us that we cannot be made righteous by works and deeds, he says that the Almighty justifies those who have no reverence or respect towards Him, and have sinned against Him and thus are ungodly.

Now there is a serious problem with Paul's logic here. Once again, the Hebrew Scriptures contradict him to his face. Paul says that Deity justifies the wicked. What does the Almighty say about himself? Let us compare:

PAUL: "[Deity] who justifies the wicked."
THE ALMIGHTY: "... I don't justify the wicked." (Exodus 23:7)

This is a plain contradiction to what Paul is saying. Remember that his claim that we are all guilty and are unable to become righteous because we always come short, a claim that has no basis in the Jewish Bible. In the Jewish Bible, repentance, prayer, and doing what is right, forsaking wrong deeds, are ways of being righteous and getting forgiveness and justification. So we are not all wicked as Paul would have us believe. And those who the Hebrew Scriptures call wicked, the Almighty does not justify them. So Paul says Deity justifies the wicked; and the Almighty says he doesn't. I don't believe Paul has a leg to stand on here. I've seen christian commentators try to explain this, but their explanations are not cogent, weighty, or logical: the plain word of scripture, the words of the Lord himself, contradicts Paul's doctrine.

verses 6-8

Paul continues by quoting the Psalms:

(6) Even as David also says of the blessedness of the man to whom God imputes righteousness without works, (7) saying, "Blessed are those whose lawless acts are forgiven, and whose sins are covered; (8) blessed is the man to whom the Lord will in no way impute sin."
(Romans 4:6-8)

Paul here is trying to give us the impression that even David spoke of obtaining a state of being righteous without doing any deeds. But if one took the time to actually read this psalm of David, would we really get the impression that David did no deeds to obtain righteousness?

In fact, let us just take Paul at face value for now. What does it say? Basically, a man who is forgiven by the Almighty is blessed. Note that these verses, on their own, without Paul's eisegesis, tell us nothing about how this man is forgiven. The verses do not say that the Lord imputes no sin with or without the deeds of man. These verses on their own tell us nothing about the validity of Paul's claim.

Focusing on the psalm of David that Paul quotes, which is Psalm 32, what is said about this blessed man to whom the Almighty imputes no sin?

(1) Blessed is he whose transgression is forgiven, whose sin is covered. (2) Blessed is the man unto whom the Lord doesn't imputes iniquity, and in whose spirit there is no guile. (Psalm 32:1-2)

So David isn't speaking about wicked or ungodly people as Paul is. He is speaking of someone who is forgiven, in whose spirit/character there is no deceitfulness. Now how would we know that this person doesn't have any deceitfulness in his spirit? By the way he acts, not simply some hidden faith! Psalm 32:5 is a sign that David is speaking of his own blessedness, and the blessedness of anyone who would read/pray/sing this psalm with the same mindset (since the Psalms were not simply a biography of David's life, but songs for others to sing or speak or pray). It says,

My sin do I ever acknowledge to you, and my iniquity have I not covered up. I said, I will make confession because of my transgressions to the Lord: and you truly forgave the iniquity of my sin. (Psalm 32:5)

Here we see that after David does something, namely, he confesses his sin to the Almighty, then he becomes that blessed man at the beginning of his psalm, whose sin is forgiven. So he does this act of confession, which is alluded to in the law of Moses (Deuteronomy 4:27; 30:2-3, 10-20), and the Almighty forgives him. Verse 9 points to the need for obedience as opposed to rebelliousness! David says nothing about righteousness without works. David's continued motif in the Psalms is that obedience is a blessed thing (Psalm 1) and that sacrifices won't always do away with sin, but only, always, and fundamentally, obedience to the laws of the Almighty is the right way to go (Psalm 40:7-9).

So, again, Paul reads things into the Jewish Bible that aren't even there, and his argument is baseless!

The main arguments of Chapter 4

The main arguments of Paul in this chapter are as follows:

* The promise given to Abraham could not come through the law, since, in Paul's eyes, disobedience would nullify it. It can only come through faith which is separate from law.

* The fact that Abraham received the promise while he was uncircumcised, only becoming circumcised afterwards, makes him the father of all who believe, circumcised or uncircumcised, because faith is the common factor before and after circumcision. How does Paul arrive at this conclusion? Because, in his interpretation, Abraham received righteousness before circumcision (Genesis 15:6)!

The problems with Paul's arguments

Now the problems with Paul's arguments are as follows:

1.Paul distorts what the law really is by limiting it to simply a set of regulations alone with no heart, promise, or forgiveness. Thus an inaccurate view of Torah is put forward by Paul. What he fails to realise is that a holistic view of Torah law, its history and messages, totally contradicts his narrow point of view and the arguments that come from it. Where Paul sees the law as a means of annulling (making void) the promise, the Torah is actually part of the fulfilment of the promise. It is through remaining in that law covenant and the faithfulness to the stipulations of the law that the promise of Abraham would be fulfilled (Deuteronomy 29:9-14; 30:19-20). It is not simple disobedience that voids the promise or breaks the covenant but rather a wholesale rejection of both. This is seen by the fact that different means of forgiveness are given in different ways in the Law.

2.Paul attempts to separate law and faith. This in itself is a strange thing and I'll tell you why. Paul is trying to say that the promise he is trying to give to everyone is only received by faith and not by law. A verse that he repeatedly uses to show the importance of faith is Habakkuk 2:4 which, in the Hebrew, says that the righteous live by 'emunah. Paul understands 'emunah as "faith". But that word is used in a particular place that refutes Paul's doctrine, if he and his followers are consistent with the usage or meaning of the word (and that is a big if when you see their methods). In Psalm 119:86, it says that "all Your commandments are 'emunah", the exact same Hebrew word Paul is so insistent on as speaking of "faith". So essentially, using a Pauline dictionary, the verse should read "all Your commandments are faith". Thus faith is part and parcel of the law and the commandments in it, thus they cannot annul a promise. In fact, if the promise comes by faith, and the commandments are faith, using Paul's "logic", then the promise must come via the commandments, which inadvertently coincides with the previous point I made about Paul's arguments.

3.Paul narrows Abraham's essential qualities, the qualities that helped him get and keep that promise, to faith alone. It has already been shown that Abraham's essential quality that cnsured the promise was not belicf, but rather obedience, as Deity said himself (Genesis 26:3-5). But aside from that, Abraham had a different quality and direction of faith(fulness) based squarely on obedience to the laws or commands he had been given. It has little to do with the faith Paul is spreading, that of Jesus' role, office, and person. It's like saying "it's good to believe". But the proper response to that statement is, "to believe in what?" or "what actions start or follow such a belief"?" Paul is just limited to "Abraham believed, we believe, so we're all the same". Such thinking is a major oversimplification and is thus inaccurate, deceptive, misleading and untrue.

4.Through law is the furtherance of the promise of Abraham (to be heir to the world) as is seen in the law about natural circumcised Israel's link to the promised land, which was an integral part of the promise given to Abraham. This is clear in law and natural circumcised Israel, and not in πιστις, pistis, "faith". Just look in the scriptures at the progression from Abraham's initial promise through to Israel's possessing the land promised to Abraham. It wasn't just about some abstract faith. Abraham's promise includes and starts with a land that was to be his (Genesis 12:1-2), which is then promised again to his seed who are to be circumcised have the Almighty as their Deity (Genesis 17), which is brought to fruition by Israel, the literal seed of Abraham who were circumcised, who possessed and had/have a lasting link to the land promised to Abraham.

verse 17

Paul says the following:

> *(16) Because of this, [it is] out of faith so that [it may be] according to grace to the end that the promise may be sure to all the seed; not only to that which is of the law, but also to that which is of the faith of Abraham who is father of us all (17) - as it is written, "I have made you a father of many nations" - ... (Romans 4:16-17)*

Paul puts forward the idea that the promise to Abraham that he would be father of many nations is fulfilled by his applying the promise to both those who are circumcised under the covenants of Abraham and Moses, and those that are uncircumcised who simply have faith in Paul's doctrine.

Now those who know where Paul is quoting from will wonder how in the world the man would come to such a conclusion when one looks at the context of what he's quoting. Where is Paul quoting from? He is using Genesis chapter 17, in particular, verse 5. Here is what it says with a little context.

(4) [As for] me, see, My covenant [is] with you, and you shall become the father of a multitude of nations. (5) And "Abram" shall no longer be called [as] your name, but your name shall be "Abraham" because I have made you father of a multitude of nations. (6) And I shall make you fruitful with abundant abundance and I shall make you into a nation, and kings shall come forth from you. (7) And I shall establish My covenant between me and you and your seed after you for your generations for an everlasting covenant to be the Deity of you and your seed after you. (8) And I will give to you, and to your seed after you, the land of your sojournings, all the land of Canaan, for an everlasting possession; and I will be their Deity.' (9) And Deity said to Abraham: 'And [as for] you, you shall keep My covenant, you, and your seed after you throughout their generations. (10) This is My covenant, which you shall keep, between Me and you and your seed after you: every male among you shall be circumcised. (11) And you shall be circumcised in the flesh of your foreskin; and it shall be a token of a covenant between Me and you.(Genesis 17:4-11)

Now people should wonder why Paul would take a small segment of a verse like this from a chapter like Genesis 17. Why? Because Paul's argument is concerning circumcision and the law and their being overshadowed and replace by faith! Yet what is the subject of Genesis 17? The covenant between the Almighty and Abraham, a covenant marked by physical circumcision. Not one section of this chapter says anything about "children of faith" or "seed of faith". It is all about those who get to bear the covenant in their flesh by means of circumcision being part of that covenant of Abraham. That is why it is so ludicrous that Paul would use this passage to make that interpretation.

In fact, nowhere in Abraham's story does it say that his promised seed are those of faith. The very Hebrew word for seed refers to natural offspring, not disciples or followers. So the promise to Abraham is always concerning his own seed primarily. This is particularly noted in Genesis 15 where Abraham is afraid that the inheritance that he should give to a son that he didn't have yet will go to a servant of his house. But the Lord corrects him and says one from his own flesh shall be his inheritor, straight after which the Almighty shows him the stars of heaven and says that his seed will be as numerous as those stars, a promise fulfilled in Moses' day (Deuteronomy 1:10) where he refers to those words said to Abraham.

The promise that starts in Genesis 12:1-3 makes it plain that he will be a blessing to other nations, but his blessing and promise is primarily for him and his biological offspring, the nation that shall come from him, as is expressed in the chapters and books that follow Genesis 12.

Going back to Genesis 17, we see another startling difference between Paul's doctrine and the passage's natural message. In Paul's vision, Sarah seems to have very little place, if any. Abraham is the father of all due to his faith and Sarah is … She's what? The spare wheel no one uses? But in Genesis 17, as Abraham becomes a nation, so does Sarah. As kings come from him, so kings come from her. Yet, again, nothing is said about faith. Why? Because the blessing that Deity gives is generally natural and physical! I'm not saying that that is the only element to this blessing, but textually speaking, it is difficult, if not impossible, to take the segment that Paul uses in its entire context and get the message Paul does.

In essence, Paul takes scripture out of context.

Just as a small aside. Some may complain, wondering how then this promise is fulfilled. They will have in their minds that Israel is the only nation descended from Abraham and wonder how that could be a fulfilment of Abraham being father to many nations. What they may not have considered is just how many sons and grandsons Abraham had, and how many of them turned into nations. There is Ishmael, Edom, as well as the sons of Abraham's wife after Sarah died, Keturah. How many sons did she have? In fact, it seems that all the Arab nations descend from Abraham.

verses 18-22

(18)... [Abraham], who against hope believed in hope, so that he might become father of many nations according to that which was spoken, "So shall your seed be" [Genesis 15:5]. (19) And not being weak in faith, he didn't consider his body now dead when he was about a hundred years old, neither the deadness of Sarah's womb. (20) He didn't stagger at the promise of Deity through unbelief, but was strong in faith having given glory to Deity; (21) And being fully persuaded that what he had promised he was also able to perform. (22) Therefore it was imputed to him for righteousness [referring to Genesis 15:6]. (Romans 4:17-22)

This is just a minor point, but looking at the verses that Paul quotes, there seems some inconsistency in his depiction of history. He says that because Abraham didn't consider his own aged body and the deadness of Sarah's womb, therefore it was imputed to him for righteousness, i.e., that belief was seen as a righteous thing (not that Abraham was now seen as righteous because of that one thing).

The reason why this is so questionable is that Paul is pointing to a defined state of Abraham's belief whilst referring to Genesis 15; but Abraham, at that time, didn't appear to have any clue that the seed would come from Sarah's womb. This can be said because in the very next chapter of Genesis, chapter 16, Sarah is unsure that the promise extends to her, so she advises Abraham to take Hagar as a wife and to have seed through her, to which Abraham agrees/consents. He listens to what Sarah says and takes her advice. This is not the actions of a person who believed that Deity could re-animate Sarah's dead womb.

So Paul's logic doesn't really follow and is not in accordance with scriptural history. But this was only a minor point against Paul.

Chapter 5

verses 6 and 8

Paul touches upon a very significant subject in these two verses, in which he says the following:

> *(6) For Christ - we were yet weak - still, at that time, died on behalf of the impious/ungodly. (7) For scarcely would one die on behalf of a righteous one; also on behalf of a good person one might possibly dare to die. (8) But the Deity exhibited his own love to us that while we were still sinners, Christ died on our behalf. (Romans 5:6-8)*

Now these verses are extremely loaded where it concerns the difference between the christian and Jewish view of forgiveness and atonement. Here we have Paul putting forward the idea that Jesus died on "our" behalf, meaning, in our place. He is literally saying, where we should have been punished with death, Jesus received that punishment. Not only this, but this was done while "we" were still in the state of being "ungodly" and "sinners".

Essays could be written on the ways that this message of Paul contradicts the message of the Tanakh on so many levels. But in order to maintain a certain length to this work, I will only summarize the main weaknesses with Paul's doctrine.

First I'll deal with the claim of Paul that Jesus died on our behalf. The plain message of scripture is that each person is responsible for their own sins and the punishment for that sin. There is no mention in the law of Moses or the rest of the Jewish Bible of a man dying in the place of another. In fact it says the opposite:

Fathers shall not die for sons and sons shall not die for fathers. A man shall die for his own sin. (Deuteronomy 24:16)

The soul that sins, it shall die. A son shall not bear the iniquity of the father, and a father shall not bear the iniquity of the son. The righteousness of the righteous shall be upon him, and the wickedness of the wicked shall be upon him. (Ezekiel 18:20)

In the Law of the Lord and in the Jewish Bible, the clear message is that everybody is responsible for their own sin. The principle shown by the above verses is that of personal accountability. Vicarious atonement - "a human life for a human life" - has no place in the Hebrew Scriptures! Christians will use unclear or out-of-context passages to support their view, but, after investigation, such proof-texting falls down, especially before clear and overt scriptures like these.

So Jesus couldn't die on our behalf, and his death would have no impact on the guilt or innocence of anyone else.

What about him dying whilst we are "ungodly" and "sinners"? Now if we are going according to the normal usage of words, we hit upon a problem here. Basically, Paul is saying that Jesus is the sacrifice for ungodly people. Now the Greek word in the new testament translated ungodly is ασεβης, asebes, meaning "without reverence, irreverent, impious, ungodly". In the ancient Greek translation of the Jewish Bible, it is normally used in the place of the Hebrew word רָשָׁע, rasha', which means a wicked person, a moral criminal, a wrong-doer. The question should be whether Deity accepts the sacrifice of asebes, rasha', ungodly and wicked people.

The book of Proverbs gives the answer:

The sacrifice of the wicked is an abomination to GOD ... (Proverbs 15:8 - see also 21:27)

The reason why this verse is so relevant is that in the Hebrew version, the word for wicked is rasha', and in the Greek, the word for wicked is asebes: exactly the same word Paul is using to say that his sacrifice of the wicked is acceptable!

You see, in the Jewish Bible, if you are ungodly, then there is no point in offering sacrifices because they won't be accepted! Repentance is the core necessity in the Jewish Bible. See Isaiah 1 where the people offer all sorts of different sacrifices and prayers, and yet it was all useless because they hadn't changed their hearts and actions! In fact, the Almighty was sick and tired of all their services because repentance, a return from wrong actions to doing what is right, wasn't there. And there was no point in looking to Jesus figures, because, according to the last point, everyone is responsible for their own sins: some "righteous" person couldn't take the punishment for a wicked person!

It should be made very clear that the execution or death of an innocent person for a crime he or she never committed is not justice, nor is it mercy. Nowhere in the Jewish Bible is it commanded that the innocent person die or be punished for crimes and sins he or she never committed. This is especially true for crimes demanding the death penalty; this is the penalty that christians claim every human deserves. To repeat myself, Jesus' supposed sacrifice, the life of a human (or godman) for humanity, has no basis in the Jewish Bible. God nowhere says that the animal sacrifices were only types and analogies.

That is the fundamental weakness of such thinking as Paul's. Paul has Jesus dying for unrepentant people. In the Tanakh, you must be repentant before the sacrifice! Or even at the sacrifice! But in the new testament view, humanity in general was ignorant of Jesus' very existence! And the majority of those who did know Jesus saw no sacrifice in Jesus' death. Basically, Jesus' death has no place or basis in the Law or the Hebrew Scriptures. Its root concepts are foreign to the methods and processes given in the Hebrew Bible, as if a man could die in another's place in the eyes of Deity.

The essential fact with Paul's logic is that he has twisted things so badly that even people who are repentant and wanting to change are, in his eyes, classed amongst the wicked and ungodly. Those who live their lives according to Torah and strive to please Deity are also seen as wicked by Paul and his disciples throughout time.
Thankfully, the Torah and the rest of the Hebrew Bible does not give such condemnation. And since the Hebrew Bible is the foundation of truth, and Paul's logic is foreign to it, then no one really needs to fear Paul's condemnation, nor that of his modern day acolytes.

Chapter 7

verses 1-6

I'm just gonna put this in front of you just to let you think about it.

(1) Or are you ignorant, brothers - for I speak to those who know law - that the law rules the man for so long a time as he lives? (2) For the wife under a husband is bound, by law, for the lifetime of the husband. But if the husband die, she is made void [discharged] from the law of the husband. (3) Therefore if there be another man during the time of the husband, she shall bear the title "adulteress"; if the husband die, she is free from the law so it won't be that she becomes an adulteress with another man. (4) So too, my brother, also we have died to the law through the body of Christ to the end that we may be[long] to another who was woken from the dead, so that we may bear fruit to the Deity. (5) For while we were in the flesh, the influences of sin which are through the law were actively working in our body-parts in order to bear fruit for death. (6) But now, we have been made void [been discharged] from the law, being dead in that which we were held fast by; so too we serve in the newness of spirit and not in the oldness of the letter. (Romans 7:1-6)

Just read this and think about Paul's process of argument. What is the analogy? What is the reality that the analogy is describing? Does it really fit?

Whether you've done that or not, I'm gonna show you the analogy in simple terms with the reality that it is trying to describe so that we can come to some conclusions about what it is trying to say.

ANALOGY: As long as husband is alive, the wife must stay faithful to his law/rule until he's dead. After that she can marry another without guilt.

So this is the analogy. Question: Who dies? The husband! And who gets freedom by the husband dying? The wife!

OK, now let's look at the reality that the analogy describes.

PAUL'S REALITY: The believer [in Jesus] is dead to the Law (v.4) so that the believer can "marry" someone else, someone who has risen from the dead, i.e Jesus. The believer has been discharged from the law, since the believer is dead (v.6).

Now, that is the "reality". Question: who dies? The believer! And who gets freedom by the believer dying? The believer???

Wait there! The analogy is talking about the HUSBAND dying so that the WIFE can be discharged to marry someone else. But the "reality" has the BELIEVER being dead so that the BELIEVER can be discharged to marry someone else!?!

Now I believe you should be able to see the difficulty. One has the one person dying so that another can be free. In the other, we have someone dying in order for that same person, who is dead, to marry someone else. In order for an analogy to work, it has to be comparable with the reality it is trying to reflect. Paul's logic doesn't do that. To put in another way, in order for the analogy to work, the husband that should reflect the analogy, the law, should die; but instead, Paul kills the wrong person!

In essence, he is making no sense.

He compounds his error by seeking to deliver his readers and followers from the law, since it is old and decrepit in comparison to his "newness of spirit". Remember, he is saying that the believer is dead to the law. As you know, dead people don't uphold or keep laws. In fact, to be true to Paul's analogy, believers are discharged from being faithful to the law so that they can be married to Jesus! And this is odd considering the fact that in the same book of Romans, chapter 3 verse 31, Paul says that he doesn't make the law void, but rather, he upholds it! Yet he is saying that believers are dead to it and no longer need to be faithful to it. There is little difference between making the law void, and making void a person's commitment to it, which is what Paul's analogy ultimately points to: the discharging from, the making void of that relationship. The Greek in verse 2 and 6 of chapter 7 means to render idle, both referring to a nullifying of a relationship.

Now some may argue that they somehow fulfil the law by believing in Jesus. But there's a severe problem with this logic created by Paul himself. He is not advocating a righteousness that has anything to do with law! He is promoting a righteousness that only comes from belief in Jesus. It's as if Paul is saying that righteousness is the end goal, no matter how you get to it; thus you can get it [according to Paul, only theoretically] by law, or you can get it by faith. Now, assuming that this is true - which it isn't - Paul is by no means upholding law since he is still advocating a break away from it. His message never promoted law-keeping, but rather became foundational to both Jews, that is Jews that became christian, and non-Jews to move away from law-keeping and seeing large portions of it as abolished, redundant, surpassed, done away with, etc., which undermines the whole thing.

So looking at Paul's words here presents me with a mixed up picture of having one's cake and eating it too: essentially forsaking the law and yet claiming to fulfil it.

verses 7-10

(7) Therefore, what shall we say? Is the law sin? May it not be so! But I didn't know sin except by means of the law; for I didn't know also the lust unless the law said, "you shall not lust". (8) But the sin, taking opportunity by means of the commandment, accomplished within me all [sorts of] lust. For apart from law, sin is dead. (9) But I lived without the law for some time, but when the commandment came, sin became animated, (10) and I died and the commandment that [should be] for life was found to me [to be] for death. (Roman 7:7-10)

Paul here is speaking of supposedly the human experience, or at least it is interpreted as such by many christians. To him, once law is brought into the picture then the desire to break it arises within him. To him, without law, there wouldn't be sin! Although Paul says that the law is holy and good, but sin uses that law to kill people by making them do bad things and consigning them to death by the judgement of Deity by means of the law. In the context, Paul says that there is no good thing within him and thus it is impossible to keep the law, a law which gives life and strength to sin (1 Corinthians 15:56). Now this is only the personal sense, namely, Paul seems to be speaking personally.

Yet in Romans 5:13, Paul makes a similar claim that before the law, sin couldn't be "imputed". The word "imputed" is a translation of the Greek verb ελλογεω, euloge-o, which means "to put to a person's account; to lay a charge against someone". In this context, it means when there was no law, no one could be called a law-breaker, i.e., a sinner. Why? Because there was no law to break! But yet sin, somehow, existed. And Paul is clear to point out that he means "before the law of Moses" because, in Romans 5:12-14, he makes it a point to say that death came from sin, but although there was no law between Adam and Moses, death was still around!

Unfortunately, for all of Paul's arguments and logic, on both counts he is dead wrong.

With regards to the notion that sin could not be imputed before the law of Moses, a glance through the book of Genesis would set a person straight on such a notion. You see sin was "imputed" by the Almighty to the inhabitants of the earth in the days of Noah which is why the earth was destroyed by a flood (Genesis 6:5-7). According to Genesis 13:13, the people of Sodom were called wicked sinners, and in Genesis 18-19, they are held to account and killed because of that sinful status by Deity. The sons of Judah, Er and Onan, were killed because they did evil in the sight of Deity. Abimelech, in Genesis 20, and Joseph, in Genesis 39, were both afraid of the sin of adultery and knew it was a sin against Deity to commit such an act. All these are clear evidence that sin not only could be, but actually was charged against certain people and acts.

So on the first point about sin not being imputed, scripture shows Paul to be dead wrong!

With regards to the second point, Paul gives his own experience with sin and law. In his eyes, the holy law of Deity gives sin life and strength. But for others, the holy law of Deity gives a person strength to escape from sin by knowing and doing what is right in the eyes of Deity. Just read David's psalms, Psalm 19 and 119 and compare its glorious words about the law with Paul's essentially condemning words. It is the words of David that show the law to be holy, good, and righteous. It is the words of Paul that make it flawed, condemning, and essentially the cause of death.

Let me just show you a comparison between the words of Paul, and the words of the Law itself and David.

PAUL:

... and the commandment that was meant to be for life was found to me to bring death. (Romans 7:10)

For when we were in the flesh, the sinful passions which came about because of the law worked in our body parts to bring forth fruit that brought death! (ibid. 7:5)

The sting of death is sin, and the strength of sin is the law. (1 Corinthians 15:56)

Compare with the words of the Hebrew Bible:

(19) I make the heavens and the earth witnesses against you today: I have put before you life and death, blessing and curse, and you shall choose life so that you may live, you and your seed, (20) to love GOD your Deity, to obey his voice, and to cling to him, for he is your life and the length of your days ... (Deuteronomy 30:19-20a)

(8) The law of GOD is perfect, restoring the soul. The testimony of GOD is sure, making the simple wise. (9) The precepts of GOD are upright, rejoicing the heart. The commandment of GOD is pure, giving light to the eyes. (10) The fear of GOD is clean, remaining forever. The judgments of GOD are truth, all together they are righteous. (11) They are more desireable than gold, than much fine gold. They are sweeter than honey and the honeycomb. (12) Also, your servant is warned by them. In keeping them, there is great result. (Psalm 19:8-12)

(1) Blessed are they who are upright in conduct, who walk in the Law of GOD. (45) I shall walk in liberty for I have sought your precepts. (92) If Your law had not been my pleasure, then I would have perished in my affliction. (93) I shall never forget your precepts, because, by them, you have given me life. (165) Those that

love your law have much peace, there is no stumbling for them.
(Psalm 119:1,92,93,165)

Now, there is a stark contrast between Paul's view and the Hebrew Scriptures' take on the commandments. Where Paul sees essentially death, the Jewish Bible preaches essential life. Paul struggles within himself because he thinks there's no good thing within him. But the Jewish Bible teaches that there is the potential for good in creation, a good that obedience to the law brings out. Paul makes the flesh seem evil, but in the Hebrew Bible, even the flesh cries out for Deity (Psalm 84:2). As shown in the small sample above, love for the Almighty shown by keeping his law is life-giving, cleansing, liberating, life-changing, and essentially beneficial. In effect, the total opposite of Paul's words!

You see, the weakness with Paul's words is that he (or those who use his words) assumes that his experience is true for any law-keeper, or for any person in general. But the fact is that it isn't! King David is proof of that. The law helps destroy sin by aiming at both the action and the thought behind the bad things; it does not give it strength. It is not the law that gives sin strength, no more than the framework and structure of the house give strength to the forces that which to tear it down.

And to be direct and personal: the problem is not with the law - it's with Paul! The law doesn't make the "sin" inside Paul come alive: his own weaknesses do! In cases like this, maybe he should have kept them to himself. If he couldn't, maybe he should have visited the ancient version of a psychiatrist or counsellor. Unfortunately, his followers take on his weaknesses and feel convinced that they share it. Well, the law is a remedy for that sort of thinking!

verses 12 and 16

Paul makes the next two "positive" statements about the law:

(12) So too, the law then [is] holy, and the commandment is holy and righteous and good... (16) But if I do that which I don't wish to, I agree to the law that [it is] good. (Romans 7:12, 16)

Paul here seems to be saying something good about the law. It would appear that he's paying the law compliments by showing its "positive side". When he does a wrong thing, this only shows the law to be right. Those who love Paul will pounce on these few verses and say that he didn't disparage the law.

But let me give a small analogy of what Paul is actually doing. Fred goes to the doctors and finds out he has a serious illness. Shocked and dismayed, he asks his doctor for a remedy or some sort of cure or medication for his illness. The doctor gives him a bottle of pills and says that he must keep taking them regularly in order to survive the disease. He goes home and starts taking the pills. Then he receives a phone call from another doctor from another clinic who says the following:

"Hi Fred. I just had to call you because I've got some new information about the medication that old doctor gave you. That pill that you're taking is a great pill, fantastic, top of the range. In fact, the fact that you're sick shows that it is a great pill. But there's only one problem: it will kill you! In fact it can never cure you. There's a chance it was even given just to make sure that you were sick! In fact, it is known that the sickness will use the medication itself to ensure your death!"

Now Fred, who is suffering with this serious illness, would be shocked. The good things that the second doctor says about the pill would mean absolutely nothing. It matters diddly squat (i.e., not at all) that the second doctor said that the pill is great and fantastic. The important statements are that the pill is ensuring Fred's death, signing his death warrant, and dooming Fred's health and life! The words of the second doctor make the words of the first doctor into a lie. The pill essentially won't help him survive the disease: it will make sure that the disease ends him!!!

To put it bluntly, the second doctor did nothing to make the drug sound good. Those few words he gave does nothing in light of the context. He has basically said that a drug that should cure is actually a poison, and nothing can be as insulting as saying that something that was meant to give life actually brings death.

Paul does the same thing, going against the constant theme of the Hebrew Scriptures and saying that the law which "if a man does it, he shall live because of it" actually is the cause of death! There is little point in arguing that Paul is really saying that it isn't the law that brings death but sin. The fact is that such thinking still makes the law ineffective and powerless, as opposed to what the Lord himself said about the law in the Hebrew Scriptures, and makes it a tool sin uses to kill!

In essence, Paul is just paying lip-service to the law.

In this analogy, what should Fred do? The fact is that wisdom would tell Fred to check with the first doctor and his sources and clinic before he took the advice of the second doctor. In the same way, a person should check the sources first, the Hebrew Bible and its plain meaning. They'll then see the error and nigh-hypocrisy (if not full hypocrisy) of Paul.

verses 16-20

(16) But if I do that which I don't wish to, I agree to the law that [it is] good. (17) But now I no longer accomplish it, but the sin living in me. (18) For I know that in me (that is, in the flesh) dwells no good thing, for to will is present to me, but to accomplish the good thing, I don't find. (19) For I don't do the good I wish, but the evil I don't wish, that I habitually do. (20) But if I do that which I don't wish, no longer am I accomplishing it but the sin living in me. (Romans 7:16-20)

Paul here seems to be shifting the burden of guilt for his wrong doings to "the sin living in him": "It's not me, it's the sin!" That is an accurate paraphrase of verse 20. Then he says that in him, in the flesh, there is no good thing, and calls himself one bearing much suffering, distress and hardship, tortured and persecuted in verse 24 (translated as "wretched" in the KJV). Sin seems to take on a life of its own, making Paul do what he doesn't want to do, as if, without Jesus, he doesn't really have a choice.

Once again, Paul's words and views can be contrasted with the scriptural view of sin and choice. I'm not going to repeatedly quote scriptures that I have used numerous times before, but it just answers so many arguments Paul is spouting. In Deuteronomy 30, the message is clear that not only has a choice been placed before the people, but they have the power and ability to make that choice! Moses says that they cannot complain that the law is somehow beyond them since it is near to them in order that they can do it. He adds further that good and evil have been placed before them and plainly makes it known that they can choose which way to go and what actions to do (Deuteronomy 30:11-20). Again referring to Psalm 119, the psalmist says a significant number of times that he has chosen or taken the way of truth and righteousness (Psalm 119:30,111,173).

There is no point in saying that somehow Israel was somehow superior to the nations in this ability to choose, because from Cain, in the first chapters of Genesis, to Nebuchadnezzar and Nineveh in the books of the later prophets and writings, the same choice was offered! Cain was told that if he would do well, do better, then there would be acceptance, elevation, and forgiveness; he was told that sin is waiting at his door, but he can rule over it (Genesis 4:7). Nebuchadnezzar was told that he can break off from his wicked ways and do righteousness and kindness (Daniel 4:27). Nineveh was told of an upcoming judgment from the Almighty and turned away from their evil deeds, repented, and were saved (Jonah 3).

The notion that we are helpless slaves, "sold under sin" (Romans 7:14), is contradicted by the plain narratives and commands in the Hebrew Bible. Despite the negative things the Hebrew Scriptures may say about man, it always shows that righteousness is possible and that it is only a choice away. Even the flesh, which Paul condemns as a source of sin that is opposed to his "spirit" concept, can yearn for Deity (Psalm 63:1; 84:2). The fact is that in the Hebrew Bible people are responsible for their choices because they are able to make that choice. They are not forced or compelled by some "other" force dwelling within them. Each one of us has conflicting desires within us, but merit comes from exercising the choice that the Almighty gave us, even in the face of those conflicting desires. That's what makes us responsible. The flesh simply does the ultimate will of the owner of that body, be it righteous or wicked.

But just to reiterate, the scriptures show that we are not slaves to sin. Righteousness is possible, and it is just a choice away!

Chapter 9

verse 7

Paul quotes Genesis 21:12 to make the simple point that although Abraham had more than one son, it was Isaac through whom the special seed and promise should come to pass. This is one of those rare moments where, in this point alone, Paul actually seems to go with the plain understanding of scripture. But that is until we come to the next verse.

verse 8

That is, the children of the flesh these [are] not children of the Deity, but the children of the promise are regarded as offspring (Romans 9:8)

What happens a few times in Paul's writings is that he says something that actually seems to go with the plain understanding of scripture and doesn't contain much of his agenda-driven "interpretation", i.e., imposing his own doctrine onto scripture. But then he continues and reveals that really he was using it for his own devices. This is one of those times.

Once Paul makes the statement that it wasn't all of Abraham's offspring that were chosen, only Isaac, he then proceeds to say that only those offspring who continue the promise are really counted as true offspring, implying that he means those Jews in his own day that accepts his views about Jesus: they are supposed to be the true children of Deity.

But here we hit upon a snag, a problem. Paul's analogy only goes so far. In real biblical history, it is true that Isaac was chosen from all the other sons of Abraham, and that Jacob was blessed instead of Esau. But after Jacob, who was chosen or, more properly, singled out from amongst the brothers to receive Abraham's promise? None! They each became the different tribes of Israel and the promise was fulfilled through all of their children when they possessed the land and became the chosen and peculiar people of the Lord. Now although the birthright was Joseph's, the promise was shared through the 12 sons of Jacob and their descendants.

So the "children of promise" concept may have worked back in the days of Abraham, but they have no real applicability in the days of Paul, especially with his application of relying more on faith in Jesus than following the law of the Lord as given to the children of Israel in the days of Moses.

Essentially, Paul has no right to pick and choose who are the children of promise centuries after that time, especially when his words conflict with the history given to Israel.

It should be noted that Paul here is making a launchpad for his predestination message which says that some are chosen before they're even born, devoid of that person's choice in life. Let's see how this goes.

verses 11-13

The first thing that needs to be done with this little section is just to read it for what it says. This is important to deal with its claims.

> *(11) For when they [Esau and Jacob] were not yet born and not having done anything good or bad, in order that the purpose according to [the] selection of the Deity should remain - not from works but from the One that calls, (12) it was said to her that "the greater shall be a slave to the lesser" (13) even as it has been written, "I loved Jacob, but I hated Esau". (Romans 9:11-13)*

Now just look at the natural flow of these verses, taking all the words into account! What is Paul saying? Before Esau and Jacob were even born, a selection was made by Deity between Esau and Jacob without them having a choice in the matter or doing anything. Now note that Paul has said that this happened before they were born. It was for this purpose that the Almighty said that the older brother shall serve the younger, that Esau would serve Jacob. But Paul adds that it was written that the Lord hated Esau and loved Jacob. And all this is done to show that it is not about works, good or bad deeds, but just about "the One who calls". This is confirmed by the verses that follow this little passage as well.

Now it is true that one statement was given before Esau and Jacob were born, the one that says that the older shall serve the younger. That was definitely done before they were born (Genesis 25:23) and has no bearing on Deity's relationship with someone. Someone can be born into royalty and another into poverty and both have equal chance of having a good relationship with Deity.

But the next quote, the quote that says that the Lord hates one and loves the other, this was given centuries after Jacob and Esau were long dead (Malachi 1:2b-3a)! There is no statement about the sort of relationship the two brothers would have with Deity before they were born. Yet the way Paul quotes one and then the other with little distinction between is very misleading and can cause a person to think that the Lord also hated one and loved the other before they were born. What bearing does this verse have on the topic?

The context of Malachi 1:2b-3a makes the interpretation of the verses quite open. The passage is talking about the nations descended from Jacob, that being Israel, and Esau, that being Edom, and thus the Lord may be saying that he loves one nation and hates the other. But it could also be understood in the way that the Lord actually loved Jacob and hated Esau. But the main thing about this small section of Malachi is that it doesn't tell you when the Lord loved/hated either.

Plus, some may argue that Paul is just giving the one verse as a prophecy and the other as a fulfilment. But I would just ask those who make this argument to just read the verses. You'll find that one says "serve" or "be slave", and the other says "love/hate". One has nothing to do with the other, and Malachi says nothing about Esau serving Jacob. So such an argument lacks any real basis because the link between the two quotes is not strong at all in that way.

The main point of Paul is that Jacob was loved and Esau was hated independent of any deeds. But Malachi doesn't give this notion at all. The way Deity felt about either son before they were born has no part in Malachi chapter 1. Paul is actually giving a baseless and empty interpretation of Malachi, and here's why.

If one reads scripture they will take note of what the Lord loves and hates. Every single time it is an action, character trait, or a habitual way of living, a lifestyle. For example, in the book of Proverbs, the Lord hates seven things and each is an act (Proverbs 6:16-19), and, in Psalms, he loves justice (Psalm 33:5). There is a trend in scripture of the Lord responding to the deeds and ways of individual humans and groups. There is not one sign of the Lord expressing any of these positive or negative responses/"feelings" before a deed is done or a person is born.

To apply this to the verse in Malachi 1, it becomes apparent that, since there is no sign that the Lord had any "feeling" towards either person before their birth, there is another reason why the Almighty would love or hate the individual brother. If you read about the lives of Jacob and Esau, many reasons could be given as to why the Almighty would love Jacob and hate Esau. Jacob chose to desire the right things, even if he didn't always go the best way about getting these things. He obeyed the Creator and did as he was told. Esau had a powerful gift from birth in being the firstborn and having a birthright, but he despised it. And for what? For a bowl of soup! And when he found out later that his brother had taken his blessing from their father, Isaac, he swore to kill him. If you look at the actions of each nation throughout history, there are still signs as to why the Lord would still be faithful in his love for the nation descended from Jacob, and why he would despise the nation descended from Esau.

In essence, Paul has taken Malachi 1:2b-3a out of context since it has no bearing whatsoever to his argument. It says nothing about Esau serving Jacob, and gives no credence to Paul's notion that either brother was loved or hated before birth, whether we are talking about the brothers as individuals or as the nations that came from them. In fact, since his main point is how the Lord chooses to act with people regardless of their deeds, the general tenor of scripture and the history of the brothers and their nations refutes part of what Paul is saying. How? Because the Creator's love or hate of them was based on their actions, not on a choice before they were even born, which goes against Paul's point exactly!

verse 15

Paul continues:

(14) So what shall we say? Isn't there unrighteousness with the Deity? May it not be so! (15) For he says to Moses, "I shall have mercy on whomever I have mercy and I shall have pity on whomever I have pity. (16) Therefore not of the one who wishes nor of the one who runs, but of the mercy-showing Deity. (Romans 9:14-16)

Again, take in what Paul is saying. What he says here may also be applied to the previous point. Paul is saying, based on his version of what the Almighty said to Moses in Exodus 33:19, that it's not about what a person does that matters to Deity. It doesn't matter what you do! The Lord does what he wants when he wants to irrespective of the deeds or will of man. The Lord's words to Moses proves that, right?

Honestly, to some extent, on this point alone, there is some truth to this. I mean, we're talking of the Almighty Unchanging Creator who is beyond space and time. So in some ways, it doesn't matter what we do: he does as he wills (whatever that means on his level of "existence")!

But that's only to some extent! What about with this particular point? So far, Paul seems to be mixing two points: being chosen and being acceptable. I say that because so far he has talked about Esau and Isaac in both ways, and these ways are separate from one another. A person can be chosen for a particular task and be unacceptable to the Deity, and another can be not chosen for something and yet, in his station, live a life acceptable before Deity. So being part of a select group is not the same as being acceptable before Deity.

But what sort of text is Paul using here to buttress his point? Does it have to do with being chosen or with being acceptable before Deity? Since it is speaking of mercy and compassion, it has to be the latter: being acceptable.

So if Paul's point is that it doesn't matter what you do, Deity forgives who he wants to regardless, then does the context of Exodus 33:19 bear this out? The actual verse in Exodus says the following:

(18) And [Moses] said: Please, let me see your glory. (19) And [the Creator] said: I shall cause all my goodness to pass before your face, and I shall call out with the name of GOD in front of you; and I shall grant favour to whom I grant favour, and I shall show compassion to whom I show compassion. (Exodus 33:18-19)

The verse itself doesn't sound much different to Paul's version does, apart from the fact that Paul is actually saying "whomever", and the verse is just saying "whom". Paul just adds a bit more uncertainty as to who is getting the favour and compassion. Now it wouldn't be best for me to give an interpretation of this verse because there are just so many interpretations from different sides. We need to see what we can and cannot get from this verse.

What we can get from the verse is that the Almighty is speaking to his servant Moses, who has asked a favour of him, and that favour is granted. In the midst of this, the statement in question is said. Now what should be plain is that all the Almighty says, in essence, is that he does something nice to the person he wants to do it to. In this case, it is Moses. But what also should be plain is that there is no sign in this statement that it includes the notion "irrespective of what man does or wants". To clarify, the Almighty did not say, "I do what I want and it don't care what you do or want". It simply says "I show kindness to the person I show it to". This verse says nothing about whether man's will or actions have any impact on what kindness the Lord shows him. So it cannot do anything to support Paul's point. Paul is making a claim; this verse doesn't say anything about that claim; and so this verse cannot help Paul's cause at all. And it doesn't.

In fact, when it comes to mercy and compassion, it is obvious that man's action to play a role in how it is given. In the context of Exodus 33, the Almighty is showing compassion to Moses by answering his prayers and showing him his glory. So he shows his kindness to a righteous man. In the context of Torah, the relationship between Israel and Deity depends on Israel (Leviticus 26;

Deuteronomy 11,28,30; Jeremiah 3:12,13; 2 Chronicles 7:13,14) to the point where the nation can choose to do what the Lord says and be blessed, or disobey and be cursed. In the context of the whole Hebrew Bible, the Almighty shows mercy to people dependant on what they do (Ezekiel 18,33; Proverbs 28:13). So these show that the Almighty's mercy can and does depend on man's will and acts, which contradicts Paul's words.

So Paul's contention that mercy and compassion are given irrespective of deed is false. Also Paul takes a verse out of context to make a point, since the verse in context gives no support to what he's claiming.

verse 17

Paul continues:

(16) So therefore, it is not of those who wish nor of those who run but of the mercy-showing Deity. (17) For the scripture speaks of Pharaoh that "for this, this, I raised you up so that I may demonstrate in you my power and that my name may be declared in all the earth. (18) So therefore, whom he wishes he has mercy, and whom he wishes he hardens.(Romans 9:16-18)

Before I begin, it's necessary to reiterate the point that Paul is trying to make, i.e., that it doesn't matter about the will, desire, or actions of man; the Almighty does what he wants. He has mercy on who he want and, here, he makes stubborn whomever he wants, regardless of whether a man does good or evil. Paul's argument here is that the Lord set up Pharaoh up in order to make him stubborn, irrespective of whether that king of Egypt had done good or bad. This was preordained even before the guy was born.

But look at what the scripture actually said:

(14) For in this time, I'm sending all my inflictions to your heart and upon your servants in order that you may know that there is none like me in all the earth. (15) For now, I could have stretched out my hand and struck you down and your people with an epidemic, and you would have been destroyed from the earth. (16) However for this reason I have caused you to stand firm [other translations say "preserved you alive" or "maintained you" or "caused you to remain"]: in order to show you my might, and so that my name may be recounted in all the earth. (Exodus 9:14-16)

Now look at the verse in context! The Almighty is talking, saying that he could have destroyed Pharaoh and his people already. But there is a reason why Pharaoh still exists. Because the Almighty is using him to make his might known throughout the world! But what does it mean, to cause to stand firm? Well in this context, we only have to use the previous verse to help us understand the current one. In this case, we find that the Lord could have destroyed Pharaoh already, whilst he was still king. But rather than the Almighty destroying Pharaoh earlier, he has let or kept the king of Egypt continue in power. So this is about the king remaining in power, nothing about a plan that occurred before birth. In fact, there is nothing overt in the text that would make a person think that this was some pre-ordained plan. Well, at least, no one without an agenda to see predestination in the text.

The text and the context is rather clear: although the Lord could have killed the king of Egypt already, he has let him continue to live and stay in power so that the world may hear about his power and uniqueness. The notion that the Lord is speaking of some pre-ordained purpose before Pharaoh was born doesn't fit the context or the flow of the sentence very well.

Also let's talk about the hardening of Pharaoh's heart. Was this done irrespective of his will? Did the Almighty simply force himself on Pharaoh's will? Or did the Creator pre-programme him and the situation? Is this borne out by the story? If you actually chart the progress of the plagues that the Lord sent to Egypt and the hardening of Pharaoh's heart, you will find that for the first five plagues, Pharaoh hardened his own heart first, and only after that it is said that the Almighty hardened Pharaoh's heart. So although the Lord said that he will harden Pharaoh's heart, this process was only started after Pharaoh rebelled of his own choice. Thus, it appears that the Lord's hardening of Pharaoh's heart was a judgment against Pharaoh, rather than the Lord pulling Pharaoh's strings from the beginning. It is a consequence of Pharaoh's own rebellion.

Therefore it cannot be said that what the Lord did had nothing to do with Pharaoh's will or actions. It was Pharaoh's own rebellion which brought about the judgment in the hardening of his heart and then his downfall.

To summarize, Paul's point is that the Lord acts regardless of what people do or think. But Exodus shows that the Lord responded to what Pharaoh did and thought. Thus, in the end, it actually ends up refuting Paul's case rather than helping it. So, in the end, this is another case of Paul taking a verse out of context.

verse 25-26

Unfortunately, the situation doesn't get any better with Paul's rendering of scripture as we shall see in his next quote.

(22) And [what] if the Deity, willing to demonstrate the wrath and to make known his power, bore with much longsuffering a vessel of wrath fitted for destruction (23) And so that he would make known the richness of his glory upon a vessel of mercy which was prepared-beforehand for glory? (24) Us whom also he called not only from out of the Jews but also out of nations, (25) as also in Osee he says, "I shall call the not-my-people my people, and the not-beloved beloved..." [quoted from Hoshea 2:23] (26) "... and it shall be, in the place where it was said to them, You [are] not my people, there they shall be called sons of living Deity." [quoted from Hoshea 1:10] (Romans 9:22-26)

This is the beginning of another of Paul's lists of so-called scriptural proofs and supports for his claims. What we need to do here is to be wary of what he is quoting and where he is quoting it from in order to see if his words actually fit with what the original passages are saying.

So what is Paul saying here? He is making a claim that people who are not Jews, namely Gentiles, are now the people of the Lord. He uses a verse in Hoshea (in the Greek, it sounds like O-say-eh or O-see-eh and is spelt similarly, "Osee"). Now from what I read of christian commentaries of this verse, there is a general, majority view that Paul here is using these verses in Hoshea (or Hosea in xtian versions) and applying them to Gentiles. That means that where it says "I shall call the not-my-people my people", the "not-my-people" is the gentiles who the Almighty, according to Paul, now accepts as his people and children of living Deity.

I would implore you, the reader, to take up the book of Hoshea and read it from the beginning with the mind to let it, the book of Hoshea, speak for itself. The prophet wrote quite clearly, so I don't think you should find much difficulty. Take account of context, both in regards to time and the text itself, and you will find a startling yet obvious truth! What is this truth? It is the answer to the question of who Hoshea is talking to and who he is talking about.

I'll summarize these two chapters of Hoshea to answer that question. In the time of the kings of Judah and Israel, the Lord came to Hoshea telling him to marry and have children with a whore, because he wants to show how the nation of Israel has turned to whoredom with other gods, turning away from following Deity (Hoshea 1:1-2). So a context has already been set: we are dealing with the bad ways of the nation of Israel. Seeing that we need to find out if the subject of the topic changes to speak of the Gentiles, we need to read on.

This whore, called Gomer, has a son. The Lord tells Hoshea to call the boy Jezreel since, in the end, he is going to end the kingdom of

Israel (ibid. verse 4). So the conversation subject is still the same: Israel and what is to befall it due to its sins. The whore then has a daughter who the Lord names Lo-ruhammah (meaning, no compassion); and the Creator gives the girl this name because he's going to have "no compassion on the house of Israel" (ibid. verse 6). Again, we are talking about Israel the nation. We can know he is talking about Israel the nation because in the next verse he compares his negative treatment of Israel to the better treatment he'll give to the land of Judah. So we're talking about countries of a specific people group called Israel, the nation.

Now all this time, the Almighty has been speaking to and about the nation Israel. So we come to the final son Gomer has, and the Lord calls him Lo-ammi (not my people) because he says "you are not my people" (ibid. verse 9). Since the subject hasn't changed from the beginning, we can know that he is still talking about Israel, saying that they are no longer his people. Now continuing in the christian English version (since the Jewish version starts a new chapter here), it says the following:

And the number of the children of Israel shall be like the sand of the sea which can not be measured nor numbered. And it shall be that the place where it was said to them, you are not my people, it shall be said to them: children of the living Mighty One! (Hoshea 1:10 in xtian versions)

Note the recipient of the blessings in this verse: the children of Israel; and to them it is said that "you are my people" and "children of the living Mighty One". This is, again, made plain by the fact that the next verse speaks of the land of Judah and the land of Israel gathering together and having one ruler. In order for it to point to someone else, the text has to be ripped unnaturally from its textual context, and all meaning made fuzzy and arbitrary (based on individual [or group] choice and selfish desire). And guess what! By spiritualizing clear texts like these, Paul and his followers commit that dishonourable act to and against the word of Deity. For them, it seems like it doesn't matter what the words say, but what they want it to mean.

There are two ways in which this act of only hearing what you want applies to what Paul and his followers throughout history have done to these "proof texts". They can be described in two twists of an analogy:

It's like a man having two sons, one called Jerry and the other called Michael. The man dies and leaves behind his last will and testament that states plainly: all the house goes to my son, Michael. And Jerry, wanting to possess the house, says that his name is now changed to "Michael" and claims ownership of the house and attempts to kick the original Michael out of the house, or at least belittles his claim to it. But people outside the house still call Jerry by his original name, "Jerry", but when Jerry wants to, when he wants to be linked to something he wants that should belong to Michael, he claims again that his name is "Michael" and claims what should belong to the original Michael. That is theft, both of identity and property. Yet Paul and his followers do the same here. But that's only if - and that's a big "if" - they are paying attention to the biblical context.

If they aren't paying attention to the biblical context and just taking verses and statements out of context, then what they are doing is like Jerry, in this analogy, hearing the will say "to Michael: I leave all the house to you", and yet, because he wants the house, totally ignoring the words "to Michael" and just taking on board the words "I leave all the house to you". Thus Jerry selectively hears the words and understands it as "I leave all the house to you, namely Jerry".

In either case, it is a gross mistreatment of the word of Deity.

Now I only dealt with Hoshea 1:10 which Paul quotes. But he also quotes chapter 2 verse 23. Question: has the subject of Hoshea's prophecy changed between chapter 1:10 and chapter 2:23? Well, the passage continues by going back to the analogy of Gomer being like Israel in her whoredom, and her children pleading with her. It shows the abuse she is treated to in her harlotry, still in that Gomer-Israel analogy, and the Lord alluring Israel back to him, a state compared to when she came out of Egypt (ibid 2:15 in xtian versions). No part of the whole passage shows any sign of changing subject: from beginning to end, at the very least of these two chapters in question, it starts with Israel and it ends with Israel.

So what can I say? There is absolutely no sign that Paul has tried to explain the verse as it is written. Rather, he seems to simply use the words of Hoshea out of natural context for his own purposes as a support for claims that have no strength or basis in the biblical passages he rips to shreds.

Unfortunately, the disappointment continues.

verses 27-28

Paul then gives the following quote:

(27) And Esaias cries out concerning Israel, Even if the number of the children of Israel [is] as the sand of the sea, the remnant shall be saved. (28) For he is finishing and cutting short a word in righteousness, because the Lord shall make on the earth a word cut short. (Romans 9:27-28)

For all those wondering what "a word" is in verse 28, it is most likely a word of prophecy, i.e., the prophecy being fulfilled and its period of fulfilment cut short.

So we have Paul quoting Isaiah 10:22-23. Let's look at what that says.

(22) For though your people, Israel, be as the sand of the sea, a remnant amongst it shall return; destruction is determined, overflowing with righteousness. (23) For [it is] a destruction and it

is being decreed; Lord GOD of hosts is doing [it] in the midst of all the earth.

Now if you read both of these versions, Paul's and the translation of the Hebrew, you will see that they don't say exactly the same thing. Paul speaks of "cutting short a word in righteousness". Isaiah says nothing about this. In fact, Isaiah speaks of the opposite: overflowing with righteousness. One speaks of a cutting short and the other speaks of abundance. So Paul isn't quoting Isaiah properly here.

This is due to the fact that Paul is relying, at this point, on the Septuagint, also called the LXX, the ancient Greek translation of the Hebrew Scriptures. And it is well known that the LXX is notoriously bad when it comes to translating the book of Isaiah as can be seen here. I'm not gonna bother with some claim that the LXX may have used other Hebrew versions since that is a claim based on no real fact. It's best to use what we have. So Paul is working using a lousy translation.

But not only is Paul guilty of using a bad translation, he is again guilty of a method he makes use of so often that it seems to be his normal mode of operation. What is that method, in case you don't know? Well, if one were to look at the whole of Isaiah 10, you will see that it has very little, if anything, to do with what Paul is talking about. The constant theme of Isaiah 10 is the Lord using Assyria to discipline a nation that worships idols and the events and judgments that flow from doing that. Both before and after verse 22 and 23 in Isaiah 10, Assyria, or Asshur, is mentioned and referred to, once with the Lord telling the people how he is using that nation (vs 5-11), then how he will punish them (vs 12-19), what will happened to Israel in those days (vs 20-23), and lastly how the people of Judah should be comforted in the fact that Assyria will not touch them (vs 24-32). As can be seen, this has nothing to do with Paul's claims. The time setting is all wrong. Assyria didn't exist in Paul's day.

So basically, he has taken the verses out of context, paying no attention to what the context is talking about, but just using some of its verses to boost his own agenda.

If Paul is simply using this verse to say that a similar case exists in his time where a remnant shall be saved, he still relies on a lousy translation and it does nothing to help or prove his case, since to just say "this happened then and is happening now" is an overly-superficial, out of context, understanding of Isaiah 10:22-23, and doesn't prove any link between the two incidents. So in this case, the usage of such a scripture does nothing for Paul's case

verse 29

Paul continues his barrage of verses:

And even as Esaias said beforehand, if the Lord of Sabaoth had not left over for us a seed, we would have been like Sodom, and would have been similar to Gomorrah [quoting Isaiah 1:9]. (Romans 9:29)

Now how Paul is using this verse is uncertain. If he is saying that his situation is similar to what was said in Isaiah's time, then his usage is valid, although it does nothing to add any scriptural authority to his words. It is not as though Paul is using it to back himself up. He is just using his opinion to judge the majority of Israel as being condemned and outcasts. That's his opinion, and Isaiah gives him no authority to make such a judgment. His own opinion doesn't mean very much.

If Paul is using these words to give himself any scriptural foundation, then the rug is swiftly pulled from his feet once a person looks into the passage he quotes from. Isaiah wasn't talking about Paul's time and his, Isaiah's, words were not foretellings of the future, but rather a statement about how his people were in his time. Thus, Paul is still relying on his own opinion to judge and condemn his fellow Israelites, an opinion that has, so far, been seen to be questionable on all levels: biblical, logical, and realistic.

verse 33

So far, Paul's verses don't seem to be really proving his point. And then he says this:

Even as it has been written: See, I place in Sion a stone of stumbling and a rock of entrapment and anyone who believes on him/it shall not be disgraced. (Romans 9:33)

This passage or quote is used by Paul to show that although the nations who didn't pursue righteousness still get a righteousness based on faith, Israel, who had a law of righteousness, didn't get righteousness because in relying on the deeds of law-keeping they stumbled with regards to Jesus, who Paul sees as this stone.

Let's ask the first and primary question: where is Paul quoting from? Where is this verse taken from?

What you may be surprised to know - if you didn't know it - is that what Paul has done here is to take verses from two different chapters of Isaiah, separated by around 20 chapters, taken different bits of each verse, and glued them together in some odd unity. Here are the verses.

(13) GOD of hosts, Him you shall sanctify, and he is your fear, and he is your dread. (14) And he shall become a sanctuary and a stone for striking [the foot] and a rock of stumbling for the two houses of Israel, for a trap and for a snare to the inhabitants of Jerusalem. (Isaiah 8:13-14)

Therefore thus has my Lord GOD said: See me, he [who] set in place a stone in Zion, a tested stone, a costly corner, a firmly set foundation, the one who trusts shall not make haste. (Isaiah 28:16)

Now look at what Paul has done: he has taken a part of Isaiah 28:16, and then glued it on to Isaiah 8:14, and then glued the final part of Isaiah 28:16 at the end. This makes up his proof-text, a subtle piece of biblical editing. It cannot be said that Paul was quoting one and then the other separately; he is actually melding two verses into one.

Can such a treatment of scripture be called honest? And if Paul was mistaken, then how can the "holy spirit" have inspired his work? The holy spirit is known not to be the author of error, so who put this error into Paul's work? As far as I can see, either Paul is mistaken and thus his words cannot be inspired by the spirit of the true Deity, or he is editing the words of the Almighty which is an unnecessary and dishonest act which also means his words cannot be inspired by the true spirit of Deity. If the word of the Lord doesn't say what a person wants it to say in the way that person wants it said, that doesn't give anyone the right to chop a section here and add it to a section there, or mix up two verses to make it look as if it is one verse. The way Paul has misused these verses can only be seen as deceptive.

What makes the problem worse for Paul is that Isaiah 8:14 isn't talking about Jesus, or even a messiah. In that passage it is the living God himself who is the stone, and the time of the prophecy is set in the age of Assyrian empire. There is no overt messianic meaning to these verses. But such a thing is said when you simply try to read the passage and what it is saying, rather than having the idea of Jesus in your head and reading that idea into scripture. But in such a case, that person isn't reading scripture: they are simply reading the product of their own ideas whilst scripture remains silent.

Isaiah 28 is an ambiguous text which makes for a difficult text to use for backing up a point such as Paul's, and it still seems to refer to a time around that of Isaiah, not the distant future. Within the context (see Isaiah 28, especially verse 21), it speaks of the Lord rising up as he did when David defeated the Philistines (Perazim, 2 Samuel 5) and like he did when it aided Joshua against the 5 kings in Canaan (Joshua 10). Nothing like that happened in Jesus' day. And there is nothing overtly messianic about the text; there is nothing that shows that it's talking about anything to do with the future Davidic king. So again, Paul is walking directly on quicksand barefooted.

No matter how Paul's usage of these verse can be seen, it all comes out with the same result: being wrong and possibly being despicable.

Chapter 10

verse 4

Paul then makes a startling statement. I'll give it in the Greek first and then the English. Hopefully it won't put readers off.

τελος γαρ νομου χριστος εις δικαιοσυνην παντι τω πιστευοντι
For christ is the end of law unto righteousness for all the believers.

The key word in this verse is τελος, telos, which is here translated as "end". This has been the centre of controversy between christians who believe the law is done away with and is now ended, and those Paul-lovers who think that Paul didn't have such a hard-line, "law-is-totally-finished" view. They both have their understandings of what this word means. Part of my time in christianity included being part of this debate. And the proper understanding of this verse will tell us how people who just accept the Hebrew Bible alone, and not the christian "new testament," should view Paul.

So what does this word, telos, mean? The verbal form of this word, tele-o, means "to end", i.e., to complete, execute, conclude, dicharge a debt. It is from a primary verb, tell-o< which means to set out for a definite point or goal. Thus the word telos means "the point aimed at as a limit, a conclusion of an act, a termination point, a result, impost or levy. That is according to Strong's dictionary. It is further discussed by Thayer who confirms most of this, but adds that in general ancient Greek writings, it does mean the termination point of a state or an act, but not of time or space, where other Greek words would be used; but in "scripture", it can include those meanings. One of Thayer's definitions is "to put an end to", which, in his dictionary and in this discussion, is very relevant.

With all this in mind, let's look at the contextual meaning of Romans 10:4. Paul has been saying that law-keeping doesn't make a person righteous, and doesn't give righteousness, but rather faith, faith in Jesus, does. In Galatians, Paul compares the law - we are still talking about the law of Moses - to an ancient type of servant who would lead young children to their destination, e.g., to school. So in Paul's mind, the law leads people to Jesus. In Romans 9:31, Israel follows after the law of righteousness but cannot reach its standards. And in the verse directly before the one in question, Romans 10:3, Paul says that the Jews are ignorantly trying to get a righteousness of their own, rejecting the righteousness of the Almighty. Now if we put this together, Paul is equating Jews trying to get their own righteousness with them following the law of Moses (cf. Romans 9:31 with 10:3). So to the Jew, in Paul's eyes, law-keeping is a way of getting righteousness. This then leads us into what chapter 10 verse 4 means.

So what does Paul mean in this verse? Remember, the translation is that "Christ: the end of law unto righteousness for all the believers." The phrase "law unto righteousness" means the law towards righteousness, or "the law in order to have righteousness". In this verse, it means that Jesus is seen as the end of keeping the law in order to be righteous or to have righteousness; and this is the case only for those who have faith, who believe in him. This coincides with so much that Paul has been saying throughout the book of Romans and all his books. Those who have faith already have the righteousness which comes from faith, and thus they do not have to keep the law to get righteousness. This does match how Thayer understood this verse, when he says concerning the word telos,

... i.q. he who puts an end to: ... Christ has brought the law to an end ... (Thayer's Greek Lexicon, under the heading τελος, telos)

Remember, keeping the law to be righteous, or to get righteousness, is now finished for those who believe in Jesus. That, I conclude, is Paul's point.

But why was the law given in the first place? Not only did it maintain the holy, set-apart status of Israel, it granted them life and good, sustained their special relationship with Deity, and it was righteousness for the people (Deuteronomy 6:24-25; Leviticus 18:5). All of this can be seen just by reading the book of Deuteronomy. Later scriptural passages show that it is what a person does and how he lives that makes a person righteous, not simply what he believes (Ezekiel 18:5-9).

There is nothing at all stated in the Hebrew Scriptures that shows that the keeping of the law, even for righteousness, would come to an end. And understand that it must come to an end if what Paul is saying is true. The law's most significant purpose is to order people's lives according to the will of Deity, i.e., make them righteous. There is no point in saying that some people, like so-called messianic "Jews" - or more properly, christians editing and ripping Judaism's oral law - keep the law just to show that they are grateful to the Almighty, and not in order to be righteous, because, even logically, that is the whole purpose of law: to govern a person's conduct according to a standard, in this case, the Divine standard. In essense, law is meant to make a person righteous. If you are not keeping law to do that, then it is simply an empty gesture, since its main purpose has been terminated.

Again, the Hebrew Scriptures say absolutely nothing about the law coming to an end. In fact, it says the absolute opposite, prophesying that in the world to come, the law will be written upon people's hearts to the point where they keep what it says naturally. Remember, I said they keep the law, not that they believe in the 10 "commandments" whilst believing the entirety of the rest of the law is nailed to the cross. I don't mean those who pick and choose which "moral" law they deem to be applicable today. The law which spans across the books of Exodus to Deuteronomy comprises of hundreds of commands, not just 10. And it is that law which will be kept in the restored world (Jeremiah 31:30-33; Ezekiel 37:21-24). The very last prophet in the Jewish Bible imposed that message upon his listeners/readers amongst his last words:

> *Remember the law of Moses my servant, whom I commanded on Horeb, for all Israel, statutes and ordinances. (Malachi 4:4)*

Paul is reaching the message that says that, in one way or another, the law is terminated, that it has come to an end. But this is only in rebellion and defiance against what the word of the Almighty, the Hebrew Scriptures, say for themselves.

verses 5-8

Here comes another of Paul's "wonderful" uses of scripture. If you have read this work from the beginning, you'll know that that is sarcasm.

> *(4) For Christ is the end of the law unto righteousness for all the believers. (5) For Moses describes the law-derived righteousness, that "the man who does it shall live in it" [Leviticus 18:5]. (6) And the faith-derived righteousness speaks in this manner, "Don't say in your heart, who shall ascend into the heaven?" [Deuteronomy 30:12] - that is to bring Christ down - (7) "or who shall descend into the deep?" [Deuteronomy 30:13?] - that is to bring Christ up from the dead. (8) But what does it say? "The word is near to you, in your mouth, and in your heart" [Deuteronomy 30:14] - that is the word of faith that we proclaim: (9) that if ever you shall confess in your mouth Lord Jesus, and believe in your heart that the Deity raised him from the dead, you shall be saved. (Romans 10:4-9)*

I have stated elsewhere how Paul rapes, plunders and pillages that passage from Deuteronomy 30 which is hacked to pieces in this portion from Paul's writings, but here, I shall at least give a brief summary of Paul's "usage" of these verses.

Paul here is trying to show that the righteousness of the law speaks one way and the righteousness of faith speaks in another way. To him, the law speaks in the way that if you manage to do the law, then you can live by it. So basically, you have to work for it. A person who has already read through the beginning of Romans will see that Paul thinks this is impossible as the law just condemns people to death. But then Paul says that the righteousness of faith says, who can do anything? - who can go up or down to retrieve salvation/Christ? Rather it is close to you already, and it is the word of faith that he preaches: all you need to do is have that faith and say it! One way is based on action, the other is based on the fact that we cannot do anything, so it must be done for us and we simply accept it by faith.

The problem with Paul's interpretation of each verse can be seen in the context of each verse. In Leviticus 18, the Lord through Moses is .... wait there, let me just quote it for you:

(1) And GOD spoke to Moses saying: (2) Speak to the children of Israel and you shall say to them, I am GOD your Deity. (3) According to the deeds of the land of Egypt in which you dwelt you shall not do. And according to the deeds of the land of Canaan to which I am bringing you, you shall not do. And in their statutes you shall not walk. (4) My decrees you shall do, and my statutes you shall observe to walk in them. I am GOD your Deity. (5) And you shall observe my statutes and my judgments which the man shall do and live in them. I am GOD. (Leviticus 18:5)

What is the subject matter of this passage? The Almighty is showing the Israelites that it is HIS laws that should be kept and followed, and not that of other nations, and by keeping his laws, as opposed to those of the surrounding nations, a man would have life. So this verse is one that points more to promise than condemnation. The Almighty was not giving laws that couldn't be kept and thus consigning the Israelites to the same fate of death as if they had kept the laws of the foreigners. By that, I mean that the Lord is saying don't keep the laws of the other nations because they are wrong and lead to death, whereas his laws lead to life. But if he was asking for perfect performance of every single law, something which no human can do, then the Israelites would always fail and thus be punished with death. Thus if they keep the laws of the nations, they would die. And if they try to keep the law of Deity, they would fail and thus die. Thus they would be in a "damned if you do and damned if you don't" situation.

Let's be blunt about this idea Paul is trying to convey. It is utter nonsense to supposed that the Deity who "knows our frame, that we are dust" (Psalm 103:14) and who chose Israel out of love for their fathers (Deuteronomy 10:15) would give a law and demand impossible observance, and then punish Israel with terrible curses and death for not keeping what cannot be kept. For someone to knowingly do this is absolute cruelty. The very notion is stupid no matter what seemingly intelligent words you try to put around it. It just doesn't follow from the premise. To say to someone you care for, "I love you and know you intimately, and because of this I'll make things impossible for you and hurt you!" It doesn't matter what level you are in life, such a sentence is nonsensical and illogical based on the definitions of the words. It's almost as illogical as a square circle, so such a notion cannot exist realistically.

To sum this up, the Lord was giving the Israelites a promise and a benefit to keeping his commands and avoiding the ways of the other nations.

To summarize the problems with Paul's interpretation of Deuteronomy 30:11-14, one simply has to look at the context to see that Moses was talking about the law, and that it is near to the

Israelites and not beyond them so that they can do it. Here, let me quote it with some context for you.

(9) And the LORD your God will make you over-abundant in all the work of your hand, in the fruit of your womb, and in the fruit of your cattle, and in the fruit of your soil for good; for the LORD shall once again rejoice over you for good just as he rejoiced over your fathers, (10) when you listen to the voice of the LORD your God to guard his commandments and his statutes written in the scroll of this Torah, when you return to the LORD your God with all your mind and with all your life.

(11) Because this commandment which I'm giving you today is not beyond you and it is not far off. (12) It is not in the sky [for you] to say, "Who is going to go up to the sky for us and get it for us so that we shall hear it and do it?" (13) And it is not across the ocean [for you] to say, "Who is going to go across for us to the other side of the ocean and get it for us so that we shall hear it and do it?" (14) Because the word is so very close to you, in your mouth and in your mind {for you} to do it. (Deuteronomy 30:9-14)

Now it's very important to see what Paul has done here. Look at what the original passage is speaking of. It is only talking about obedience to God's commandments. This is the very same "righteousness of the law" he just ascribed to Leviticus 18:5. But Paul throws all that away and does a hatchet job to scripture, removing every word about law, cutting out certain sentences and phrases, and interspersing his own words about Jesus. But there is no "Messiah" or "Jesus" in the natural message of Deuteronomy 30. There is no "descending into the deep" in Deuteronomy 30, neither in the Hebrew, nor any version of the Septuagint available to me currently. It is all about the Israelites obedience to the law and the blessings that flow from keeping it and the choice and consequences involved. Yet Paul inserts his own words, an alien message, into the text. This just shows that the text itself doesn't really help his case, but rather his agenda twists biblical texts for his own purposes. Paul has essentially violated scripture.

I may repeat myself but I want you to really think about this! Where did Paul quote from to make his case? He says that the righteousness of the law speaks one way and the righteousness of faith speaks another way. But where does he quote from to show the righteousness of the law? He quotes from the Law, namely Leviticus! Now where does he quote from to show the righteousness of faith? From the same law, namely Deuteronomy! A law that Paul portrays as being void of or contrary to faith is quoted to show the righteousness of faith. Now that's a weird one! It just makes the point more serious against Paul that the quote about the righteousness of faith is edited and distorted, and the original context spoke only of law! If Paul was in any way honest and accurate, he would have to call both quotes the righteousness of the law without adding anything to it. But I guess that would be asking too much of Paul!

In essence, Paul is making things up that don't exist. He violates scripture and shows no reluctance to twisting and ripping it for his own self-righteous ends.

verse 11

(9) ... that if you confess in your mouth Lord Jesus and you believe in your heart that the Deity raised him from the dead, you shall be saved. (10) For with the heart, one believes unto righteousness; and with the mouth one confesses unto salvation. (11) For the scripture says, All who believe on him shall not be disgraced. (Romans 10:11)

Paul here quotes again the final part of Isaiah 28:16 as he did in Romans 9:33. It has already been briefly shown that the passage in Isaiah doesn't say anything about a messiah, and its description is different to anything to do with Jesus. So Paul is simply taking the verse out of context since it has nothing to do with faith in Jesus.

verses 12-13

(12) For there is no difference between Jew and Greek, for the same Lord of all [is] rich to all those that call him. (13) For all who shall call on the name of [the] Lord shall be saved. (Romans 10:12-13)

Paul here makes use of a biblical verse, Joel 2:32, to conclude his claims.

Now Paul did not say his usual formula of "the scriptures say" or something like that, so there is a question as to whether this is a proper quote or a reference. If Paul is trying to use it as a quote, then it doesn't help him when you look at the context. If you read through the book of Joel in a christian version, looking through all of chapters 2 and 3, you'll note that the words of the prophecy don't match the experience of Paul, or anyone currently in existence. The context speaks of there being deliverance in Jerusalem and Zion, but for many hundreds of years they lay in ruins. And chapter 3 says that in the day such things happen, i.e. those who call on the name of the Lord shall be saved, the Lord will return the captives of Judah who were exiled in a different land. That never happened. And the Lord negatively judging the nations, in Paul's preaching the exact opposite is happening, with the nations attaining to righteousness when the Israelites couldn't. There is no mention of "messiah" and people call on the name of the Almighty, not the name of the man Jesus. So the message of Joel as a whole is distinctly different to that of Paul.

If it is merely a reference which Paul is using for his own ends, then it doesn't really mean or prove anything.

verse 15

(14) Then how shall they call to him whom they don't believe? And how shall they believe that which they don't hear? And how shall they hear without preaching? (15) But how shall they preach if they be not sent? Even as it has been written, How timely [are] the feet of those announcing good news of peace, of those announcing good news of good things [Isaiah 52:7]. (Romans 10:14-15)

If you have been reading through this work, you won't be surprised about what I have to say next about Paul's usage of this verse in Isaiah compared to its original context.

The original context of Isaiah 52 speaks of the redemption of Israel from those who held the Israelites captive, Judah's deliverance from her physical enemies. Verse 1 speaks of no more uncircumcised and unclean people entering Jerusalem, and verse 8 speaks of the return of Zion. Verse 9 speaks of the Almighty comforting his people and redeeming Jerusalem. The context all throughout Isaiah makes it plain that we are speaking of Israel and literal Jerusalem.

But what is Paul talking about? Jews and Gentiles believing in Jesus and hearing the "good news" concerning him! But this is a totally different message to what Isaiah is giving. In Paul's day up until today Jerusalem hasn't been comforted, and it still a thorn to many a nation. There are still uncircumcised and unclean people walking its streets. The message is not the same. In fact, in total contrast to Isaiah's message, Jerusalem was under the rule of the Romans and due to be destroyed in Paul's day.

I don't need to add much more. It is just another case of Paul taking a verse out of context to forward his agenda.

verse 16

(15) But how shall they preach if they be not sent? Even as it has been written, How timely [are] the feet of those announcing good news of peace, of those announcing good news of good things. (16) But all have not obeyed the good news, for Isaiah says, "Lord, who has believed our report?" [Isaiah 53:1] (17) Then faith [is] from report, and report [is] through the word of Deity [or "word of Christ" in some Greek manuscripts]. (Romans 10:15-17)

Before I continue with this critique of Paul's use of Isaiah 53:1, a person who knows the book of Romans, or who reads it using a normal christian translation, will note a strange translation of verses 16 and 17, e.g. "faith is from report". This is just to highlight the fact that the very same Greek word is used every time the word "report" is used. This approach differs slightly from translations like the KJV which translate the first "report" as "report", and then translate the following phrase as "faith is of hearing". This definitely helps the reader understand the sentence, but the word link Paul appears to be using disappears. Other translations like the NIV just add more words to try and convey the message, but lose the fight to be a "word-for-word" translation, preferring to convey what they think it means rather than what it says. In the translation I use above, you can just replace the word "message" with "report", since the word simply refers to either the act of hearing or what is heard, namely, in this case, a message or report.

So Paul here refers to the words of Isaiah, as if Isaiah is speaking of what Paul is speaking of. That is how Paul phrases his words. But was Isaiah really talking about not all people believing the good news about Jesus?

Now it must be noted that Isaiah 53 is a hotly contested scripture between Jews and Christians (and yes, I include "Messianic Jews" under the umbrella of "christian"). I've known both sides of the issues, being once a christian, and now under the umbrella of Judaism. And it is clear that, if we base our understanding of Isaiah 53 on its context from Isaiah 40 to 53, and that of the Jewish Bible, then Isaiah 53 does not speak of any messiah figure, but rather of the nation of Israel being spoken of prophetically and poetically. This is seen by the fact that the only time the Hebrew word "anointed one" or "messiah" appears in this context, it refers to Cyrus (Isaiah 45:1), and whenever "servant" is mentioned, it refers either to Israel or Isaiah, since they are the only characters that are in the context that fit the description. And Israel is repeatedly called "the servant" throughout the context. A future Davidic king is absent from the text. Simply read Isaiah 40-54 and, based on the text, see who the servant is. It can only be Israel in Isaiah 53, the nation spoken of in the singular, as is done frequently throughout scripture.

Thus, what is Isaiah 53:1 really talking about? In the verse before, Isaiah 52:15, it speaks of the nations being startled at the servant. Note the textual signs: nations are spoken of in the plural (more than one), and servant is spoken of in the singular (just one). Thus when the next verse, Isaiah 53:1, therefore says "who believed our report", then it can be known who is speaking. Since "our" is plural (more than one), and we have a choice between the nations (plural - more than one) and the servant (singular - one), then the "our" refers to the nations: the nations are talking in Isaiah 53:1 about the singular nation, Israel. For those who may not know, the chapter and verse division in scripture are not divinely inspired and they were not part of the original texts of scripture. Thus Isaiah 52 flows straight onto Isaiah 53.

So Isaiah is talking about the nations being surprised at Israel's exaltation after they had seen his humiliation, and stating "who believed our report" as a startled rhetorical question like "who would have believed what we heard"? Paul is talking about people not believing the "good news" of Jesus. So once again, the message is not the same; Paul has taken another verse out of context.

There is even a chance that Paul's view of this verse didn't even agree with the christian understanding of what verse 53 was talking about. Some christians see the nation Israel, or Isaiah representing Israel, speaking in Isaiah 53:1, which also doesn't fit with Paul's view.

Now whether you agree with the interpretation of Isaiah 53 that I gave or not, or you accept the christian understandings of Isaiah 53 - even if you think Paul's message was right - this is just one out of many verses lifted and cut off from their natural context in the Hebrew Scriptures. So I'll just move on.

verse 18

But I say, Haven't they heard? Yes, "their sound went into all the earth, and their words unto the ends of the world." [quoting Psalm 19:4] (Romans 10:18)

Paul here quotes the psalm, but the question is in what way did he mean it? Is this a proper quote or him just taking the words and giving them a different meaning?

Let me be very very plain here. Psalm 19 has nothing to do with the "good news" that Paul preaches. It speaks very plainly of the wisdom of Deity as seen in the objects in the sky, namely, the sun and the moon. So Paul isn't even beginning to expound on the content of Psalm 19:4. The psalm goes on to praise the many benefits of the law, something Paul only gives lip service to.

What Paul has done, yet again, is take a piece of scripture out of context and give it a meaning that is foreign to its original setting. So scripture is by no means backing up Paul, no, not at all. Paul's agenda is supreme, and scripture must bow! Now the empty verse in Paul's hands speaks of the "good news" of Jesus being heard throughout the land.

I say again, the Psalm doesn't back up or support Paul at all. Paul's agenda is supreme, and scripture must bow!

verse 19

And it continues ...

But I say, didn't Israel know? First, Moses says, "I shall make you jealous with a no-nation, with a senseless nation I shall make you angry." [Deuteronomy 32:21] (Romans 10:19)

Now this is an interesting one for the following reason: christians actually base their understanding of the original verse in Deuteronomy on Paul; they would defend Paul's understanding of it whilst explaining the meaning of the verse (see Keil and Delitzsch's Commentary of the Old Testament and Gill's Exposition of the Whole Bible, both of which comment on this verse). They take the "make you jealous" hyper-literally to mean that Deity would literally make a covenant with another nation and have a relationship with that foolish nation whilst casting off Israel.

Now some may argue with my using the phrase "casting off Israel" since some christians don't believe Israel is cast off. But just understand what they are really saying and its implications. The only way Israel would be jealous is if they didn't have that relationship that the nations are now supposed to have with Deity because of Jesus. Now Israel had a special relationship with God from the beginning, a very special one. So they must have either lost that relationship in order to be jealous, or the nations get a better one. Paul's words throughout this chapter has involved being chosen and not being chosen. So it would appear that the nations are now the chosen people and the Jews are not, thus they would be made jealous.

But let's just focus on Romans 10:19 here: Paul is saying that this verse in Deuteronomy means that Deity will have a relationship with a "no-people", a "foolish nation" to provoke the Israelites to anger and jealousy. But what does Deuteronomy 32 and the rest of the Hebrew Scriptures have to say?

Firstly let's take note of what Deuteronomy 32 does and doesn't say. It says nothing clearly about how the Lord would provoke Israel using this foolish nation. But there are clues within Deuteronomy itself. Remember that the Lord is punishing the Israelites due to their disobedience and idolatry. Check out Deuteronomy 28 where it says in verse 14, 15, 33, 36, 49, and 50, that if the Israelites would go after strange gods (idolatry) and commit disobedience, then the Almighty will send a strange nation against them who they don't know, whose language they don't know, who would come and smash them to pieces. It does reflect the song that Moses is singing in some ways, and is a clue to what the Lord is talking about when he speaks about using a certain senseless nation to provoke Israel.

But what does the verse/passage say? The very same verse says the following:

They have made me jealous with a no-god; they have made me angry with their empty acts. Then I shall make them jealous with a no-people, with a foolish nation I shall make them angry. (Deuteronomy 32:21)

Now take careful note of what this verse, even on its own, is saying. When does the Almighty make Israel angry and jealous? Only after they have worshipped idols, or "no-gods", things which are not gods, concretely idols.

Now even Paul never ever accused Israel of idolatry. At best, he said that they had ignored Jesus or cast him away, but he never accuses them of idolatry. And they were not guilty of idolatry in the times of Paul; this crime is never charged against them as a whole. So if it's the case that this verse is talking about something that is supposed to be happening in Paul's day, then a very important part of it is missing, i.e., the very reason why the Lord would provoke Israel. And if the reason isn't there, then the judgment can't be happening. In other words, Paul has put the cart in front of the horse; he has tried to build the body of a house and forgotten to make sure there was a foundation. And guess what! In this case, there is no foundation. So the house, his usage of this quote, just falls down!

What else does this verse say? It says that the Lord will make Israel angry with a foolish nation. What is a foolish nation? It is a nation that is foolish. You may think I'm being a bit simple here, but it is the simplicity of this that slaps Paul's argument across the face in order to embarrass it. Israel would be provoke by a nation. Now christianity was not and is not a nation, especially now with all these conflicting and feuding denominations. Also, each christian maintains the nationality of their own nations: there are Spanish christians, Turkish christians, Chinese christians, etc. Christianity is not a nation, it is a faith, a belief system! There is no such thing as the nation of christianity, even amongst the majority of christians. There is no strong evidence of such a concept in the new testament, so there is no need to deal with made-up arguments christians may use when confronted with this argument. Their own scriptures don't give them a firm basis in order to make themselves a nation. When you hear terms such as "this country is a christian country", e.g., America is a christian country, they are not saying that some christians have banded together and made a nation of christianity, if such a thing could exist. It just means they expect the country to have christian values. Now a real nation isn't about value. There is more to England and France and Germany and New Zealand than just values, morals, or faith. In fact, there is more to Israel than just values, morals or faith. Christianity has nothing to do with birth or nationality. Using the normal understanding of the word, both in Paul's day and now, the followers of "the Way", Nazarenes, Christians, Messianic Jews, whatever they choose to call themselves, they are not a nation!

Just to finish off the point, just compare christianity to the non-Jews who fear the Deity of Israel but are not christians. They are a group of people who have the same beliefs and worldview, but they are scattered all over the world. They have a knowledge of the Almighty and faith in him. They would never call themselves a nation because they know what the normal meaning of the word is. The same is true for the people of "faith" Paul is admonishing: they are not a nation! Thus, they cannot be the people, the nation, who the Almighty would use to provoke Israel.

Secondly, the rest of the Torah (5 books of Moses) as well as the prophets help clarify what is meant here and the limits of its meaning. Leviticus 26, like the Deuteronomy 28 which I referred to above, shows the Lord using Israel's enemies to attack it and put it into exile in order to cause the nation, Israel, to turn back to him. Each time he is using the foreign nation to make Israel see its obligation to him. He never chooses and makes covenants with other nations to the same or greater extent to that of Israel in order to make them jealous. No such thing is prophesied in scripture. Such a thing is unheard of throughout the whole Jewish Bible. That Bible never says that the Lord would make a covenant with or choose another people. Every time the Creator uses another people to provoke Israel, it is not by making that other nation his people, but by having that nation trounce, mash up, and horribly defeat Israel and/or putting Israel into exile or under subjection.

So basically, the whole Jewish Bible objects to Paul's distortion of Deuteronomy 32:21. Paul makes it seem as though Moses was prophesying concerning what he was talking about. But this is nowhere near what Moses was really talking about. Again, Paul's agenda wins out.

verses 20-21

(20) But Esaias ventures boldly and says, "I was found by those who didn't seek me. I became manifest to those that didn't enquire after me." [Isaiah 65:1a] (21) But to Israel he says, "I stretched out my hands all day to a nay-saying and dissenting people." [Isaiah 65:2a]
(Romans 10:20-21)

Paul here is making the claim that even Isaiah the prophet knew and made known the fact that the Gentiles, those that didn't seek the Almighty, would find him, whilst Israel would reject him. But I think we should stop right here and quote Isaiah 65:1-2 with some context just to see what is really being said.

(9) GOD, don't be angry greatly, and don't remember iniquity continually. Behold - look please! - your people [is] all of us. (10) Your holy cities have become wilderness: Zion has become a wilderness; and Jerusalem a desolation. (11) Our holy and beautiful house where your fathers praised you has become a burning of fire; and all our coveted things have become waste. (12) Will you restrain yourself based on these things, GOD? You are silent and have

afflicted us greatly. (65:1) I granted access to "they don't ask"; I allowed myself to be found to "they don't seek me". I have said, "I'm here, I'm here" to a nation not called by my name. (2) I have spread my hands all the day to a contrary people those that walk in the way not good after their thoughts. (Isaiah 64:9-12 in xtian versions; 65:1-2)

Now when one reads the context, it becomes obvious that Paul's interpretation makes no sense. I've only shown you this small section of Isaiah which starts and finishes speaking about Israel, and no other nation. Zion and Jerusalem belong to the Jews and that is who Isaiah was talking to. There is no split between verses 1 and 2 of Isaiah 65. There is no sign that the Lord has started speaking about the Gentiles. In fact, his words are a response to the previous prayer (Isaiah 64:9-12) and he is still speaking to and about Israel.

In fact, if chapters 64-66 are read allowing the natural meaning of the words to speak for themselves, then it will be seen throughout the whole passage, the main direction to which this prophecy is focused is Judah/Israel. The main flow of the passage is for no other nation!

Now some may pounce on the words "I have said "I'm here, I'm here" to a nation not called by my name". They would say to themselves that Israel is supposed to be called by the Lord's name. They would use verses like 2 Chronicles 7:14 which, speaking of Israel, says "if my people which are called by my name" to prove that point. They would then say that since Isaiah is talking about a people not called by the Lord's name, then that must mean not Israel, i.e., the nations! These people would then accept Paul's words and apply these to christians.

But I would ask the reader to just do one thing before jumping into such a crowd. I would ask you to think! Stop and think! First think on one level: the context! The context points irresistibly to Israel. Thus the question can be asked if this is wholly literal. Is the Lord literally talking about another nation? Or has he just seen enough wickedness by his own people, in that they are not acting like a people called by his name, that he just calls them that: "a people not called by my name"? This would be the same as a father seeing his son do terrible things and say that this boy is not his son. He doesn't mean it literally, but shows how far the boy has departed from the right way he was taught. Or it could be that the rebellious boy doesn't want to be regarded as the father's son. Thus, due to context, it should be understood that this phrase about not being called by the Lord's name is not about another nation.

But then think on another level: the actual words used in this phrase: "a nation not called"! Understand that it doesn't say "not a nation", but rather "a nation". This is one of the greatest advantages Israel has over nations that would try to usurp this verse: Israel is actually a nation. But the nations are not "a nation"! And, as has been shown before, neither christianity nor christians are "a nation". In their minds, they may imagine that on some "spiritual" realm they are a nation, but here, in real life, they are no nation. They are just a group of believers who loosely share the same belief: that Jesus is the promised anointed Davidic king.

Did you know that many nations could respect the sovereignty of a king and still be classed as different nations? So the fact that all these christians accept Jesus as their king does not make them a nation.

All in all, once again, Paul shows himself either to be only concerned with his agenda as opposed to honest interpretation of scripture, or to be a deceiver twisting scripture to entice people into a snare. Either way, the truth of scripture doesn't shine through Paul's misusage of it.

Chapter 11

verses 2-6

Although this quote has some length to it, I think it needs quoting.

(1) Therefore I say, Hasn't the Deity rejected his people? May it not be so! For also I am an Israelite, from the offspring of Abraam, tribe of Beniamin. (2) The Deity didn't reject his people whom he foreknew. Or didn't you know in Elias what the scripture says how he entreated to the Deity against Israel saying, (3) Lord, they killed your prophets, and they have destroyed your altars, and I alone remain, and they seek my life [1 Kings 19:10 or 14]. (4) But what does the divine response say? I have left behind for myself seven thousand men who haven't bent knee to Baal [1 Kings 19:18]. (5) Therefore also in the now time there has been a remnant according to the selection of grace. (6) And if of grace [it is] no longer out of works, else the grace is no longer grace and if out of works [it's] no longer grace, else the work is no longer work. (Romans 11:1-6)

Paul uses these experiences of Elijah to show that, even in the past, Israel had forsaken the Creator, but the Lord had reserved for himself 7000 men. And this reserving, based on what Paul is saying, had nothing to do with the actions of the men: it was just out of grace, i.e., just on the Lord's decision to give, paying no attention to the lives and lifestyles of the men he had "reserved".

But yet again, Paul's "interpretation" falls in light of the natural context of the experiences of Elijah.

Before I get into why and how Paul's interpretation falls and fails, it is interesting to note a slight change in what Paul seems to be quoting here. Now normally, if you were to have access to the ancient Greek translation of the Hebrew Scriptures, the Septuagint or "LXX", you would note that so far, Paul has generally been quoting in agreement with this translation. Yet all of a sudden, with this passage, he seems to be comfortable to paraphrase, ignoring certain words that can help in understanding the verse properly. Also, whilst ancient commentators and translations, including the LXX, put 1 Kings 19:18 in the future tense ("one shall leave 7000"), Paul, followed by his christian followers and translators, put it in the past tense ("I have left 7000)". It's a strange pick-and-choose policy Paul has when it comes to referring to scripture in whatever version or translation.

But getting back to the issue at hand, what is the contextual understanding of the verses that Paul quotes from? Has Paul been explaining scripture or making it say what he wants? Do these verses provide support for his point? First I'll deal with the contextual interpretation of the verse Paul uses, and then we'll look at the very words that is in the verse.

Now Paul's depiction of 1 Kings 19:10 (or 14) where Elijah complains about the way the Lord's sacred institutions have been undermined and about his being left alone alive of those that serve Deity. There's nothing too wrong with Paul's representation of that verse.

But when you continue reading through to the 18th verse of 1 Kings 19, then you will see a sequence of events that the Lord puts into motion:

1. He tells Elijah to anoint a new king of Syria;
2. He is also to anoint Jehu as king of Israel;
3. Elijah was also sent to anoint Elisha as a replacement prophet for Elijah himself;

After all this, whoever escapes the death the new king of Syria will cause, then they will fall to Jehu. And if not Jehu, then Elisha. And from all this, the Lord will leave remaining 7000 men. These men will survive this slaughter. This agrees with the Jewish interpretation, the form of the Hebrew verb, and, amazingly, the LXX with its odd translation of this verse. It flows with the context of what will happen, rather than some abrupt and odd recollection of what has happened already.

In fact, even christian commentators accept this interpretation, even when using the past tense that the King James and other christian versions use!!! (But to no surprise they still think Paul has some validity!)

So the context of 1 Kings 19 shows no sign of grace devoid of works. There is no clear sign in the passage that shows this "salvation by grace". In fact, it is quite inconsequential. But it is the words of the verse that Paul uses that messes up his plans. Why? Because the verse specifies who exactly will remain alive from all these slaughters, and it is not simply anybody. According to the verse in 1 Kings, all who haven't worshipped Baal will be spared. So it is people who have done something who will be saved. If it were just 7000 people irrespective of deeds, then why even mention this deed of refraining from Baal-worship? The very same verse Paul uses to say that these people were "reserved" based on grace alone devoid of deeds shows that these people were set apart from those who were to die by the very deed of refraining from Baal-worship!!!! I guess, based on Paul's logic, it isn't really grace then!?! Thankfully, we don't have to be so limited in our thinking!

The fact is that 1 Kings 19 says nothing to back up Paul's logic that if grace is involved, then works can have nothing to do with it. The verses he uses contribute nothing positive to his point. In fact, they may be spitting in his face whilst he's using them.

verse 8

(7) Therefore what? Israel searches diligently for this and he didn't chance upon [it] and the selection chanced upon [it] and the rest were hardened, (8) Even as it has been written, the Deity has given to them a spirit of slumber, eyes that they don't see, ears that they don't hear, until this day. (Romans 11:7-8)

When I first began to realise that there was something wrong with Paul, and that his method of scriptural interpretation is highly suspect, I thought that it was only in Romans 9:33 where he takes two verses, chops them up, sticks them together and offers them as if they are one. I held this opinion for years. But when I actually decided to do this deeper look at all of Paul's usages of scriptures, I found this other "quotation" that I had overlooked for some time.

Now remember, throughout Paul's books, especially in Romans, whenever you hear the phrase "as it has been written" or something similar like "and this bible character says..." or "the scripture says", that normally means that a reference or quotation is coming next. Now look again at Paul's quotation. If you looked for those words being contained in the same verse in about the same order, then you would come up with nothing! There is no scripture that contains all these words in this order! And even in the much-adored Septuagint, that "blessed" ancient Greek translation, you wouldn't find such a verse!

So is Paul getting this all out of his head? Actually no! If you do a search for some words from each half of this quote, you will find that there are two verses in the Jewish Bible that carries traces of each part. I'll show you them.

For GOD has poured over you the spirit of deep-sleep, and he has firmed up your eyes. He has covered your prophets, and your heads, and your visionaries. (Isaiah 29:10 - Hebrew version)

(2) And Moses called to all Israel and he said to them, You, you have seen all which GOD did before your eyes in the land of Egypt, to Pharaoh, and to all his servants, and to all his land; (3) the great trials which your eyes saw, the great signs and miracles. (4) But GOD didn't give to you a heart to know, and eyes to see, and ears to hear until this day. (Deuteronomy 29:2-4)

Also, just for the sake of argument, let me also quote the Septuagint version which Paul loves to use, when he feels like it.

Because [the] Lord has made you drink a spirit of slumber and he shall close the eyes of them, and their prophets, and their rulers, the ones that discern the hidden things (Isaiah 29:10 - LXX version)

(2) And Mouses called all the sons of Israel and he said to them, You, you have seen all which [the] Lord did in the land of Aigupto [that's Egypt - DD] in front of you to Farao and to his attendents and to all his land, (3) the great trials which your eyes saw, those enormous signs and wonders, (4) and [the] Lord the Deity didn't give to you a heart to know nor eyes to see nor ears to hear until this day (Deuteronomy 29:2-4 - LXX version)

Now look at any version of these two quotes, and compare them to Paul's "quotation". Here it is again:

PAUL:

The Deity gave to them a spirit of slumber, eyes that they don't see, ears that they don't hear, until this day.

Now you should be able to see the editing and distorting that Paul has done to these two verses which talk of two different things at two different times. I'll focus on wording first and then context.

It should be rather plain that Paul is using both of these passages. If you look at the middle part of Isaiah 29:10 in the Greek version of the Jewish Bible and Paul's verse, they both speak of a spirit of slumber, with Paul using the same Greek words as the LXX to describe this sleepy and comforted-to-the-point-of-tiredness state (note, one of the words is in a slightly different form). But before and after this Paul departs from every ancient version of scripture. At the beginning he says "the Deity gave to them" whereas the Hebrew and Greek speak of the introduction of a liquid to a human body, the Hebrew saying "For GOD has poured out over you", and the Greek version saying "Because [the] Lord will make you drink". This says a lot more than Paul's version.

But where does he get "the Deity gave to them"? Look at the Septuagint version of the Torah in Deuteronomy 29:4 and you will note that it says something almost similar to Paul's words but it says it in a way opposite to what Paul saying. Both the Hebrew and Greek versions say that the Lord did not give them certain heart or eyes. But Paul says the Lord did give them a certain heart and eyes. Again, this is Paul's editing as opposed to the pure word of scripture. In Deuteronomy, the Lord did not hardened Israel's hearts and eyes, but Paul says that the Lord did!

So it can be seen that Paul has chopped certain texts and combined them, as well as switch words around to make up a verse that doesn't exist. That is called distortion.

But if you also look at the context of both scriptures, you'll see that Paul really had no right to combine the two passages. They are talking about two different subjects and times, both being limited to the time period of the author. In Isaiah's time, he was prophesying about a coming spirit of deep-sleep which was part of a punishment upon Israel because of disobedience (see Isaiah 29:13). In Moses' day, he was speaking those words as he was giving the Israelites the re-iteration of the law, and the covenant at Moab. There is no contextual proof that disobedience was the cause of their not having ability to truly understand what they had seen. The text simply says that the Lord did all these acts in Egypt and that although Israel saw them, the Lord hadn't given them "a heart to know and eyes to see and ears to hear" until this day.

Now the question is this: what does "until this day" mean? It can mean Israel doesn't have these things "until this day" and even now (without any change in the situation). Or it can mean that Israel didn't have these things "until this day" but now they do have these things (showing a change in the situation). The context shows that in this case it means the latter, that they did not have these faculties before, but now they do. This is shown by the following verses which show that the Almighty didn't give them these assets but led them through the desert those forty years in order for them to gain such a knowledge and understanding shown in their knowledge of him (Deuteronomy 29:5-6). It's as if the Almighty is speaking here of the experience that the children of Israel had to go through and all of their trials that needed to be accomplished for them to get that heart of understanding.

So what does this all have to do with Paul's point? Paul is saying that Israel have a spirit of slumber and eyes that don't see and ears that don't hear and a heart that doesn't understand even to his day. But Moses never lengthened Israel's inability to fully perceive the knowledge of Deity up until Paul's day, only until the end of the forty year trek in the wilderness. Isaiah said nothing about the condition of the people in his time period lasting until Paul's day or anyone else's day. Unfortunately, all of the "classic" (in age, not in popularity) christian commentators I read interpret "until this day" to mean even until their and our present time, i.e., the Jews are blinded and dulled to the "good news" of Jesus until now, showing that they have inherited the error of Paul.

Now this in itself, the wording and the context of both scriptures that Paul uses, should show that Paul is guilty of editing scripture to his own whims and personal agenda, and taking it out of context. The Jewish Scripture which Paul quotes do not contextually speak of anything similar to what Paul is talking about. If there were such passages, he would use much clearer scriptures, rather than having to splice verses together that are contextually alien to each other.

verses 9-10

(9) And Dabid [David] says, May their table become a snare and a trap and a trip-up and a recompense to them. (10) May their eyes be darkened that they not see and may their back constantly be bent down. [Psalm 69:22-23] (Romans 11:9-10)

Paul is speaking of none other than the Jews, those Jews who rejected his "good news", who he sees as being blinded and made dim-witted as he has claimed in the previous verse (Romans 11:8). Again, the question should be asked whether Paul is expounding scripture or going with his normal mode of operating and taking verses out of context in order to prove a point of his choosing. His christian followers have taken his words very seriously to the point of calling Psalm 69 a messianic psalm, by which they mean that they think it speaks of Jesus. But have they just been led astray by Paul and their own preconceptions?

The only way to know this is to look at the original psalm of David. First we can see if this is messianic, and then we can see if it has any bearing on Paul's discussion.

We can quickly lay to rest any idea that it is talking about the sinless Jesus imagined by Paul and his christian followers. Verse 5 clearly states that the person experiencing everything in the psalm had foolishness and had committed trespasses/sins (Psalm 69:5). So much for the idea of a sinless man!

Let's now see if it has anything to do with Paul's point where he curses Jews that don't believe him or Jesus with these words from the Psalms.

Now although it can be seen that Paul does not quote from the Hebrew version and thus has numerous errors in his translation, there is still a more fundamental problem with Paul's interpretation. The problem is that the Psalm's introduction already tells us who is most likely talking: king David! And if not him, then someone around his time who would give the psalm to be added to David's collection so it could be called a psalm belonging to David. This at least tells us who is talking when words like "I" and "me" are used. There are no overt signs whatsoever that this psalm has anything to do with Jesus when all of it is read. In fact, the psalmist is simply writing a "praise passage" that anyone can sing or pray. There is no specific prophecy in it that would point to a specific time or place. If a person wishes to make more of this Psalm and force some literal quality to it, then it can only speak about the person who wrote the

Psalm, namely, David. He is the one that goes through his turmoils, acknowledges his sin, and prays for his foes to be ashamed and defeated.

With nothing in the Psalm to point to Paul or Jesus or the Jews of their time specifically, then it cannot be classed as some deliberate prophecy against them. Rather, Paul takes these words and purposefully curses those he sees as his enemies: those Jews who don't believe. Now Paul is entitled to see as an enemy anyone he wants. Unfortunately he has no scriptural authority behind his words.

To just make a small but still important point, this is just another example of christians wanting a text to speak about their messiah-figure, and then reading those ideas that they already accept into scripture. Some would call this eisegesis, reading ideas into the text; others would call it painting Jesus onto scripture where he's not there. Whatever you call it, it is an unfortunate form of scripture distortion which the "new testament", especially the Pauline letter, is full of. It is always such a shame that such notions have been swallowed whole by so many people of the nations who originally had no link to the Hebrew Scriptures and tradition, and also by those misguided Jews who forsake their rich and divine heritage to embrace so horrible and unjust a way of interpreting scripture.

One more reason to dislike Paul!

verses 11-25

I'm not going to quote this section, but in it Paul says that the Gentile believers are grafted onto a tree. What tree? I don't know, the text never really says. Israel? It would seem to be so. If we take for granted the idea that Paul was saying that somehow Gentiles become part of Israel just by believing, then Paul's claim must be a lie or a claim without foundation or support from the Jewish Bible, which can be seen by the fact that he doesn't quote anything in this section.

Not much more can be said about a foundationless claim.

verses 26-27

(25) For I don't wish you to be ignorant, brothers, [of] this mystery so that there may not be amongst themselves those conceited that there has been a hardness/stubbornness of parts to Israel up until the fulness of the nations shall come in. (26) And in this manner shall all Israel be saved, even as it has been written: The deliverer shall come out of Sion, and he shall turn ungodliness away from Iakob [Jacob]. (27) And this [is] a covenant with me for them whenever I may forgive their sins. [Isaiah 59:20-21a] (Romans 11:25-27)

Another quote from Paul which he is using to show that Israel will turn to his doctrine, i.e., "be saved", when "the deliverer", who Paul sees as Jesus, comes. This deliverer would remove ungodliness from Israel. This may be a sign of the second coming in Paul's eyes.

But have you seen what the actual text of the Hebrew says?

(20) And a redeemer shall come to Zion, and to those turning away from transgression in Jacob, declared GOD. (21) And me, this [is] my covenant [with] them, said GOD: my spirit which [is] upon you, my words which I have set in your mouth, they shall not depart from your mouth and the mouth of your offspring and from the mouth of the offspring of your offspring, said GOD, from now and unto everlasting. (Isaiah 59:20-21)

Let's note the obvious differences between Paul's "quote" and the actual Hebrew Scriptures. Now according to Paul and the version he uses (this time he does agree with the LXX), the deliverer to come would "turn ungodliness away from Iakob". So it is the deliverer doing the turning. But the actual Hebrew version, the original language says that a (not "the") redeemer shall come to Zion and that's it! In this instance, he is coming to those who are already turning away from their sins, i.e., repenting. So it is the people who are turning away from sin/trespass, not the coming redeemer.

Also, Paul has the line "whenever I may forgive their sins". Neither the Hebrew version nor the LXX has this line. It seems as if Paul just adds it from who knows where. And it is an addition to the passage because he continues talking with the "I" and "me" fashion as the verse properly starts as if the Almighty is speaking. So this is an unscriptural addition by Paul.

So what do we make of this proof-text of Paul? In each of its important points, Paul's "quote" fails miserably. He's wrong when he says that the deliverer removes ungodliness from Zion, since the scriptures say that a redeemer will come to those who are already turning away from sin. And the part about this happening whenever the Lord forgives their sins is not even part of that scripture.

So basically, Paul has nothing to go on here.

verse 28

Please note carefully what Paul says:

> *(28) Certainly, according to the good news, [they are] enemies because of you, but according to the selection, [they are] beloved because of the fathers. (Romans 11:28)*

A verse full of double talk and serious meaning! The Jews have no merit of their own, but only due to the fathers. But they themselves are enemies, because of and to the Gentile believer in Jesus. This verse does nothing to promote peace and paints the Jews as having no good to them except that of their fathers. Paul seems to preach both hatred and love at the same time. So at least on one level, he curses the people chosen by the Most High, regarding them as enemies. But the Almighty said to Abraham, with a promise that was given to his descendants also, "I will bless those who bless you and curse those who curse you", or in another way "your friends are my friends, and your enemies are my enemies". If Paul has become an enemy to the Jews, then he may have a greater Enemy to deal with: the Almighty himself.

verse 32

For the Deity has shut everyone up together into disobedience [impersuadability, obstinancy, rebellion] so that he may have mercy on all.

This seems to be consistent with the apparent doctrine of Paul concerning the ineffectiveness of man's will and the irresistible power of the Creator over man's will. In this verse, the Creator has everyone closed in and trapped in a state of disobedience just to have mercy on them.

I, for one, am thankful that this idea has no basis in the Jewish Bible, and that this is just Paul blowing out hot air and writing vanities.

Why the Septuagint always loses to the Hebrew version

Just an aside: Some may wonder why I keep on relying on the Hebrew and I don't seem to pay the Septuagint much mind, only using it to say whether Paul's quoting agrees with it or not. There may even be those who think that I should be treating the Septuagint with much more respect.

But to be blunt, there is no reason to pay too much respect to the Septuagint or any other translation into any other language, including English, especially in such important matters as proving biblical interpretation and doctrine. Now although there is some accuracy and a lot of general truth in translations, their eternal weakness will be that they are translations! What are translations? They are the attempt of a translator to bring across what he believes to be the meaning of a word and passage. It is at this point where we hit upon the problem on two levels.

Firstly, although the original words of the prophet in their original language (Hebrew) were divinely given and inspired, the translator does not have this divine guidance! Thus he (whether by himself or in a group of translators and scholars) cannot claim perfection! And thus secondly, and linked to that first point, the translator must use his own knowledge of both languages and his own judgement regarding words with more than one meaning in order to convey the meaning of the words from the original language to his target language. This is basically the same as a commentator who looks at a text and tries to explain its meaning to those he is communicating with. That's why translations will always be on the level of commentaries. They may be authoritative commentaries, but they can still be toppled if they disagree with the natural reading of the Hebrew text and the traditional and cultural understanding of the words by those who have always had and maintained the language, i.e., the Hebrews or the Jews. Just like you don't go to Spain or China to get an authoritative ruling about or interpretation of British laws and texts, you don't rely on people of different nations to get an authoritative understanding of the Hebrew text.

Even if the translator is from the same place as the mother language, many factors are involved in translation that adds subjectivity to the process, like the choice of which, for example, Greek word to use in the place of a Hebrew one. Just dealing with the translations in this work showed me the difficulties involved in translating Greek or Hebrew into English. And rulings/interpretations based on different translations will always be weaker than rulings/interpretations based on the original language, especially when in reference to or in the context of the original culture.

A third point is that Hebrew words don't mean exactly the same thing as Greek words. Therefore when a word or passage is translated, although some main gist can be carried across, important details can be missed because of the inability of one language to exactly replicate the other. You can miss some of the important points that come from word order, from missing letters or seemingly superfluous ones.

In essence, the closer you are to the original, the closer you are to truth. The further you are from the original, the closer you are to error. Translations are a few steps and levels away from the original.

For these reasons, the Hebrew copies we have, no matter how young or old people may say they are, will always have a higher authority than a translation, no matter how ancient! This is regardless of the fact that the Hebrew versions were maintained, kept, and copied in a highly scrupulous and painstaking fashion, keeping an extremely high level of uniformity (sameness) in every copy we have, whereas most translations, including the Septuagint, were not kept with such care, with evidence of several versions, revisions, and editing of those translations. The Septuagint itself has a jaded and ambiguous history and uncertain origin which makes claims about its authority extremely doubtful.

So that's why it doesn't matter too much if the Septuagint/LXX differs with the Hebrew: the Hebrew version will always take a superior place whether it is compared with the Septuagint or Paul's writings or any other translation.

Chapter 14

verses 10-11

(10) But why are you judging your brother? Or why do you despise your brother? For we all shall be presented to the judgment seat of Christ. (11) For it has been written, [As] I live, says [the] Lord, because every knee shall bend to me, and every tongue profess to the Deity [Isaiah 45:23]. (Romans 14:10-11)

Now here is a puzzling piece of writing. It's amazing that even in this seemingly innocent area of his letter, Paul still uses an illogical basis to back up his point. Note the logical flow of this:

* We'll all stand before Jesus' judgement seat;
* Because it is written that we'll worship and acknowledge Deity?!?

Now it is illogical for two reasons. Firstly, Jesus can't be the Creator. I'm not going to go into the scriptural and logical reasons here, but the Creator cannot be a created thing. Jesus was, at whatever time, a man, a created thing. Therefore he can't be the Creator. The Creator said that He is not a man (Hoshea 11:9) and that his characteristics are different to that of humanity and all created things. So Jesus cannot be the Creator, and the Creator cannot become Jesus. So Paul's description here cannot logically mean that Jesus is Deity and that everyone will bow to Jesus.

The other problem with Paul's quote is that it has nothing to do with Paul subject. Let me show you why by quoting the verse he uses with a little context.

(21) Declare and draw near! Even deliberate together! Who has caused this to be heard from ancient times? He has declared from then! Is it not I, GOD? And there is no other deity apart from me - a righteous Mighty One. And a saviour? There is none except me. (22) Turn to me, and be saved, all the ends of the earth, for I [am the] Mighty One, and there is nothing else. (23) By myself I have sworn - a word has gone out [with] righteousness and shall not return, for to me, every knee shall bend, and every tongue shall swear. (24) Surely in GOD, [one] has said about me, Vindications and might. And to him all that were angered against him shall come and go pale with shame. (25) In GOD, all the seed of Israel shall be justified and be praised. (Isaiah 45:21-25)

The context I quote here is much like the wider context of this chapter 45. Not one mention is made of the Davidic king to come! The only time the word "anointed one" or "mashiach" is used, it refers to a gentile king, Cyrus. Apart from that, all that is being talked of here is the Lord, the Creator, himself, and that particular verse quoted by Paul refers to no one else.

So what business has Paul to use it to back the notion that everyone is gonna get judged by Jesus??? None whatsoever! Context gives him no basis to use this verse for that purpose. So once again, he's taken a verse out of context.

verse 14

(14) I know and am persuaded in Lord Jesus that no [food] is common of itself except to the one regarding anything to be common, to that one [it is] common. (20) Don't, for the sake of food, demolish the work of the Deity since all things [are] clean, but it is bad to the man eating due to stumbling. (Romans 14:14)

So, to Paul, all foods are pure and nothing is profane/common.

But even a glance over the first 10 chapters of the Jewish Bible should show a person that Paul's statement is wrong. When Noah was loading the ark in Genesis 7, he had to collect different numbers of certain animals, i.e., the clean ones. The ones that were not clean went in two by two, whilst the clean ones went in seven by seven (Genesis 7:2). So, despite what commentaries may say about the implications of these clean/unclean states, there is still a natural statement in scripture that distinguishes between those animals that are clean and those that aren't.

This distinction is made even clearer in Leviticus 11 and Deuteronomy 14 where animals are called disgusting and abominable to eat, being unclean. Even food that is not slaughtered properly, being eaten whilst alive, is forbidden (see Genesis 9:4).

So scripturally we can confront Paul and those who regurgitate his words and say: no, Paul, you're dead wrong! - The scripture says that certain meats are unclean and forbidden, and you have no authority to change that! It's not just based on the views of a man or the person to whom something is unclean, but is based on the word of the Creator who made these animals and distinguishes between clean and unclean!

So, again, Paul has it wrong!

Chapter 15

verse 3

(2) Let every one of us please his neighbour for his good, to build up. (3) For even Christ did not please Himself; but as it is written, "The reproaches of those who reproached You fell on Me." [Psalm 69:10] (Romans 15:2-3)

Paul is using this verse in Psalm 69 to show how the person he views as "christ" took upon himself the reproaches or the disgraceful expressions/insults of christians.

Now there is no need for me to do any in-depth interpretation of Psalm 69 or Romans 15 to show their difference in meaning. Why? Because Paul has used another verse from this same psalm already in Romans 11:9-11! There it was clearly shown that it cannot refer to a sinless Jesus, since the person writing/speaking in that psalm speaks of his own sin and iniquity (Psalm 69:5). So it has nothing to do with Paul's idea of Jesus or the "christ".

There is no need to say more than this. Paul again takes a verse out of context to make a baseless point.

verse 9

(8) And I say, Jesus Christ has become a servant of the circumcision for the truth of Deity, to confirm the promises of the fathers, (9) and that the nations might glorify God for mercy, as it is written, "Because of this I will confess to You amongst the nations, and I shall give song to Your name. [2 Samuel 22:50; Psalm 18:48]" (Romans 15:8,9)

Now both Psalm 18 and 2 Samuel 22 are lengthy scriptures and are two copies of the same song of David. I just want you to consider how this psalm starts, and the verse in question.

(1) And David spoke to GOD the words of this song in the day GOD had delivered him out of the hand of all his enemies, and out of the hand of Saul.... (50) Based upon this I shall give thanks to you, GOD, amongst the nations, and shall sing to your name. (2 Samuel 22:1,50)

For those who wish to check, you can look through the whole passage between verses 1 and 50 which I quoted. All you will see is David speaking about his experiences and how God rescued him. There is no sign of Jesus in this verse. So Paul, once again, takes this verse out of context.

Just to make sure no one comes up with some strange ideas, I'll just deal with something that a person may say. One may say, Hey! Isn't an anointed one mentioned in the next verse? I would say, yes, sure there is! But it has no connection to what is being said in the verse that Paul uses, since it is David talking about himself! And since there were many anointed ones, including all the high priests, and all of David's descendants who ruled Israel - which Jesus never did - then there is nothing in the verse that distinctly points out Jesus with the exclusion of all others.

So to reiterate, this is another example of Paul ripping a verse out of its context to suit his own purposes.

verse 10

Paul continues with his verse picking and quotes from Deuteronomy 32:43. What I'll do next is show you how he quotes it both in the English and Greek, and then compare it to the other versions.

PAUL:
And again he says, Rejoice, O nations, with his people. (Romans 15:10)

PAUL (in the original Greek):
ευφρανθητε εθνη μετα του λαου αυτου

SEPTUAGINT/LXX:
ευφρανθητε εθνη μετα του λαου αυτου [exactly the same as Paul's so the translation would be the same]

HEBREW BIBLE (in the original Hebrew):
עַ_מֹו גֹוִ_ם הַ_רַ_נִ_ינוּ

WORD-FOR-WORD TRANSLATION OF HEBREW (with no regard to English grammar or ease of understanding):
Sing nations his people

Again, Paul is seen to be quoting directly from the Septuagint (LXX) which mistranslates the Hebrew by adding the extra word "with". Not surprisingly, most christian versions, followers of Paul, follow Paul and the LXX in his mistranslation when they "translate" Deuteronomy 32:43. For example:

King James Version: Rejoice, O nations, [with] his people ...

Modern Young's Literal Translation: Sing you nations -- with his people ...

World English Bible: Rejoice, you [pl.] nations, [with] his people ...

American Standard Version: Rejoice, O ye nations, [with] his people ...

Rotherham Emphasized Version: Shout for joy O ye nations [with] his people ...

New International Version: Sing, O nations, with his people ...

Now I'm not going to quote all of them, but you should get the main idea that the followers of Paul throughout time have simply followed him and the Septuagint version in their translations. As this version has passed mostly through christian hands and there are signs of alteration and editing, one can never be too sure which follows which sometimes, whether the writings of Paul are following the Septuagint, or whether the christian Septuagint is following Paul. But regardless, the christians side with Paul and the Septuagint. For those that don't believe me about editing, then please research the different Greek manuscripts of the last verses of Daniel 9.

Also not surprising is the fact that the Jews, ignoring the desires of the christians, translate the verse as follows.

Jewish Publication Society 1917: Sing aloud, O nations, of his people ...

Rashi: Let the nations extol his people ...

Isaac Leeser's 19th Century Translation: Speak aloud, O ye nations, the praises of his people; ...

New Jerusalem Publication Society 1986: Acclaim, O nations, his people ...

Artsroll Stone Edition Chumash: O nations - sing the praises of his people ...

Targum Onkelos:

שַׁבַּחוּ מַיָּא עַמְמֵהּ עַמְמַיָּא

Literal Translation (as close as word-for-word equivalence can be): Praise, o nations, his people ...

Just a little warning about translations of the Targums: beware of christian translations of the Targum. I've looked at the Aramaic of the Targums, and still they have no "with" or "and" in that clause. I say this because I've seen a translation online of the main Targums - those of Onkelos and Pseudo Jonathan - and the translator follows the christian tradition of adding "and" or "with". So just be careful! And a useful piece of information is that although the writing of the Targum may be around or after the 3rd century CE, their oral tradition seems to have been around before that, before 1BCE.

As you can see, the Jewish versions see no need to add the word "with" to their translations, not even the old Aramaic Targums., The Hebrew version of the books of Moses have a much better track record when it comes to preservation and standards of accuracy. this being the version originated with and was preserved by the people of Israel. This is the version that can be relied on. It has no "with" in Deuteronomy 32:43, and Jews are more faithful in their rendering, having a better, natural understanding of their own language.

All this is to show that in order for Paul's argument and use of this scripture to stand, a lot of weight is needed with that word "with". If it wasn't so, then the christians that followed Paul wouldn't have had to follow in Paul's error. And the problem is that this word is not in the original Hebrew which makes at least a significant difference. The word "with" cannot be so important if it's not even in the Hebrew.

But even if we can barely imagine that the word "with" was stuck on that verse, would it still have any agreement with the message of Paul? So let's add to this analysis the context of Deuteronomy 32:43. What exactly is Paul trying to say in his quote of this verse? Paul started this section in Romans 15:8 speaking of Jesus being sent to the Jews to fulfil the promises to the fathers, and so that the Gentiles may glorify Deity for his mercy upon them. Therefore, as he understands it, the Gentiles rejoice with Israel. And why? Because Jesus has been sent to the Jews fulfilling an old promise. But does Deuteronomy 32:43 and its context have anything to do with this?

In the verses surrounding Deuteronomy 32:43, we see the Almighty destroying his enemies, those who have held captive his people, and atoning for the land and his people. So basically, we have scenes of vengeance, battle, blood, and the redemption of both the land and people of Israel. It has nothing to do with Jesus who did absolutely none of these things, and the Gentiles are not rejoicing about mercy that has fallen upon them but about the way the Lord, through battle, has defeated his enemies and redeemed his people Israel.

Now I don't want people spiritualising my words, since I mean what I say literally. Jesus took part in no battle; Israel was dispersed from the land in a matter of decades after his death, and the land was desolate for centuries. This is the exact opposite of the context of Deuteronomy. Let me show you.

(40) For I lift my hand to heaven, and say: "As I live forever, (41) If I sharpen my glittering sword and my hand take hold on judgment, I shall return vengeance upon my adversaries, and shall recompense those that hate me. (42) I shall cause my arrows to be drunk with blood, and my sword will devour flesh, with the blood of the slain and the captives, from the first breach of the enemy. (43) Sing aloud, O nations, of his people, because he will avenge the blood of his servants and will return vengeance to his adversaries, and has cleansed his land and his people. (Deuteronomy 32:40-43)

As you should see, this passage had nothing to do with the ministry of Jesus or Gentiles singing aloud about mercy. This is about vengeance. And at the end, the land and people of Israel and in a good condition. After Jesus' death, things went from bad to worse for Israel. Instead of the enemies of Israel being destroyed, Israel was destroyed and its people dispersed. So the Pauline explanation turns things on its head.

And as I mentioned before, I know the tactics of Paul's followers. They will spiritualise the words of Moses to take away Israel's promises and apply it to themselves. I hope those who are more honest with the context and will appreciate the audience that Moses was talking to when he gave this song, this prophecy.

So, essentially, we're back where we have been so often in Paul's writings: we find him taking a verse or clause out of context to make a point that is absent from the context of the Jewish Bible.

Another aside: How many times?

Now I've got to add a point here. Normally, when studying a text or an author, you normally have to spot a few serious errors for you to realise that you cannot trust a writer's conclusions or interpretation skills. After 3-5 times of seeing serious errors, you should at least be wary of taking a person at their word.

Yet so far in this study - and I haven't even finished going through even the first major book of Paul - almost every time he has put scripture forward to prove or support his point, he has been guilty of one serious error or another. Either he takes a verse out of context and gives it a meaning that is different to, and normally against, the natural meaning of the original passage; or he mistranslates a verse; or, rarely, he has no problem with taking two verses from contextually different passages, and merging and editing them.

He is supposed to be a Hebrew of Hebrews, meaning a super Jew or the best quality Hebrew, yet he is apparently bound to the Greek translation of the scriptures. This shows that he had little knowledge of the original Hebrew Scriptures or he felt that the Greek translation suited his purpose better. This further separates him from the original language and tone of scripture, and from those Jews that know their Hebrew Bible and who could and can easily see his mistakes and the inaccuracies of the Greek translation.

But regardless of his use of versions, his greatest weakness is the following: his skill at and common practice of taking verses out of context to make distinctly different points from that of scripture. Along with his other erroneous methods, the amount of times he is wrong in his usage of scripture still brings home the point: how many times must a person do wrong for his words to be, at best, distrusted, or, at worst, thrown in the garbage? It is a miracle that his words are even seen as the word of "God" by anyone.

But the fact is that Paul preached to the right people to get his following: the uneducated gentiles. Once he has distorted their view of the Hebrew Bible before they even could fully read a translation of it, they were already trapped. And the same method is used by modern day christians. They will teach a person the new testament first, giving the idea that the Jewish Bible only or fundamentally speaks of Jesus. Once that emotional mindset is fixed in the potential convert's mind, once those tinted glasses are fixed firmly on their eyes, they can only read the Hebrew Bible in the "colour", the interpretation, that is fixed in their minds. And it is so difficult to escape.

verse 11

And again, Praise the Lord, all nations; and commend him, all the peoples. (Romans 15:11, quoting Psalm 117:1)

On the surface, this is one of the most applicable quotes that Paul has ever done. At the very least, it actually has the nations worshipping Deity, unlike Paul's previous quote. The only significant problem with this quote is that the passage says nothing to prove Paul's point that Jesus is the reason for this worship. If this is not a case of taking a verse out of context, it is definitely either putting a different meaning to a verse than what it naturally has, or Paul is just using a verse that doesn't really back up his statement.

Another way of saying this is that he's taken a verse out of context. Just because it says that the nations worship, it says nothing about it being a prophecy about the "messiah".

verse 12

PAUL:

εσται η ριζα του ιεσσαι και ο ανισταμενος αρχειν εθνων επ' αυτω εθνη ελπουσιν

Translation: It shall be, the root of Iessai [Jesse] even the one standing up to rule nations, upon him shall nations put their hope. (Romans 15:12 quoting Isaiah 11:10)

LXX:

εσται εν τη ημερα εκεινη η ριζα του ιεσσαι και ο ανισταμενος αρχειν εθνων επ' αυτω εθνη ελπουσιν

Translation: It shall be, in that day, the root of Iessai [Jesse] even the one standing up to rule nations, upon him shall nations put their hope. (Isaiah 11:10)

HEBREW TEXT:

גּוֹיִם אֵלָיו עַמִּים לְנֵס עֹמֵד אֲשֶׁר יִשַׁי שֹׁרֶשׁ הַהוּא בַּיּוֹם וְהָיָה יִדְרֹשׁוּ

Translation: And it shall be, in that day, a root of Yishai [Jesse] that stands as a flag of peoples, to him nations shall seek/enquire. (Isaiah 11:10)

Don't ask me why the English tradition has made the name of King David's father almost unrecognisable compared to the original sound of the name. It's a messed up story that just shows how tradition is more important to bible translators than bringing us closer to the rich ancient Hebrew culture where bible history takes place.

Anyway, as you can see, Paul mostly follows the LXX translation, although he misses out the words "in those days". There may be a reason why he misses out these words when one looks at the contexts of the passage. Paul here is trying to link the future Davidic king to the nations in his own time. To him Jesus came to make the nations give thanks for the Lord's mercies. But looking at the context of Isaiah 11, you will see that none of that is fulfilled. There is no world peace; ravenous animals and humans don't dwell in peace; the knowledge of Deity does not cover the world; and the exiles of Israel haven't all been brought back to Israel.

Isaiah's prophecy speaks of the future, not Paul's time. Thus, Paul has taken the verse out of context. In fact, the main point of this prophecy is that regardless of whether a person tries to use this to prove Jesus or not, it is unfulfilled! So it does nothing for Paul's point.

verse 21

To finish off Paul's quotes in Romans, we come to verse 21 of chapter 15 where Paul quotes Isaiah 52:15 as follows:

(20) And in this manner I have been eager to preach the gospel, not where Christ was named, so that I don't build on another man's foundation; (21) but as it is written, "To whom nothing was said about Him, they shall see. And they who have not heard shall understand." (Romans 15:21)

Paul is saying that he wants to preach the gospel where no one else has, and then applies the verse in Isaiah to himself where he preaches to those who don't know and haven't heard.

Again, Paul has taken leave of the context. In Isaiah 52:15, it is speaking of a special servant of the Lord who shall startle many nations and cause kings to shut their mouths by showing them what hadn't been seen or heard of before. Now I'm not going to go into a big discussion over this, I'll just lay out the facts. Throughout Isaiah 40-52, the nation of Israel is mostly called the servant of the Lord (e.g., Isaiah 41:8-9, 42:1, 43:10). There is not one single time in this section where the word "servant" is overtly linked to the future Davidic king. In fact, the word meaning "anointed one" (moshiach, or messiah) is only used once to refer to Cyrus (Isaiah 45:1), and that's it! This is all about the condition and redemption of Israel. And in chapter 53, the passage goes on to show how Israel will surprise the nations with its ascendancy from humiliation and humble beginnings to an exalted state.

So where in all this does Paul fit in? Absolutely nowhere! In fact, where does Jesus fit in? Same answer! So what has happened? Basically the same thing that has happened throughout the majority of Romans. Paul has taken a verse out of context and used it for his own purposes, disregarding what the original message of the passage was.

So as the book starts, so it ends! Let's see what the next book has to say!

1 Corinthians

Chapter 1

verse 19

Now some may have wondered why, in my analysis of Romans, I kept on comparing Paul's quotes with the LXX, the Septuagint, the ancient Greek translation of the Jewish Bible. They may have thought that in most cases Paul's quotes agreed with the Septuagint, so it was quite needless. There are a number of reasons why I continued to keep the LXX in the conversation as I was discussing Romans. One reason was that a good number of more knowledgeable christians and secular scholars cherish that Greek version, thinking they could use it to find or reconstruct some hidden or lost original Hebrew manuscript, or that the Greek version itself is as holy as the Hebrew version. So it's interesting to see if Paul, their main teacher, treats it with the same respect. He may have done so in the book of Hebrews if he wrote it, although he still cuts and edits where he wants to.

Another reason is that Paul's quotes do not always agree with the Greek version, especially as we go through his different books. As we go through 1 Corinthians, you'll see that the "revered" Paul chooses to go his own way when it comes to quoting scripture, regardless which version you would look at.

So we start here, in 1 Corinthians 1:19, where Paul refers to Isaiah 29:14.

PAUL:

απολω την σοφιαν των σοφων και την συνεσιν των συνετων αθετησω

I shall destroy the wisdom of the wise and neutralize the understanding of those understanding.

LXX:

και απολω την σοφιαν των σοφων και την συνεσιν των συνετων κρυψω

I shall destroy the wisdom of the wise and hide the understanding of those understanding.

HEBREW:

תֹּ,ס,תְּ,תֵּ,ר נ,ב,ר נ,יָ'ו וּ,בֵ,ינַ,ת חֲ,כָ,מָ,יו חָ,כְ,מַ,ת וְ,אָבְ,דָ,ה

The wisdom of his wise ones perishes and the understanding of his "understanders" shall hide itself.

Although Paul retains much of the LXX language, he does change one word to suit his notions, changing the word "to hide" to "to neutralize, or set aside". Apparently, for Paul, it is not that understanding is simply hidden: it is given no place at all. We also see that he has, for all intents, simply forgotten the original Hebrew. The structure and meaning of each of the words has changed. The Hebrew just says that wisdom and understanding are gone; whereas the Greek has the Lord himself destroying wisdom and hiding understanding. Instead of Isaiah speaking of Israel's wise men and "understanders" losing their wisdom and understanding, it is just some set of wise and understanding people who have lost it. Things have changed! Of course, such a translation paves the way for Paul's applying it to any group of wise and understanding people, be it Jew or Greek.

What is the point that Paul is trying to make? He is saying that the message of the cross, the execution of Jesus, is foolishness, stupid, to those who are "perishing". In case you don't know, according to Paul, anyone who doesn't accept Jesus as their "Lord", as one who died for their sin, is perishing. So Paul's message is that the Almighty himself has purposefully and actively used the execution of Jesus to baffle people, to destroy wisdom and understanding. Is this what Isaiah is talking about?

Those words of Isaiah speak neither of Paul's subject or his time. Isaiah 29 contains descriptions of war time and Jerusalem being surrounded by her enemies. Whilst in this condition, the people experience this blindness and drunkenness where their prophets are senseless and their wise men can't make heads or tails of the situation. The next chapter (Isaiah 30) speaks of the desire to join with Egypt, giving us some idea of the times they are facing. There is no mention of a dying man, or a "god" that is killed. Neither crucifixion nor execution has a place in this chapter whatsoever. There is nothing in the context that would point to Paul's idea that a dead man makes people confused, or, to put in a more polite way, that the "messiah" dying would be confusing. There is no mention of the future Davidic king in these passages.

Now don't get me wrong! Am I saying that these messages and passages can't have lessons for us today, or for any time in history? No! Am I saying that Isaiah's words are only relevant to people in his time so no one can take a message from it? No! All I'm saying is that if you are going to use a verse to support your point, make sure that the context can also support your point. To take a verse, isolate it, and then make it seem like some sort of prophecy about Messiah is pointless if the whole context isn't pointing in the same direction, and Isaiah 29 is by no means pointing to Paul's notions or ideas. So it's the same old story of Paul taking a verse out of context.

What makes things worse is the commentaries of Paul's writings, those which are written by those who love and follow Paul. For example, the Jamieson, Fausset, and Brown commentary would make it seem that the spirit of "God" guided Paul's hand and understanding. I'll quote them commenting on this verse we're looking at, 1 Corinthians 1:19:

> 19. I will destroy - slightly altered from the Septuagint, Isa 29:14. The Hebrew is, "The wisdom of the wise shall perish, and the

understanding of their prudent men shall be hid." Paul by inspiration gives the sense of the Spirit, by making God the cause of their wisdom perishing, &c., "I will destroy," &c. (emphasis mine)

Just like many other Pauline christian commentators and readers, they base their interpretation of Paul's methods on their faith in the "truth of Paul", as opposed to honesty and sincerity with the original passage, i.e. Isaiah 29. That way of commenting on scripture can never lead to truth!

verse 31

(27) But God has chosen the foolish things of the world to disgrace the wise; and God has chosen the weak things of the world to disgrace the things which are mighty; (28) and God has chosen the base things of the world, and things which are despised, and things which are not, in order to bring to nothing things that are; (29) so that no flesh should boast before his presence. (30) But you are of him in Jesus Christ, who became to us wisdom from God, righteousness also and purification and a ransom; (31) so that, just as it is written, "He who boasts, let him boast in the Lord [Jeremiah 9:24]." (1 Corinthians 1:27-31)

I believe the context is important here for us to get an idea of what Paul is talking about before he does his "quote". In a nutshell, the Almighty has messed up the wisdom of the world using stupid and vile things so that no one can have any pride before him. Jesus is now the wisdom that christians should use. And that fulfils what is written.

Now I will say that what Paul quotes is nowhere in scripture. The words he uses, in the order he uses them, is nowhere in the Hebrew Bible or the jaded Septuagint. Now some may be surprised to hear this, especially if they have a christian bible with references that universally point to Jeremiah 9:23 or 24. I don't want to overload you with Greek or Hebrew, but there is no point in me making a claim if I can't back it up. So here it is. I shall once again compare

Paul's words with that of the Hebrew and Septuagint. I do this because normally when Paul says "as it is written", he actually attempts to quote, not just paraphrase, a scripture.

PAUL:

ο καυχωμενος εν κυριω καυχασθω
TRANSLATION: The boaster, let him boast in [the] Lord.

LXX:

αλλ' η εν τουτω καυχασθω ο καυχωμενος συνειν και γινωσκειν οτι εγω ειμι κυριος ποιων ελεος και κριμα και δικαιοσυνην επι της γης οτι εν τουτοις το θελημα μου λεγει κυριος
TRANSLATION: But rather, let the boaster boast in this: to understand and know that I am [the] Lord, doing mercy and judgement and righteousness upon the land, because my will is in these [things], says [the] Lord. (Jeremiah 9:23 LXX verse numbering)

HEBREW VERSION:

אָ‌נֹ‌כִ‌י כִּ‌י אוֹ‌תִ‌י וְ‌יָ‌דֹ‌עַ הַ‌שְׂ‌כֵּ‌ל הַ‌מִּ‌תְ‌הַ‌לֵּ‌ל יִ‌תְ‌הַ‌לֵּ‌ל אַ‌ם־בְּ‌זֹ‌את כִּ‌י
חָ‌פַ‌צְ‌תִּ‌י כִּ‌י־בָ‌אָ‌רֶ‌ץ וּ‌צְ‌דָ‌קָ‌ה מִ‌שְׁ‌פָּ‌ט חֶ‌סֶ‌ד עֹ‌שֶׂ‌ה יי
נְ‌אֻ‌ם־יי

TRANSLATION: But rather, let the boaster boast in this: to know and understand me, that I, GOD, do lovingkindness, judgement, and righteousness in the earth, for I delight in these [things] - a declaration of GOD. (Jeremiah 9:23 Hebrew verse numbering)

It may be a lot to take in, but just see the simple point I'm making. The words "let the boaster boast in the Lord", in that order, is not in the text. Even the Septuagint does a better job of portraying the Hebrew than Paul, to the point where Paul's words are not even in that ancient Greek version. In fact, Jeremiah is making a much more specific point than Paul is. Whereas Paul leaves it wide open, "boast in the Lord", Jeremiah is actually talking about understanding, doing, and observing the things that the Lord delights in, i.e., judgement, lovingkindness, and righteousness. Jeremiah's message has nothing to do with the words of Paul who is trying to make out that Jesus has become wisdom to shame the world. All Jeremiah cares about is letting people know that they should do and keep these good things, saying nothing about - and therefore caring nothing about - any "Jesus", any "cross", and such alien messages such as Paul is trying to give out.

What makes things that more confusing is Paul's use of the word κυριος, kurios which Paul uses for Jesus and sometimes for "God". The point of the context of this passage is that Jesus is the cause of the christian "foolishness", i.e., what is supposed to appear foolish to Jews and Greeks. Because of this, some christians interpret Paul's quote to be referring not to the Almighty, but to Jesus. For example:

> *He that glorieth, let him glory in the Lord; not in his own wisdom, riches, and strength; but in Christ, as his wisdom, righteousness, sanctification, and redemption. (John Gill commenting on 1 Corinthians 1:31 in his "Exposition of the Whole Bible")*

Unfortunately, Paul doesn't do a good job of clarifying the matter, especially with statements like "there is one Deity, the Father ... and there is only one [κυριος] Lord, Jesus Christ..." (1 Corinthians 8:6).

But after all is said and done, Paul's method of arguing his point attempts to destroy any basis of defence against his teaching. He seeks to make all argument against his point impossible since wisdom and sign-seeking (or more properly, looking for evidence) - both normal ways of finding out things - become invalid: Jesus is the wisdom. The only way you can understand or know is Jesus. And all you can have in Jesus is faith or belief.

But, at least, the study of the Torah, the books of Moses, can prepare one for such teachings as that of Paul. Knowing passages like Deuteronomy 13 and knowing the eternal role of the Law of the Lord as given by Moses from its own statements, as well as reading the Hebrew Bible for oneself can protect a person from the idea that understanding and wisdom are vain if you don't believe in Jesus.

But what about people who cannot read for themselves? In essence, Paul's source is supposed to be the Hebrew Bible. So there are at least two choices: that person can either find a knowledgeable Torah-keeping Jew who can read the passages for you; or, he or she can learn to read it for themselves. Actually, in this day and age, you can even listen to the whole bible in audio form. Such Torah-derived lessons and laws as well as trust in its source, the Creator, can inoculate a person from Paul's deceit/conceit or cure one from his poison.

Chapter 2

verse 9

Paul quotes Isaiah 64:4. Let's see how well he does with this one in comparison with the Hebrew Bible and the Greek source he is supposed to be using.

PAUL:
α οφθαλμος ουκ ειδεν και ους ουκ ηκουσεν και επι καρδιαν ανθρωπου ουκ ανεβη α ητοιμασεν ο θεος τοις αγαπωσιν αυτου
... things which eye hasn't seen and which ear hasn't heard and has not gone up upon the heart of man, which the Deity has prepared for those loving him.

LXX:
απο του αιωνος ουκ ηκουσαμεν ουδε οι οφθαλμοι ημων ειδον θεον πλην σου και τα εργα σου α ποιησεις τοις υπομενουσιν ελεον
From the age, we have not heard, nor have our eyes seen a deity apart from you and your works which you shall do for those awaiting mercy.

HEBREW VERSION:

אֱלֹהִים לֹא־רָאָתָה עַיִן | לֹא־הֶאֱזִינוּ לֹא־שָׁמְעוּ וּמֵעוֹלָם
לְמִחְכֵּה־לוֹ יַעֲשֶׂה זוּלָתְךָ.

And from old [or from the age] they haven't heard, they haven't hearkened. Eye hasn't seen a Deity except you - He shall act for the one that waits for Him.

After going through the texts that Paul has used so far, it is easy to get the impression that he is almost allergic to actually dealing with scripture as it is. It's almost like he has to do something or other to rip himself from the natural language of the Hebrew Bible. We have another classic example here. He almost ignores both the Hebrew Bible and the LXX to create for himself a brand new message. While the passages in both versions of Isaiah focus on the Deity who is doing the giving, Paul focuses on what is being given. Isaiah looks towards the person of Deity whereas Paul looks for the hand of Deity and what is going to be given to those who follow his, that is Paul's, doctrine.

(6) But, we speak wisdom among those who are perfect; yet not the wisdom of this world, nor of the rulers of this world, that come to nothing. (7) But we speak the wisdom of God in a mystery, which God has hidden, predetermining it before the world for our glory; (8) which none of the rulers of this world knew (for if they had known, they would not have crucified the Lord of glory). (9) But as it is written, "Eye has not seen, nor ear heard," nor has it entered into the heart of man, "the things which God has prepared for those who love Him." (1 Corinthians 2:6-9, Modern King James Version)

So Paul's focus is the wisdom, that hidden wisdom.

Let's just take a step back here. What is Paul going on about? What are the Hebrew Scriptures going on about? To take the latter question first, the prophet Isaiah is talking retrospectively about what happened in Sinai in the verse before (Isaiah 64:3) and then gives a general statement in verse 4, that no other nation has seen a god like the Most High who takes care of those who wait on him. There is nothing that prophetic (in the "speaking of the future" sense) about Isaiah's words here. There is nothing messianic about it.

But then here comes Paul! He speaks of "God's wisdom in a mystery, the wisdom that has been hidden with God foreordained before the worlds ... which none of the rulers of this world has known". Huh?!? Totally different! Isaiah is going on about stuff that was done by a deity not known by the nations, and Paul is going on about some wisdom that makes smart people look stupid. It takes an awful lot of twisting and shifting to even get to Paul's view from Isaiah's.

In essence, Paul goes his way with his interpretation; and the Almighty and Isaiah go theirs. And never the twain should meet! [Translation: there's no agreement!]

verse 16

Paul quotes Isaiah 40:13. He depicts it as:

For who has known the mind of [the] Lord that would teach him [Isaiah 40:13]? But we have the mind of Christ. (1 Corinthians 2:16)

Now when I first read through 1 Corinthians and passed this verse, I thought that Paul had used this verse in a fair manner. You know, sometimes you can look at Paul's "quote", and then look at the original verse on its own, and then think that it is translated fair enough. But when you actually look at the verses in Isaiah that surround this verse that Paul "quotes" .... Well, I did, and my opinion changed quickly.

Paul has been building up the notion that just as the spirit of a man knows "the things of [that] man", so the spirit of God knows "the things of God". In Paul's eyes, his followers have the spirit of God and therefore know "spiritual things". So when he writes what he does in 1 Corinthians 2:16, as quoted above, he is actually saying that because they have the mind of Christ, they essentially know the things of God. To reiterate, as Paul and his followers are supposed to have the spirit of God, therefore they know "the things of God", i.e., his mind.

Here's the problem with Paul's logic. There have been great prophets in the Hebrew Scriptures, men having a much closer relationship with Deity than Paul, for example, Moses, who not only had the spirit of Deity, but also spoke with him face to face. Yet, he said, "the revealed things are for us, but the hidden things belong to Deity" (Deuteronomy 29:29). This means that even though he had the spirit of Deity, he never claimed to know the mind of Deity, only that which was revealed. Then we have Isaiah himself, a prophet who was a channel of the divine message, a man who had the spirit of Deity, and yet when we let him speak for himself, he says the following:

(12) Who has measured in the hollow of his hand the waters, and meted out the heavens with the span, and comprised in a measure the dust of the earth, and weighed in the scale-beam the mountains, and the hills in balances? (13) Who has meted out the Spirit of GOD? and who was his counsellor that he could have caused him to know? (14) With whom did he take counsel, that gave him understanding, and taught him the path of justice, and taught him knowledge, and caused him to know the way of understanding? (Isaiah 40:12-14 - Translation of the Hebrew Version)

Just in case you didn't know (hey, I had to look in Webster's 19th century dictionary for this as well), "to mete out" means to measure something. The exact same word is used in verse 12 when it says "meted out the heavens with a span."

But Paul was using the LXX, the Greek version of the Hebrew Bible which says the following:

(12) Who has measured the water in His hand, and the heaven with a span, and all the earth in a handful? Who has weighed the mountains in scales, and the forests in a balance? (13) Who has known the mind of the Lord? And who has been His counsellor, to instruct Him? (14) Or with whom has He taken counsel, and he has instructed Him? Or who has taught Him judgment, or who has taught Him the way of understanding; (Isaiah 40:12-14 - Septuagint)

Now although the Septuagint is slightly different, the message is similar enough for what I say next to be valid, no matter which version you read.

For those who may not understand, Isaiah here is asking questions that have an obvious answer, i.e., rhetorical questions. And the answer to each of these questions is this: "Absolutely no one". No one has measured the waters in the palm of his hand! No one has weighed the mountains and hills in balances! No one is the Lord's counsellor! No one taught him knowledge!

So within this context, when Isaiah asks "who has meted out the spirit of GOD?" or "who has known the mind of the Lord?", this question has the same answer as all those questions around it: Absolutely no one! Remember, these are the words of the prophet, Isaiah, a man who had the spirit of Deity in a much more intense way than any christian in history or existence, including Paul. On one hand, Paul had to try to argue his point through argumentation and using the Hebrew Scriptures as proof and could hardly say "thus says the Lord", at one point saying "I think I have the Lord's spirit" (1 Corinthians 7:40). On the other hand, Isaiah could boldly say and write that the Lord had spoken to him and had definitely given him a message. If I have both writings in front of me, that of Isaiah and that of Paul, and Isaiah teaches that no-one knows the mind of Deity, and Paul says, referring to Isaiah's words, that he does know or even insinuates such a thing as he does in this verse, it should be clear that Isaiah, who was closer to Deity, had his spirit and spoke his word, would be right and Paul would be speaking foolishness.

[ASIDE: I just want to confront something that some christian commentators have said about this phrase of Paul, "I think I have God's spirit." They seem to have the idea that the Greek word δοκεω/δοκω [dok-e-o or dokow] translated as "I think" - when Paul says "I think I have God's spirit" - can mean "I know for certain" or "I am certain" (see Wesley's and Adam Clarke's commentary of 1 Corinthians 7:40). I will just put this bluntly: there are a good number of Greek words that simply mean "I know" or "I am sure/persuaded" or "I acknowledge": that Greek word, dokow, isn't one of them. It means what it says on the tin: "I think" or "it seems like this to me." I know and see what the christian commentators say in order to defend their hero of the faith: Paul. But for all their reasoning and logic, one thing seems to stand: the word simply means "I think" or "I hold the opinion that" or "it seems to me". Rather than try to twist the meaning of the word, it would be more reasonable to say that it means what it means, but it depends on how authoritative the readers of Paul's letters would have thought Paul to be. If you are a believer in Paul (not necessarily in Jesus) like the Corinthians he was writing to, then you would believe his opinion to be very authoritative. If you are either a believer in Jesus who didn't accept Paul or anyone else, then you would think that such an opinion needs to be tested or rejected.]

So, just to reiterate, Paul has taken this verse out of context and given it a different meaning. The original meaning of the verse in Isaiah gives Paul no basis for the phrase "but we have the mind of christ" which only strokes someone's ego, i.e., the person following Paul.

Chapter 3

verses 19-20

Paul continues:

(19) For the wisdom of this world is foolishness with the Deity. For it has been written, He takes the wise in their own craftiness [Job 5:13]. (20) And again, The Lord knows the thoughts of the wise, that they are vain [Psalm 94:11]. (1 Corinthians 3:19-20)

So Paul is using these verses to prove his claim that "the wisdom of the world is foolishness with Deity". We'll see if Paul's quotes back him up.

Firstly, Job 5:13. It must be noted that Paul's translation does not agree with the Septuagint. Almost every word is different. Because of the nature of this essay, it is best to provide evidence of this.

PAUL:
>   γαρ ο δρασσομενος τους σοφους εν τη πανουργια αωτων
>   *Translation: for he catches the wise [people] in their villainy.*

SEPTUAGINT:
>   ο καταλαμβανων σοφους εν τη φρονησει
>   *Translation: for he seizes wise [people] in high-mindedness.*

You don't even have to know ancient Greek to see that the words are different. And just to compare it with the original Hebrew:

HEBREW BIBLE::
בּ עֲ ר מַ ם חֲ כׇ מ ים ל כׇ ד
>   *Translation: He captures/seizes wise [people] in their craftiness.*

As you can see, Paul's translation isn't too bad. He is more forceful in showing the wickedness in what these "wise people" are doing, but still he is not too far off the mark. The verse itself, Job 5:13, doesn't really show that the wisdom of the world is foolishness with Deity. Why? Just because a person traps someone else with their own devices and plans, that doesn't really make those devices and plans stupid or dumb. But the verse does at least show that the Lord's wisdom is superior to man's wisdom, no matter how smart they think they are. So although the verse doesn't really back up Paul's point, it is not so far off the mark that we can add it to the many other misuses of scripture Paul is guilty of.

But what about the other verse Paul quotes? That would be Psalm 94:11.

PAUL:

κυριος γινωσκει τους διαλογισμους των σοφων οτι εισιν ματαιοι
Translation: [the] Lord knows the reasonings of the wise that they are vanity.

SEPTUAGINT:

κυριος γινωσκει τους διαλογισμους των ανθρωπων οτι εισιν ματαιοι
Translation: [the] Lord knows the reasonings of the men that they are vanity.

Once again, we'll compare this to the original:

HEBREW BIBLE:

יי ע ֵד ֹת בוֹ ֽשׁ ֵח ַמ ָם ָד ָא י ִכ ה ָמ ֵה ַל ֶב ָה

Translation: GOD knows [the] reasonings of man that they [are] vanity.

What may strike you is that Paul seems to follow both the Septuagint and its pretty decent rendering of the Hebrew, except for one word. Paul changes a word. He changes the word that means "men" for the word which means "wise". Since Paul's point is that the wisdom of the world is foolishness with Deity, then it would seem that Paul has changed the words of scripture to go along with his point as opposed to accurately bringing across the words of scripture.

But some may say that it doesn't really matter about Paul's alteration of scripture because the message is the same regardless of whether you use "men" or "wise": that man's wisdom is folly to Deity. But stop and think! If the verse would back up Paul's point without him changing any words, then what's the point in him changing that word? Why not just keep it as it is? If the verse naturally backs Paul up, then there is no need to change it! Well, there is no need to change it unless Paul felt that the wording of scripture wasn't good enough. Or he made a mistake. But christians who believe that the new testament is inspired by "God" cannot accept that Paul made a mistake because that would affect their claim that Paul's words are "spirit-filled" and infallible, i.e., without error or mistake.

Now it should be noted that the context of this verse is pointing to wicked or foolish people as opposed to every single human, or even wise people (see Psalm 94:2-11). It is pointing to wicked people. Although the verse we are looking at, verse 11, speaks of "man", its context limits it to wicked men.

So does this verse, in its untampered state and when read in context, really back up Paul's point that the wisdom of the world is foolishness with Deity? No, not really, unless you equate "the wisdom of the world" with "the reasoning of wicked men"! It takes a limited and arbitrary interpretation to use this verse.

All in all, Paul's usage of verses don't really help his case. His scriptural evidence is either not conclusive or off the mark.

Chapter 5

verse 7

Here's one of the central themes of christianity:

So purge out the old leaven so that you may be a new lump of dough, even as you are unleavened. For even Christ our passover was sacrificed for us. (1 Corinthians 5:7)

According to Paul himself, Jesus died for them, on their behalf. The technical term for this is "vicarious atonement", which means that Jesus dies as a substitute for people, in their place. Paul, in this short statement, gives his support for human sacrifice. Before anyone argues with what I said there, let's just use some basic logic. Whatever people may think of the "divinity" of Jesus, he had to be human, according to christian doctrine and the new testament. And according to this verse and others in the christian bible, he was sacrificed for sin. So let's put that together: we have a human; and that human was sacrificed; therefore we have a human sacrifice. That is the basis of christianity.

There are two significant problems with this concept and with Paul's linking Jesus to the Passover.

Firstly, there is no textual basis for Paul's interpretation of the Passover in Exodus 12 as pointing to Jesus. The text says nothing about sin or a cleansing of sin. There is nothing prophetic within the text and no sign that it is in any way messianic. There is nothing that suggests that it is speaking of man at all. The links between the Pascal lamb and Jesus are non-existent. The first passover sacrifice was, in summary, about a symbol for protection as opposed to a sacrifice for sin. The passover celebrations that happen yearly afterwards were as a constant reminder of the deliverance of the Israelites from Egypt.

Now some christian will say something like this: "Yeah, Jews are reminded of the deliverance of Israel from Egypt, and Jesus was our deliverance from sin." But there are still significant problems with this sort of thinking. One problem is that anyone being delivered from anything could use the passover as a symbol for their deliverance. It can be interpreted in so many contradictory ways that the christian interpretation becomes meaningless. Just because the christians pin this symbol onto the death of their messiah figure, that gives it no truth or credence, neither does it make their messiah any sort of sacrifice. Another problem is that the passover lamb and its blood were symbols and signs. The passover lamb and its blood did not deliver Israel from Egypt. According to christians, Jesus' death couldn't be simply a sign or a symbol, and it was he who supposedly delivered christians from sin. That is the opposite of what the Passover lamb and observance was for.

The second and possibly most significant problem with Paul's interpretation is that human sacrifice is totally eschewed, avoided, and shunned in the Torah, in the law of the Lord. Throughout the Jewish Bible, EVERY clean and good literal sacrifice/offering was either of an animal or some inanimate object, like flour or grain. It always went down in the food chain, meaning that Jews didn't go around killing their equals, humans, but rather they went to what they ate, like domesticated animals or bread. That is what was always commanded in the Hebrew Scriptures, in the Torah. Sacrifices for sin were done in very specific ways in very specific places, and always by the command of Deity. The animals had no blemish. The blood was only spilt on a specific altar by specific people: the Levitical priests. After the giving of the Law in completion, it could not be added to or diminished.

But Jesus' "sacrifice" had absolutely none of these characteristics. It was essentially an illegal sacrifice. Rather than fulfilling the law, Jesus' death, if seen as a sacrifice, broke the law. There was no Levitical priest involved (I'll deal with the Melchizedek idea later); he died outside of Jerusalem, away from the legal place, the temple grounds; his body was mutilated and therefore blemished; his blood just dripped to the floor; he didn't die of bloodloss; and, worst of all, he was human! In every way, Jesus' death is outside of legal limits that the divine law provides. It was outside of the aspects of the Passover offering which had nothing to do with sin. Basically, it is an illegal entity, like an outlaw.

So in every way, Paul's idea fails. Unfortunately, it never stopped his Gentile followers, who were not versed in scripture, from drinking up his words.

verse 11

But as it is, I wrote to you not to associate with anyone who is called a brother who is a sexual sinner, or covetous, or an idolater, or a slanderer, or a drunkard, or an extortioner. Don't even eat with such a person. (1 Corinthians 5:11 - World English Bible)

Now here, I don't really have much to say about the morality of Paul's command to his followers. What is significant here is the amount of christians who actually take this advice, especially with regards to those who fall under the category of "slanderers", where the Greek word means to revile or rail, which means to criticize severely or spread negative information about someone. I had been part of a church for a long time and hardly anyone got shunned and socially isolated for gossip or slander, even though it were a common occurrence.

I guess this advice fell of deaf ears generally. Or people can pick and choose the seriousness they put on Paul's words.

Chapter 6

verse 3

(2) Don't you know that the saints shall judge the world? And if the world shall be judged by you, are you unworthy to judge the smallest matters? (3) Don't you know that we shall judge angels, not to speak of this life? (1 Corinthians 6:2-3)

Not much needs to be said about the plain words of Paul. He believes that he and his followers will judge angels!!! Such a view had no basis in scripture, and speaks more of Paul's arrogance than anything else.

verse 16

Or don't you know that the one who bonds [sexually] to a prostitute is one body? for they two, he says, shall become one flesh [Genesis 2:24]. (1 Corinthians 6:16)

Paul says that if a man is joined sexually with a prostitute, then they become "one flesh", based on Genesis 2:24. Now the quote of the verse is quite accurate. Superficially, it may even sound reasonable to use this verse since the words of Paul accurately depict this portion of Genesis 2:24. The only problem comes when you actually look at the context, and you have some knowledge of the Jewish Bible.

Let's first look at the whole of Genesis 2:24.

Based on this, a man shall leave his father and mother and cling to his wife, and they shall become one flesh.

Even looking at the plain rendering of this verse, a problem can be seen with regards to Paul's usage of this verse. A man's normal relationship with a prostitute has nothing to do with leaving his mother and father. This verse implies a lasting relationship where the man actually stays with his wife building a home, whereas a prostitute is a temporary business, or possibly religious, arrangement where one comes and goes as he pleases without any commitment. They are not the same thing.

According to this verse, it is only after a man leaves, with intended permanence, his father and mother, and clings to the person he intends to be his wife, it is only after that where they become one flesh. This says nothing about a paid worker, the prostitute. The context of Genesis 2:24 makes nonsense out of Paul's words. The sexual act by itself doesn't make the two one. Compare this with Exodus 22:16, where a man seduces a girl to have sex with him, and it is only once it has been accepted by the father of the girl that she becomes his wife. If the father refuses, the girl doesn't become the man's wife. This shows that just having sex with a girl/woman doesn't make her your wife or make two people become one.

Note also that the verse starts with "based on this" or "therefore". This is because what this verse states is based on what came before it. What happened before it? After the Lord said that it wasn't good for man to be alone, and after a little test with the animals, the Lord took a rib or a side from Adam and created the woman, who he recognised as his own flesh and bones. So they were absolutely one and the Lord separated them making them two. Therefore a man leaves his mother and father to become one with his wife. Now looking at what came before and the oneness that Adam and the woman originally had, and noting that sexual interactions are not even mentioned, how can it be interpreted that this verse simply refers to a sexual encounter??? The fact is that it can't and that sex is not essentially part of this verse's meaning.

In essence, there is no such concept in Genesis 2 or the whole Jewish Bible as that of an isolated sexual act making married couples or making two people one.

Once again, Paul takes a phrase out of context.

Chapter 7

verses 1-2, 6-9

> *(1) Now concerning the things whereof ye wrote unto me: [It is] good for a man not to touch a woman. (2) Nevertheless, [to avoid]*

sexual immorality, let every man have his own wife, and let every woman have her own husband... (6) But I speak this by permission, [and] not of commandment. (7) For I would that all men were even as I myself. But every man has his proper gift of God, one after this manner, and another after that. (8) I say therefore to the unmarried and widows, It is good for them if they abide even as I. (9) But if they cannot contain, let them marry: for it is better to marry than to burn.
(1 Corinthians 7:1-2, 6-9)

Paul tells his readers that marriage is to help a person avoid sexual immorality, but only advises marriage as a concession, something to be done because it has to be done, rather than something to be desired. He says that he prefers that people remain single like himself, but that if they simply can't control themselves, then "it's better to marry than to burn" (I'll leave "burn" open to interpretation). So essentially, according to Paul, it is better to be single!

How different is the message of the whole of the Hebrew Bible?!? In the beginning, the Almighty says it is NOT good for a man to be alone, so he makes woman and institutes marriage so that they may be whole as they were in the beginning, one flesh. Every patriarch was married. Most of the prophets were married. And marriage wasn't instituted just to fulfil sexual appetites, but for wholesome togetherness, companionship, and, if possible, raising godly children.

Apparently, Paul has other ideas about the divine institution, ideas based on something alien to scripture. He carries it on even in v.28 of chapter 7 where he says that virgins who marry will have "oppression/trouble/affliction in the flesh", but Paul, in his mercies, is gonna be lenient with those virgins.

Another example of Paul reversing the message of the Hebrew Bible, calling the righteous wicked, and making positive experience, which was seen as good by God himself, such as marriage, into something negative and dark.

verses 12-40

This is what Paul says after he gives his "advice" on marriage.

> *... and I think also that I have the Spirit of God. 1 Corinthians 7:40*
> *(King James Version - 1769)*

I've dealt with this previously when commenting on 1 Corinthians 2:16. It's clear that some christians think this is still Paul speaking with the spirit of God. But when I read the words of Paul, I don't think even Paul seems so certain.

Critique of Chapters 8 and 10 - Paul and his discussion on eating things sacrificed to idols

Paul writes at length about things offered to idols. He writes about the subject in chapter 8, seemingly digresses for a time in chapter 9 although there are still subtle links to the main topic, and then returns in a direct manner to the subject matter in chapter 10. Rather than recite the whole thing, in its multiple Greek versions, let me just summarize.

To Paul, food is nothing and an idol is nothing. Therefore, there is nothing wrong with eating food offered to idols in and of itself. The only reason, he advises his followers, that they should really be careful about eating such meat is in case they are seen eating such food. Other people may be weak who see the idol as something and who are therefore affected when they see someone who has [Paul's] knowledge eating such food.

I will not be too callous with Paul. He does admit that those who serve idols are doing something wrong, even though, in his eyes, they are serving "demons" (there are no such things as these demons that Paul is talking about in the Hebrew Bible). He also says that he doesn't want his followers to have anything to do with "demons".

But Paul's philosophy appears to be "all things are lawful (permissible) for him, but not everything is beneficial".

And after this small interlude (i.e., chapter 9), Paul returns to his essential argument: don't eat such things because of other people's consciences. Unfortunately, we see Paul, because of his self-proclaimed authority, missing the mark by trying to reason people into obedience. Yet the Law of Moses, the Torah (Exodus 34:15-16; Numbers 25:2 [see context]) speaks against it, even commands against it. And even in the christian bible, James condemns such a practice for non-Jews (Acts 15:20) along with sexual immorality and the eating of blood and things strangled. James gives that as a command to be put on non-Jewish believers in Jesus.

So these actions were condemned and there were commandments (not just rational arguments) against them years before Paul. Yet to Paul, these commands and condemnations are nothing, as he tries to rationalize all of this. You don't have to think about what the Law warns, or what the leader of the church, namely James, says. All Paul's followers have to think about is what their fellow man thinks. That in itself is not bad. To be concerned about how one's actions will impact one's fellow man is good. But it's just the total absence of the higher authorities in Paul's writing. His disregard for these authorities makes him the start and finish of these recommendations he's giving his followers. The commandments given by the Law, and, for those who follow Jesus, the commandments by James govern a person's public and private life, in front of people and when one is by oneself with only the Almighty watching. Whatever praise might be given Paul for teaching people to be aware of their neighbour is negated when he ignores and rubbishes laws and ancient divine principles, calling their condemnation "nothing", for the sake of his own rationalizations.

All things are lawful? I don't think so, Paul. Not according to scripture, either for Jew or Gentile.

If Paul is said to only be attempting to reason with the intellectuals amongst his followers, or even using some sarcasm to appeal to them, the same condemnation of his methods spoken of above applies in the same way, with the additional remark that neither Paul nor the Corinthians left a tradition about how the words of this letter to the Corinthians were meant to be interpreted. That means that when christians read it today, they basically have to guess, infer, use logical reasoning to deduce what Paul is most likely saying and if he is using different communication tools, such as sarcasm. So they are not on the most solid of grounds for this sort of argument.

In case I lost you, let me summarize the issue with Paul's teaching. Meat offered to idols is forbidden to eat by the law of Moses and, for those who follow Jesus, the commandment of James for all non-Jews. It has nothing to do with whether other people see you or not. Regardless of whether you are seen, a person is not supposed to eat meat offered to idols. Paul changes the nature of the commandment to this: don't offend your weak brethren if you are seen eating food offered to idols. Whereas the commandment makes the food offered to idols forbidden, Paul says food is nothing, it's ok to eat any food, even food offered to idols. But his issue is offending others. So Paul's teaching contradicts that of the Torah and that of James, the leader of the Jerusalem church.

Chapter 9

verse 2

(1) Aren't I an apostle? Aren't I free? Have I not seen Jesus Christ our Lord? Aren't you my work in the Lord? (2) If to others I am not an apostle, yet doubtless I am to you, for you are the seal of my apostleship in the Lord. (3) This is my defence to those scrutinizing me: ...(1 Corinthians 9:1-3)

What is interesting about Paul's claim to apostleship is that it was questioned. The people who had actually seen Jesus in real life, according to the new testament, those who were chosen at the beginning of the book of Acts because they had seen the man in real life, their claims to apostleship were unquestioned. But Paul, who had never seen Jesus in real life and only could rely on his supposed vision, had his apostleship questioned and rejected.

A question to ask would be whether a person's rejection of Paul but acceptance of Jesus would have raised the same questions regarding his faith as a person today who rejects Paul. Some of Paul's words in another place would seem to suggest that you don't necessarily have to accept Paul to still be a follower of Jesus (1 Cor 1:12-14; 3:3-7). But after looking through the words of Paul, this openness from Paul doesn't stop his word and his judgment being law and giving him the right to condemn those greater than him, like the original apostles and anyone else that would happen to disagree with him. It's probably such an attitude that made his brand of christianity, the christianity that survived and is believed by essentially all christians throughout history, so exclusively Pauline, where Paul's words are the words of God and none can condemn them.

verses 19-23

(19) For though I be free from all men, yet have I made myself servant unto all, that I might gain the more. (20) And unto the Jews I became as a Jew, that I might gain the Jews; to them that are under the law, as under the law, that I might gain them that are under the law; (21) To them that are without law, as without law, (being not without law to God, but under the law to Christ,) that I might gain them that are without law. (22) To the weak became I as weak, that I might gain the weak: I am made all things to all men, that I might by all means save some. (23) And this I do for the gospel's sake, that I might be partaker thereof with you. (1 Corinthians 9:19-23)

Now, I just have to be clear on something. I know that these verses have been used by some to claim that, here, Paul openly admits duplicity, meaning that he wears whatever mask he wants, maybe even breaking laws to win people over to his gospel. And it is a possible interpretation; it is similar to the code of liars and deceivers who will be one thing to some people and another thing to other people.

But although it is a possible interpretation, I don't believe that is what Paul is saying. He seems to be saying that he tries to communicate with people from all walks of life in order to convert them to his way of thinking about the gospel. Although that can still be exactly what deception is, or what a deceiver is, I don't think Paul would openly reveal his deceptive nature.

Chapter 10

verses 1-4

(1) But I don't want you ignorant, brothers, how that all our fathers were under the cloud, and all passed through the sea; (2) And all were baptised unto Moses in the cloud and in the sea; (3) And all ate the same spiritual meat; (4) And all drank the same spiritual drink: for they drank of that spiritual rock that followed them: and that rock was the Christ. (1 Corinthians 10:1-4)

So according to Paul, the ancient Israelites who escaped Egypt "were baptised unto Moses", and ate from a rock which was "the Christ". But what must be brought out from this mystical interpretation of Paul's is the fact that it is total fantasy, a work of imagination not based on either reality or the Jewish Bible. I'll show you where my conclusion comes from.

Baptism is a sign of conversion into a religion, the christian religion. But the Israelites were not converting to any religion when they passed through the Red (or Reed) Sea. In fact, the Israelites didn't receive any new laws until they were on their way to Sinai. And the fact that the waters of the Reed Sea stood on either side as the sea was split, and that they walked on dry land shows that the Israelites themselves remained water-free throughout this miracle. That isn't similar to christian baptism which was historically the act of immersion, being covered over with water, or, later on, sprinkling; both of these acts involves the intentional contact between a person and water, i.e., you have to get wet!

The Israelites never went through or in the cloud, especially when they went through the sea. In fact, it was behind them, sometimes as a pillar of fire, to prevent the Egyptians from attacking them. And before and after that, it lead, went ahead of, them. So there was no "going through" or "being baptised" by the cloud!

Also, note the distinct opposite characters of christian baptism and the Reed Sea experience:

* Christians must believe in their religion FIRST and then get baptised;
* But the Israelites went through the Reed Sea FIRST and then they believed the Lord and Moses (Exodus 14:31, see context).

So basically, Paul has an upside-down, twisted approach to bible interpretation. But then again, that's been evident throughout Paul's usages of scripture.

And with regards to "the spiritual rock" being "the Christ", it must be stated that this is nothing more than straight out idolatry or a baseless forced "reading" of scriptures that say nothing about messiah in that way. Actually, I correct myself. It isn't an either-or scenario: it's both! It's both idolatry and a forced "reading" of scripture. It is idolatry because Israel's only Rock was their immortal, invisible, eternal God, a God without form or physical features, whereas what is known about the "christ" is that he was a man who was visible and who died. Saying that something else, other than this God, was the

Rock of Israel is idolatry, putting something other than God in the place of God.

I'll quote the following verses to forcefully kick Paul's notion to the proverbial kerb!

> *(3) For I shall call out the name of the Lord; ascribe greatness to our God: (4) the Rock; his work is perfect; for all his ways are judgment: the God of truth and without iniquity, he is just and upright. (Deuteronomy 32:3-4)*

> *(37) Then he will say, Where are their gods, the rock in whom they trusted, (38) who ate the fat of their sacrifices, drank the wine of their drink-offerings? let them arise and help you, let them be a protection over you. (39) See now that I, I, am he, and there is no god with me: I kill, and make alive; I wound, and I heal; and no one can deliver out of my hand. Deuteronomy 32:37-39 (1853 Leeser Old Testament)*

> *Fear not, neither be afraid; have I not caused you to hear it from past time, and declared it? And you are My witnesses. Is there a God beside Me? and there is no Rock; I know not any. (Isaiah 44:8)*

There is no rock with Israel except the one true God. No "christs"!

Chapter 11

verses 2 and 23

> *(2) But I praise you, brothers, because you remember me in all things, and you keep the doctrines as I delivered them to you ... (23) For I received from the Lord what I also delivered to you, that the Lord Jesus in the night in which he was betrayed took bread ... (1 Corinthians 11:2,23)*

The passage then goes on to describe the little ceremony Jesus is said to have instituted just before his capture and execution.

That which Paul received from Jesus? Interesting. He claims that his teachings come from "the Lord", i.e., Jesus, not from the apostles, those who, according to the christian bible, walked with Jesus. He doesn't even say he got this teaching from an eye-witness! No, he gets it "from the Lord".

This is interesting for a few reasons:

Firstly, Paul never followed Jesus in the flesh according to his own admission (Galatians 1). When the reader of the new testament meets Paul for the first time, he is persecuting christians. Before that, he claimed, dubiously, to be an unconverted Pharisee. So he couldn't have received his message from the Jesus that was visible to everyone who saw him.

So if he claims to get this teaching from Jesus, and he never had contact with the visible fleshy Jesus, then he opens the door to his "spirit-Jesus", the Jesus that supposedly appeared to him on the road to Damascus. This leads to the second point.

According to christian chronology, the books/letters of Paul were written some time before the gospels. The gospels were written at least decades after Paul had distributed his thoughts throughout the early christian sect. But all the synoptic gospels, that would be the first 3 gospels, have versions of the pre-death ceremony that match up quite well with Paul's "record". So that leaves a question open. What was the source of the gospel narratives of the "Lord's supper"? Was it the reports of eye-witnesses who were there at the time? Or was it the report of Paul's "spirit" communications? It doesn't help that no one knows who wrote the gospels since their authors didn't identify themselves in their gospels. All there is is tradition, which is interesting since Protestants reject tradition, except when it suits them, of course. They prefer "sola-scriptura", to use the scripture alone to determine doctrine. Unfortunately, the original translated words of the new testament didn't include words like "the gospel according to Matthew". You begin to see the limits of their approach right there.

Chapter 14

verse 21

Paul quotes Isaiah 28:11-12 to say that "other [unworldly] languages are for a sign to the unbelieving". Let's see how he does this.

PAUL:

οτι εν ετερογλωσσοις και εν χειλεσιν ετερων λαλησω τω λαω τουτω και ουδ' ουτως εισακουσονται μου λεγει κυριος

TRANSLATION: Because with those of another language and with lips of others I shall speak to this people, but not even in this manner will they listen to me.

LXX:

δια φαυλισμον χειλεων δια γλωσσας ετερας οτι λαλησουσιν τω λαω τουτω λεγοντες αυτω τουτο το αναπαυμα τω πεινωντι και τουτο το συντριμμα και ουκ ηθελησαν ακουειν

TRANSLATION: By the insulting manner of lips, by other languages, because they shall speak to this people, saying to it, this [is] the rest for him who is hungry and this [is] the destruction, and they didn't want to listen.

HEBREW BIBLE:

כִּ֚י בְּלַעֲגֵ֣י שָׂפָ֔ה וּבְלָשׁ֖וֹן אַחֶ֑רֶת יְדַבֵּ֖ר אֶל־הָעָ֥ם הַזֶּֽה׃
אֲשֶׁ֣ר ׀ אָמַ֣ר אֲלֵיהֶ֗ם זֹ֚את הַמְּנוּחָה֙ הָנִ֣יחוּ לֶֽעָיֵ֔ף וְזֹ֖את
הַמַּרְגֵּעָ֑ה וְלֹ֥א אָב֖וּא שְׁמֽוֹעַ

TRANSLATION: (11) For with stammering lips and with another language he shall speak to this people, (12) to whom he had said,

"This [is] the rest - give rest to the weary! this [is] the pause". And they didn't want to listen.

If you don't understand the languages, it is still enough to look at the translations.

First, what should be noticed is that, if this LXX (ancient Greek translation) was in existence in Paul's time, then Paul neither cares for it or the Hebrew and edits out the bit that doesn't go with his agenda. He is not too worried about changing the words of scripture.

Also, note the context of Isaiah's words is this: that the prophet is talking to Israel, not believers of one religion speaking to those who don't believe. The chapter speaks of Ephraim which is a part of Israel (Isaiah 28:1-3), but no part of the christian church. It also speaks of Jerusalem in natural terms (verse 14). As it is with a great many verses that christians, including Paul, attempt to use, the natural context is ignored. The prophet is primarily talking to the people around him about the situation they are facing. There is no sign in the context of these words that Isaiah is speaking primarily of the distant future (Paul lived centuries after Isaiah).

The most important thing to see is that the words themselves of the verse in Isaiah do not go with the message Paul is trying to convey. The language in which the people in Isaiah 28:11 spoke could have been understood by the Israelites, but they didn't want to listen. They chose not to listen. Yet, the languages, or tongues, of Paul's day couldn't even be understood by Paul himself. According to verse 2, no-one understands! In my past experience as a christian, even people who want to understand what is said by tongue-talkers are at a loss. Reading all of 1 Corinthians chapter 14, it is plain that the "tongues" of the Corinthians were unknown and couldn't be understood by men. This is not what Isaiah was talking about at all. So Paul cannot be using the scripture according to its natural context and meaning.

It is commonly understood by Jewish scholars and other commentators that Isaiah here is speaking of Israel's disobedience and its desire to have a covenant with death, i.e., Egypt. The whole message of Isaiah 28 has nothing to do with what Paul is talking about.

Out of context! Again, out of context!

verse 34

Wives/women should keep silent in the assemblies for it has not been permitted for them to speak; but let them be under subjection, as the law says. (1 Corinthians 14:34)

This verse has struck the nerve of many a woman. It has been bent, reinterpreted, modernized, anything to make women feel more welcome in church. It has been the point of much contention.

Now I myself am not one for total equality between men and women. Why? Because they are not the same in many ways, so why should they be treated the same in all ways? That approach makes little sense to me. But there is a reason why someone like me would find a problem with this verse.

Paul says that women should act like this because the law, the Law of Moses or the Hebrew Bible, says so. The question to ask is: where in the Law does it say this? To someone who reads the Hebrew Bible, they would have difficulty finding this. But thankfully we have christian commentators to clarify things for us! According to them, the source of Paul's words are in Genesis 3:16 which says:

... and your [the woman's] desire shall be for your man/husband, and he shall rule over you.

Before I deal with this claim by the christian commentators of Paul, I just want to make it very plain that it is not Paul who says he's referring to Genesis 3:16. No christian, especially of the many sects of Protestant christianity, can claim to have a tradition directly from Paul of what law he is referring to. It's just the guess of the commentators who had no contact or communication with Paul for clarification.

After stating that, let me deal with the actual text in Genesis.

It is not a law! The context is about punishments upon mankind. And the verse isn't letting you know things you should do, like a law that says "you shall not murder" or "you shall not murder" or "honour your parents." It is simply stating what the nature of the physical world would be like. For example, the text says that thorns and thistles will grow from the soil. Does this mean that one should purposefully plant them if he doesn't find any growing in his garden? It also says that man shall eat food with sweat and toil. Does this mean that we should seek to sweat whenever we eat or work for our food? The answer to both questions is "NO". These are not commands. So although we are impacted by the fact that there will always be struggle between husband and wife, man and woman, it does not have to be this way. Paul has no basis in the Law on which to give this instruction.

A christian commentator called John Gill attempts to point to the Talmud, i.e., the Oral Law, as a basis for Paul's treatment of women. But what is obvious is that Paul rejected the oral traditions of the Jews and taught based on his own convictions and his conversations with his spirit-Jesus. In fact, his words that he counts his history and law keeping in Judaism as dung can be seen as a rejection of the tenants of Judaism (Philippians 3:4-8). [NB. It should be pointed out that Paul is saying that he counts all things as dung for Jesus, and he distinctly refers to his keeping of the law, so it is not far-fetched or irrational to conclude that he sees his former life and the doctrines of it as rubbish.] So the oral law of the Jews, if it could be blamed, which is doubtful, has nothing to do with this discussion.

Once again, Paul doesn't really have a foot to stand on with this teaching.

Chapter 15

verses 3-4

(3) Because I passed down to you at first what also I received: that Christ died for our sins, according to the scriptures; (4) and that he was buried, and was raised on the third day, according to the scriptures. (1 Corinthians 15:3-4)

This verse reminds me of the gospels. When it comes to places where they make critical, important statements about Jesus being the christ, or that he had to die, and that he was to rise from the dead, they would say that these things happened "according to the Law and the Writings", or "according to scripture" like Paul. And then, they would give NO references, no quotes to prove it. So all that leaves us with is an empty statement, no stronger than saying "Michael Jackson will rise again, rule the world and we would all be his slaves, according to scripture". Yes, it is an empty statement, and it is only "full" or "apparently full" of meaning to those who already have been predisposed to the notion that Jesus is the promised anointed one.

Into this gap flies the christian commentators who try to fill Paul's mouth or mind with all sorts of scriptural references like Genesis 3 or Isaiah 53. Again, we must, must point out the fact that Paul left no tradition as to how these words were meant to be understood. He never made sure the proper interpretation of his writings were passed down throughout the generations up to the time of the modern Protestant church. Christian commentators living hundreds and thousands of years after Paul try to guess what he meant by using verses and passages from the Hebrew Bible that they are convinced point to what Paul and the gospels are claiming. But from Paul himself, we have no clue. From the gospels, we have a number of verse quotations that smack of Paul's method of butchering scripture and hacking off the context in order to promote their view. And aside from that, they also offer little insight into how the Hebrew Bible is full of their "Jesus", their "messiah".

But let me make some plain factual statements. There are no verses in the Hebrew Bible that clearly and unambiguously state that the coming "messiah" would die for sins; there are no verses in the Hebrew Bible that clearly and ambiguously state that the coming "messiah" would be buried and be raised on the third day. These are facts! Even Isaiah 53 lacks the focus to point to the future Davidic king, only mentioning "the servant". And the context of Isaiah 53 pulls the subject matter even further away from the person of the Messiah and focuses more on another child of God, another servant, namely the nation of Israel (Exodus 4:22; Isaiah 43:10). I've devoted my time going through every single one of the 300+ so-called messianic prophecies promoted by christians, and I know from experience and research using the context of scripture that no verse in the Hebrew Bible clearly backs up these claims of Paul and the gospels.

It is not within the scope of this book to go into the messianic prophecies. All I will say about these statements of Paul is that just saying "according to the scriptures" doesn't make something accord to scripture. I said it once, and I'll say it again: Paul just makes empty claims.

verse 6

> *After that, he was seen by above five hundred brothers at once, of whom the majority remain unto now, but some have fallen asleep.*

What truth there is to this claim we will never know. The gospels and the books of Luke don't appear to back Paul up when it comes to the number of people witnessing the resurrected Jesus going up to the sky. So all we have here is Paul's word. The reader of this letter to Corinthians would just have to take Paul's word for it.

Now some would attempt to use the Jewish Kuzari argument to support Paul's claim of 500 people witnessing Jesus' ascension saying that because a lot of people saw it, then it must be true, which is a horrible oversimplification of the Kuzari argument. I refer you to Jewish websites to tell you exactly what the Kuzari argument is (e.g., Living up to the Truth from Rabbi Dovid Gottlieb at www.dovidgottlieb.com). But the christian argument has two problems: 1) Jesus' resurrection was not an event that would leave enormous easily available evidence, due to the fact that the resurrection itself was witnessed by no one, whereas Sinai would have been witnessed by a nation of over 2 million people; and 2) there is no evidence that the 500 men even existed since they left no unbroken line of tradition to show that they even existed, whereas the Jews have an unbroken line of written and oral tradition, a knowledge the community had that was passed down from generation to generation, that makes the claim of the event of Sinai too strong to ignore.

So there is an enormous difference between the event at Sinai and anything that Paul or his followers can bring up.

verse 55

Paul attempts to quote Hoshea 13:14.

PAUL:
> που σου, θανατε, το νικος; που σου, θανατε, το κεντρον;
> TRANSLATION: Where [is] your victory, death? Where is your sting, death?

LXX:
> που η δικη σου θανατε που το κεντρον σου αδη
> TRANSLATION: Where [is] your right/justice, death? Where [is] your sting, Hades?

HEBREW BIBLE:

שׁ,אוֹ ל קׇ,ט,ב,ךָ,אֶ,הׅ,י מִ,וׅ,ת,דׅ,בׇ,רׅ,ךׇ,אֱ,הׅ,י

TRANSLATION: I shall be your pestilences, death! I shall be your destruction, grave! [or Oh, your pestilences, death! Oh, your destruction, grave! - Translated by Jewish Scholars: I will be your words of death; I will decree the grave upon you.]

It is amazing how different the Greek is from the Hebrew. No surprise, though. It's well known that there is a varying level of quality of translation within the ancient Greek version of the Hebrew Bible, the LXX. But again, context is different. The context of Hoshea 13 gives this promise to a sinning Ephraim and a rebellious Israel. There is no promise of an end of death here. This isn't a promise of resurrection. This is the punishment of Israel for going against God (v9). The verse before and the verse after only speaks of punishment against the people for going to idolatry (see also the first few verses of Hosea 14). Again, Paul rips the verse from its natural context and changes the meaning to suit his own agenda. If some are going to use the lame excuse that he is reciting from memory then that makes things worse for a person who they claim is filled with the spirit of the Most High, whose words are meant to be infallible, but are again and again shown to be anything but!

This process of going through Paul's writings, even at this early stage, is somewhat frustrating. I don't take pleasure in ripping apart and shredding someone else's efforts, but this guy ... spewing out such distortion and deception which is gobbled up by his followers! Every time he seems to get something even partially right, in some other way, he, seemingly purposefully, goes horribly wrong!

verse 56

Paul says:

> *The sting of death is sin and the power of sin is the law. (1 Corinthians 15:56)*

I asked a christian what this meant; they said they didn't know. But a little focused thought can help a person find the answer. Death has a painful impact on reality, much like a bee-sting, and that impact is sin. Sin is linked to and leads to death. But where does sin get its strength? According to Paul, sin is made strong by the Law, the Law of Moses, the law of righteousness. Without the law, sin has no strength. With the law, sin has strength (compare with Romans 7).

A person having some knowledge of what the Lord has to say about his own law through people such as Moses and David would have to throw out this statement of Paul with the trash. To have the law, which is the wisdom of the nation, the means of being righteous, that which renews life and makes the simple person wise, etc, to have this law - the law of God, by the way - called "the strength and power of sin" is insulting the God who gave it and called it good. And insulting God and his deeds is the definition of blasphemy.

Unfortunately, Paul twists the meaning of the law, and his lackies, like the commentator John Gill, make excuses for him!

2 Corinthians

Chapter 3

verses 6-12

Take careful note of the words of Paul, who, as some claim, loved and respected the Law of Moses.

> *(5c) ... but our ability/competence is of God; (6) Who also has qualified us [to be] ministers of the new testament; not of the letter, but of the spirit: for the letter kills, but the spirit makes alive. (7) But if the service of death, written and engraven in stones, was glorious, so that the children of Israel could not gaze intently at the face of Moses for the glory of his face - the glory of which was to be abolished/nullified - (8) how shall not the service of the spirit be more glorious? (9) For if the service of condemnation is glory, the service of righteousness shall exceed much more in glory. (1 Corinthians 3:5c-9)*

You can look at the context of these verses, just to make sure that what I say next is accurate.

It is a fact that all the underlined terms are being used by Paul to clearly point to the covenant of Sinai and the Law of Moses. The "service of death, engraved in stone" can only refer to the Decalogue, the 10 Words, or "the 10 commandments", which were written in stone. "The letter" would refer to the written letters of the law and the strict adherence to those written words. It is called a service that brings condemnation. The goodness, the glory, of such a service, according to Paul, is "passing away, being nullified". If the glory of something or someone is being diminished, dwindling away, then that entity is no longer of any importance or use and will be replaced by whatever or whoever comes next. How any of this can be seen as respectful to the Law of Moses is beyond reason.

Note that the phrase "the glory of which was to be abolished/nullified" doesn't refer to the glory of Moses' face. Verse 9 confirms that the comparison is between the different "services" or "ministrations", or covenants, not how Moses' face looked at a certain point in history.

Paul's emphasis is the nullifying, the abolishing of the letter and the coming of the "glorious spirit", the passing away of the "service of death written in stone" and the coming of the new testament. But Paul's words are bitter, hollow, and void in light of the main passages in the Jewish Bible that speak of the everlasting nature of the law. Ceremonial services involving the sanctuary and the priests are everlasting, (e.g., Exodus 27:21; 28:43; 6:18; Numbers 18). Festivals and their laws were everlasting (e.g., Exodus 31:17; Leviticus 16:29). Just look throughout the Law of Moses and note the amount of times words like "everlasting", "perpetual" and "forever" are used, and you'll see the foolishness in Paul's interpretation.

And Paul's words are nothing less than insulting to the first giving of the covenant of Sinai, turning the thing that was to give and ensure the freedom of Israel and gave life and good, into some old, condemning, deadly entity, ready to give up the ghost. See how he calls the Law of the Almighty "the service of condemnation" and his own thing "that of righteousness". This is the reason why Paul's words must be seen as arrogant, wrong, and full of deception in light of the Jewish Bible.

verses 12-13

(12) Then since we have such hope, we use great plainness of speech. (13) And we are not like Moses, who put a veil over his face

so that the sons of Israel could not steadfastly look to the end of the thing being done away with. (2 Corinthians 3:12-13)

To Paul, the covenant of Law is done away with, nullified. He uses the Greek word καταεργεω, kataerge-o, which means to nullify, render idle or useless, or abolish. A number of points can be made:

The way Paul twists what happened with Moses: He claims that, unlike Moses, he can use freedom of speech, due to the fact that Moses had covered his face. But Moses never covered his face because he had no freedom of speech. But rather, he covered his face because, unlike Paul, he had had the most direct contact with Deity and his face shone with divine brightness. Unlike Paul, who has to form logical arguments based on a strange interpretation of other writings, Moses spoke to Deity face-to-face, and spoke the word of Deity himself.

What actually happened to Moses: Paul says that Israel couldn't gaze intently at his face due to its brightness. Such a thing never happened and is written nowhere in scripture. I'll point to Exodus 34:29-35. This is where the event happens. You'll see nowhere where it says that the children of Israel couldn't gaze upon his face. All it says is that, at first, when Moses comes down the mountain with his face shining, the people were afraid to come close to him. This says nothing about not being able to look at him. Then he called to them, and then Aaron and the rulers went to him. Note that at this point, Moses' face was still uncovered and shining. Then the people drew near to him. And his face is still uncovered and shining. It is only after he finishes speaking to them that he puts a veil on, having nothing to do with an inability to look at him straight. In fact, Exodus 34:35 makes it clear that "the children of Israel saw the face of Moses that the skin of Moses' face sent forth beams", i.e., they could see the skin of his face. It is only after giving the commandment of the Almighty to the children of Israel that he could put the veil on, until he spoke to Deity again. So Paul just makes up this part of his argument.

The end of the law: Paul says προς το μη ατενισαι τους υιους ισραηλ εις το τελος του καταργουμενου "... so that the sons of Israel wouldn't gaze intently into the end (compare with Romans 10:4) of that which passes away." This refers to the law of Moses passing away. In Paul's eyes, something about Moses' brightness caused the people not to see the end of the law. And the only way people can see this end is to accept Jesus who is supposed to be the end of the law. It is only then when you see the law passing away. But this is vastly different to what the Jews at Jerusalem thought. In Acts 21:18-26, the Jerusalem church, led by James, the brother of Jesus, and where many of the real apostles (those who walked with Jesus) appear to have resided, had "many who were zealous for the law", i.e, eager to keep the law. Apparently they didn't see this "end" that Paul speaks of. Yet they accepted Jesus. Maybe they just didn't do it Paul's way.

The general message of 2 Corinthians 3 can be seen to be deceptive, insulting, and wrong when a person actually takes time to check out the sources.

Chapter 4

verse 4

(3) But also if our gospel has been hidden, it has been hidden to those who are doomed, (4) in whom the god of this age has blinded the minds of the unbelievers, so that the light of the glorious gospel of Christ, who is the image of God, should not beam on them. (2 Corinthians 4:3-4)

Some have to wonder about Paul's state of mind for him to refer to "the god of this age who blinds the minds of the unbelievers". It is obvious that he is not talking about the one true Deity, the Creator of everything. So he must be referring to another being as "the god of this age".

Who is this "god"? This has historically been understood by christians to be referring to the devil, Satan. But seeing this with the glasses of the Jewish Bible, which states that there is no other deity except the Creator of the universe, Paul leaves the door wide open for idolatry, i.e., other spiritual beings who control the world. In the modern christian mind, there are only two forces you can worship, either God or the devil. If you don't serve God in a christian way, then, by default, you must be worshipping the devil. If you don't worship the devil, then, by default you must be a christian. Now this point should be stressed. To many christians, and the message is strong in the new testament, if you are not a christian, you are worshipping the devil. If you are not worshipping God through [the belief in] "jesus christ", then you are doomed, lost, and worshipping the devil!

What a different message there is in the so-called "old testament", the Jewish Bible!!! There are no grounds for this duality there. God controls all and the "adversary", the satan, is his servant. In the Jewish Bible, you can either serve God or you don't. But if you choose not to serve God, then, according to those holy scriptures, there is no default spiritual opponent or opposite of the Almighty as christianity claims. The only thing that has happened is that you've disobeyed an essential commandment. There is no other "god" like Paul claims.

To be very blunt, such thinking is pure and simple idolatry at worst! At best, it's just a doctrine that has no basis in the Jewish Bible, and thus has no foundation.

verse 13

(13) For we, having the same spirit of faith - according as it is written, "I believed, and therefore I have spoken" [Psalm 116:10] - we also believed and therefore speak, (14) knowing that He who raised up the Lord Jesus shall also raise us up by Jesus, and shall

present us with you. (2 Corinthians 4:13-14, Green's Modern King James Version)

So Paul here quotes Psalm 116:10.

This is one of the few occasions where Paul actually manages to quote the LXX, that ancient Greek translation, word-for-word. Then again, in the Greek, the phrase "I believed and therefore I have spoken" is only three words. But still, give credit where credit is due.

But that's where the credit stops!

Now it could rightly be pointed out that the word "therefore" that Paul uses is a mistranslation of the Hebrew word which doesn't mean "therefore". This is not just my opinion and not just a result of my meager experience with the Hebrew word. In Keil and Delitzsch's commentary on this verse, they also say the same thing. So Paul is going along with the LXX's mistranslation of this whole verse. But again, that is not the problem here. A familiar motif will raise its ugly head.

If a person would just read Psalm 116 in its entirety, it should be plain that the subject of the song is not a belief in Jesus, but rather the writer's experience of struggle, whilst giving thanks to God. The words of the whole verse in Psalm 116 is, "I believed/trusted even when I spoke: I am greatly afflicted". The verse has nothing to do with Paul's message. The chapter of Psalm 116 has nothing to do with Paul's message.

Paul is not explaining what the verse means; he is just pulling some words from the Psalms that he can use to make a point, to express his own feeling. It has nothing to do with interpretation in order to understand the original intent. Paul has his own message, separate from that of scripture, and these out-of-context words agree with a sentiment that he is feeling, so he just uses them with no regards to context. It's similar to me seeing a stranger who is rooted to the spot and not moving, and then saying "it's just like the verse that says 'he shall be like a tree'." Those who know their bibles, or look it up, will see that I'm quoting a portion of Psalm 1. The whole chapter is about the righteous man who loves Torah, the Law of the Lord, and speaks about how prosperous he is, using the tree metaphor. My usage of the scripture had absolutely nothing to do with the righteousness of this stranger, only that he was standing still. Paul uses the scripture in much the same way where what scripture is actually saying is put aside for the sake of the moment.

So once again, Paul takes the verse out of context.

Chapter 6

verse 2

Paul here quotes Isaiah 49:8, agreeing with the LXX version. Let's just compare Paul's words with the Hebrew Scriptures.

PAUL:
> *At the approved time, I heard you, and in the day of salvation, I helped you.*

ISAIAH:
> *At the time of favour, I answered you, and in the day of salvation, I helped you.*

For one of the very few times, Paul actually quotes something that is very similar, if not the same, as the Jewish Bible. This is a pretty good rendering by Paul.

BUT ... (unfortunately, there had to be a "but")

Paul's great weakness again comes into view. The problem, as usual, is the context. Isaiah 49:7 onwards is referring to Israel as a nation. The Almighty is saying that he saved and answered them, i.e., Israel the nation. The context speaks of saving from slavery and maltreatment at the hands of other nations. This is a salvation in real life, something visible. This is a prophecy to a nation, not a religious sect.

But Paul is not referring to the salvation mentioned in Isaiah, but rather an invisible "spiritual" salvation. Whereas Isaiah was speaking of the redemption of a real nation, called Israel, from other nations, Paul is referring to a spiritual deliverance from sin given through faith in Jesus separate from works of obedience. So basically, Paul is ignoring context again and speaking of his own message, not bringing across anything from Isaiah himself.

verse 13

Paul appears to use another quote in this verse, apparently Leviticus 26:12. Once again, we'll look at the comparisons, comparing between Paul's Greek, the LXX Greek, and the Hebrew standard.

PAUL:

οτι ενοικησω εν αυτοις και εμπεριπατησω και εσομαι αυτων θεος και αυτοι εσονται μου λαος

TRANSLATION: I shall dwell amongst them and I shall walk amongst [them] and shall be their God and they shall be my people.

LXX:

και εμπεριπατησω εν υμιν και εσομαι υμων θεος και υμεις εσεσθε μου λαος

TRANSLATION: I shall walk amongst you and I shall be your God and you, you shall be my people.

HEBREW BIBLE:

וְ אַתֶ ם לְ אֵ אל הׅ ים לְ כֶ ם וְ הׅ יׅ יתׅ י בְ תוֹ כׇ כֶ ם וׅ הׅ תׇ הׅ לַ כֶ תׅ י
לְ עׇ ם תׅ הׅ יוׅ-לׅ י

*TRANSLATION: And I shall walk about in your midst, and I shall be
your God and you, you shall be my people.*

We can either call this a bad translation from Paul, or he is just
editing the words, but still, it doesn't really change the message of
the verse in the original version. So Paul can only be criticized for
changing the words, but not really moving too far from the message
of the verse.

But Paul again applies promises meant for Israel to others, to those
who he chooses, who are in his camp of believers. He appears to
spiritualise the intent of the scripture which refers to God dwelling
amongst the nation of Israel as a people. In Leviticus 26:11, it speaks
of the tabernacle being set up, but the verse which Paul uses refers
more to God walking amongst his people, not simply residing in the
temple. So Paul seems to misapply verse 12 to refer to the
tabernacle/temple and then apply it to his group as if they are the
temple or the people Israel. The context of the verse also has nothing
to do with Paul's message of rejecting unbelievers, but rather of the
care that the nation Israel should take when they enter the land of
promise and the punishments that would befall them should they sin.

At the very least, this interpretation by Paul is questionable. It has
the merit of still requiring people to live holy lives which is not too
distantly removed from the message of Leviticus. But the link is not
strong. I wouldn't blast Paul for the way he uses this verse. But I
wouldn't pat him on the back either. The link to the context is also
quite weak, so he doesn't help himself very much.

verse 17

Paul here quotes from Isaiah 52:11,12. Let's see how this goes.

PAUL:

εξελθατε εκ μεσου αυτων και αφορισθητε λεγει κυριος και ακαθαρτου μη απτεσθε καγω εισδεξομαι υμας

TRANSLATION: Get out from their midst and be excluded, says [the] Lord, and don't touch an unclean thing, and I shall accept you.

LXX:

αποστητε αποστητε εξελθατε εκειθεν και ακαθαρτου μη απτεσθε εξελθατε εκ μεσου αυτης αφορισθητε οι φεροντες τα σκευη κυριου οτι ου μετα ταραχης εξελευσεσθε ουδε φυγη πορευσεσθε πορευσεται γαρ προτερος υμων κυριος και ο επισυναγων υμας κυριος ο θεος ισραηλ

TRANSLATION: Distance yourself! Distance yourself! Get out from there and don't touch an unclean thing! Get out from its/her midst! Be excluded, those carrying the vessels of [the] Lord! Not with trouble shall you be liberated, nor with hasty flight you shall go. For [the] Lord [is] in front of you and the one gathering you [is the] Lord the God of Israel.

HEBREW BIBLE:

סוּרוּ סוּרוּ צְאוּ מִשָּׁם טָמֵא אַל־תִּגָּעוּ צְאוּ מִתּוֹכָהּ הִבָּרוּ נֹשְׂאֵי כְּלֵי יְיָ: כִּי לֹא בְחִפָּזוֹן תֵּצֵאוּ וּבִמְנוּסָה לֹא תֵלֵכוּן כִּי־הֹלֵךְ לִפְנֵיכֶם יי וּמְאַסֵּפְכֶם* אֱלֹהֵי יִשְׂרָאֵל

TRANSLATION: Depart! Depart! Get out from there and don't touch an unclean thing! Get out from its/her midst and be pure, those carrying the vessels of HaShem. For not in haste shall you go forth and in flight you shall not go, for the Lord is going before you and the God of Yisrael [is] your rearguard*.

מְאַסֵּף me'asef: in the Hebrew version, both in the Hebrew and the English, you'll see a word with a star (*) next to it. It's not a common verbal form. The same verbal form is used in Numbers 10:25 and Joshua 6:9,13. The word means "rearguard", someone who watches the rear of a group of people.

Now this is significant. Why? Because Paul, not only edits the verse, cutting out the bits he doesn't want, but he mistranslates the final clause as the Lord receiving or accepting a person into his favour.

But the actual text of Isaiah 52:11-12 speaks of God delivering Israel and being both in front of them, and being behind them, being their "rearguard". Again, Paul makes up a totally separate message from that of the prophet of God, Isaiah.

Now some may say "but Paul quotes from the LXX". And I would reply that Paul quotes what he wants and cuts out the rest. And the words of the Septuagint for the most agrees with the message of the Hebrew Bible, but this time saying that God is gathering Israel, leading it from captivity, . Even though this is a mistranslation, it still goes with the general message of the context, unlike Paul who makes up a brand new message for these words.

So either way, whether we refer to the Hebrew or the Greek version of the Jewish Bible, Paul has both mistranslated, edited, and taken out of context the portions of these verses that he uses. It has little to do with believers and unbelievers, but rather Deity delivering his captive Israel from their captors. Again it's Paul's agenda speaking and not scripture.

verse 18

And I shall be to you a father and you, you shall be to me sons and daughters, says [the] Lord Almighty. (2 Corinthians 6:18)

It is important to know that the word "you" in Greek refers to the plural "you", as in speaking to a group of people as opposed to an individual.

Now in this verse, Paul seems to be quoting God. But search as I like, these words do not appear in the Jewish Bible. We can ignore the claims that Paul is quoting 2 Samuel 7:14 or 1 Chronicles 28:6 because they are both speaking of Solomon, an individual. So basically, Paul isn't quoting the Hebrew Scriptures here.

And if he isn't quoting scripture, the only other conclusion is that he is attempting to speak for the Almighty. And if we even attempt to accept the claims of those who follow Paul that he is quoting scripture, then it only shows the fallacy of Paul's method, in that he totally distorts scripture for his own pleasure. And his attempting to speak for God shows his own arrogance in making himself a prophet.

Chapter 8

verse 15

(12) For if the eagerness is present, it is acceptable [to give] according to what one has, and not according to what one does not have. (13) For it is not that others may have relief, but you [have] affliction; (14) but by equality in the present time; your abundance for their need, that their abundance also may be for your need; so that there may be equality; (15) as it is written, "The one [with] the much didn't exceed; and the one [with] the little didn't get less. [Exodus 16:18]" (2 Corinthians 8:12-15)

Paul uses the verse in Exodus to support his argument that the Corinthians should give what they have in support of those in need; maybe those in need will one day supply the needs of the Corinthians when they need it. This is so that there will be "equality".

Now for those who don't know, Exodus 16 is about the children of Israel getting manna, a special food given by Deity whilst they were in the desert. They were commanded that each man should gather a certain amount for each person that would last for the day. Some gathered more than they should, and others gathered less. But, amazingly, when it was all measured out for their family, everyone in Israel had the same amount for each person (see Exodus 16, especially verses 14-18). That's why it was said that "he that had much did not have extra, he that had little didn't lack."

So we have Paul talking about giving to someone in need and sharing; and we have Exodus talking about people gathering food for themselves and having enough no matter how much they took. It should be plain that Paul had taken the verse out of context. Even the link between Paul's message and the message of Exodus is weak. I would have said that there was some link in the message of equality Paul was giving, but even that isn't enough. In what way were the Israelites equal? They had the same amount of food each. How were the Corinthians equal with those who they would help? The way Paul seems to phrase it, the Corinthians help those in need, so that when those in need are out of desperation and in a better position, they'll help the Corinthians. Maybe the equality comes in the Corinthians giving enough so that everyone would have the same amount, both Corinthian and the poor people. And then there would be a constant sharing between the two so they help each other out in making sure that everyone has the same amount of funds or food. But still, only on the very superficial level, everyone may have the same amount of funds or food, but that's only by sharing. That has nothing to do with the equality that the people of Israel had with regards to the manna. So the link between the two is weak and superficial and is still a case of Paul ignoring context.

Now I have read the christian commentaries on Exodus 16, especially that of John Wesley, who claims that the people in Israel would share their manna to make sure that they all had the same amount. There is just one main problem with that: it is not what the text says; he is adding too much to what the verse actually mentions. I wonder if he is using his christian methods of interpretation and using Paul to interpret Exodus, i.e., going backwards, as opposed to letting the words of Exodus speak for themselves and determine if Paul is really agreeing with its message.

Chapter 9

verse 9

(8) And God is able to make all grace abound toward you; so that in all things, [at] all times, having all self-contentment, you may abound to every good work - (9) as it is written, He has dispersed; he has given to the poor; his righteousness remains for ever [Psalm 112:9]. (2 Corinthians 9:8-9)

Give credit where it's due! Paul actually translates the verse quite well, and his usage of it is quite fair. The verse in Psalms is an open verse meant to describe a righteous man. Paul isn't trying to give controversial doctrines in this instance. So there's nothing much to say here apart from the fact that this is rare. If only all, or even most, of Paul's quotations were this accurate. Unfortunately ...

Chapter 10

verse 17

But the boaster, let him boast in [the] Lord. (2 Corinthians 10:17)

See my comments on 1 Corinthians 1:31. It's basically the same thing apart from the addition, in this verse, of the word "but".

Chapter 11

verse 2

(1) Oh, that you would bear with me a little in senselessness. But also bear with me. (2) For I am zealous for you with a zealousness of God. For I have espoused you to one man, to present you, a pure virgin, to Christ. (2 Corinthians 11:1-2)

This is a very telling verse since it shows Paul's aim in contrast to that of biblical Judaism. No matter how authoritative a messenger or agent is, even the mighty Moses, the aim is to get the people connected to God. Paul's aim is to link people to an intermediary, someone between God and man, i.e., "messiah". It has always been possible for even a non-Jew to have relationship with Deity without an intermediary. Paul simply puts something in between a man and his God. Unfortunately, at any level, if your aim is to link someone to an intermediary rather than link that person directly to the Source, it only becomes a barrier, a further separation, as opposed to a bridge, something which is a common, but false picture of Jesus and his death in christianity.

verse 4

For if, then, the one coming proclaims another Jesus, whom we have not proclaimed, or if you receive another spirit, which you did not receive, or another gospel, which you never accepted, you might well bear [these]. (2 Corinthians 11:4)

As will be shown later in Galatians, but is seen in this verse, the only message of Jesus to be accepted is Paul's! Thus, because the mainstream church adopts Paul's version of Jesus, modern christianity is the product of Paul as opposed to Jesus' own disciples/apostles, the 11 plus the one chosen by the apostles in Acts 1, those who had actually walked with the man Jesus. But as can be seen later in this chapter of 2 Corinthians, Paul sees himself as nothing less than equal to them (verses 5-6).

verses 1, 16 and 17

(1) Oh, that you would bear with me a little in senselessness. But also bear with me... (16) Again I say, let no one think me to be senseless. But if otherwise, you receive me as senseless, so that I may also boast a little. (17) What I speak, I do not speak according to the Lord, but as in senselessness, in this assurance of boasting. (2 Corinthians 11:1,16-17)

Some use these verses to warn readers not to take Paul too seriously with the words that he uses in this chapter. But Paul never said that he was lying! The only thing Paul is doing is "boasting", but his "boasts" are not baseless lies. Why? Because some points, such as verse 4 which I commented on before, are repeated in other books where he is not speaking foolishness, at least his kind of foolishness. Also he is still boasting as others do to show his "fleshy" superiority or his qualities that make him at least equal to his opponents. And he is using factual evidence!

I say this just to put the rest of the chapter into some context. Paul's words can be commented on and criticized without the answer coming back that he shouldn't be taken too seriously.

verses 22-23

(22) Are they Hebrews? Me too! Are they Israelites? Me too! Are they the seed of Abraham? Me too! (23) Are they ministers of Christ? - I speak being deranged, Me, more so! I have been in labours more abundantly, in whippings above measure, in prisons more abundantly, in deaths many times. (2 Corinthians 11:22-23)

These verses seem to point to the fact that Paul's enemies in this context are other Jews professing Jesus, but in a way different to Paul.

Although friends and followers of Paul, those who try to interpret this in a pro-Paul way, say that they were simply Judaizers, those who would make Gentile christian believers into fully fledged Jews, being circumcised and following the law of Moses. But here I will show another possibility. Seeing Paul's strained relationship with the law-keeping apostles (Acts 21:18-26; Galatians 2), apostles who preached the keeping of the Law of the Lord, it could well be that those who Paul sees as enemies are those who preached the apostles' version of Jesus and his message as opposed to Paul's version. Some may not like such a possibility, but unfortunately for them, it will always be a possibility, a possibility with evidence that can be drawn from the christian bible itself.

verses 32-33

(31) The God and Father of our Lord Jesus Christ, who is blessed forever, knows that I am not lying. (32) In Damascus the governor of Aretas the king guarded the city of the Damascenes, desiring to arrest me. (33) And I was lowered in a basket through a window through the wall, and escaped his hands. (2 Corinthians 11:30-33)

It is interesting to compare this, Paul's words, with the way Acts 9:22-25 depicts it. I'm sure Paul-loving christians (that is said just to highlight the point that not all people who claim or claimed to follow Jesus loved or followed Paul or even accepted his self-proclaimed apostleship) could find a way to harmonize these two accounts. But on certain levels, they do not agree. The source of Paul's harassment is different in each account, one being this governor of Damascus; and the other being the Jews of the city. Again, Paul lovers see the harmony and exclaim that these differences show the "new testament's" truth since things too similar can smack of forced agreement caused by distortion or collusion. But sometimes an obvious disagreement can be exactly that: a disagreement/contradiction. The choice of harmony or contradiction I leave to the reader's judgment.

Chapter 13

verse 1

This third [time] I am coming to you. Upon the mouth of two witnesses and three, every word shall be established. (2 Corinthians 13:1).

Now Paul doesn't say that he's quoting anything in this verse. But his words do reflect Deuteronomy 19:15. For that reason I just want to quote the 3 sources that are said to be the source of Paul's words: the Hebrew Bible; the Septuagint; and, based on the commentary of Adam Clarke, Matthew 18:16. Why am I quoting these sources? Because some say that Paul is quoting from one of them and I want to show you how his version compares to them in order to judge such a claim.

PAUL:
... επι στοματος δυο μαρτυρων και τριων στηθησεται παν ρημα
TRANSLATION: ... on the mouth of two witnesses and three every word shall be established.

LXX:
επι στοματος δυο μαρτυρων και επι σοματος τριων μαρτυρων στηθησεται παν ρημα
TRANSLATION: ... on the mouth of two witnesses and on the mouth of three witnesses every word shall be established.

MATTHEW:
επι στοματος δυο μαρτυρων η τριων σταθη παν ρημα
TRANSLATION: ... on the mouth of two witnesses or three every word may be established.

HEBREW BIBLE:
דְּבָר יָקוּם שְׁלֹשָׁה־עֵדִים עַל־פִּי אוֹ עֵדִים שְׁנֵי עַל־פִּי
TRANSLATION: Upon the mouth of two witnesses or upon the mouth of three witnesses a matter shall stand.

Now, as you can see, there are slight differences between all the Greek versions. And all of the Greek versions add or take away something from the Hebrew version. But whereas all the Greek versions says "every word", the Hebrew version of Deuteronomy only says "a word shall stand", not "every word shall stand". But these are just slight differences and the message is generally the same. It would seem that Paul does get his statement from Deuteronomy 19, even if he simply alludes to it, rather than overtly quoting it.

But Paul uses this verse in a strange way. He makes it seem like his coming to the Corinthians three times is similar to the three witnesses of Deuteronomy 19:15. But the link is weak, if there is any. In Deuteronomy, the two or three witnesses are three different eye-witnesses, three different sources. And they are to help judge matters of law in Deuteronomy in the case of a crime that is reported to have been committed. Paul's coming three times, the appearance of the same man, has no similar authority. I'll give an example.

If there is a court of law, and three witnesses are called, and there one person comes once, and then again, and then a third time giving the same or similar testimony, that three part testimony is not considered as three witnesses. It is one witness. And nothing can be firmly established by one witness, whereas, according to the law of the Hebrew Bible, three different witnesses establish a matter. That's why the whole verse in Deuteronomy 19:15 says:

One witness shall not stand against a man for any [case of] iniquity or for any sin, in any sin where he shall sin. By the mouth of two witnesses or by the mouth of three witnesses, the matter shall stand.

The principle taken as a whole invalidates Paul's usage of it.

So how Paul's coming to the Corinthians three times relates to Deuteronomy 19:15 is mysterious unless we fall back to Paul's usual mode of operation, i.e., taking a verse or phrase out of context and twisting it for his own purposes.

One may say, "Isn't the word "twisting" a bit too strong? I mean, don't we all do something like what Paul's doing at times: using a verse or a phrase from the Bible without care of its context; and sometimes even using it in a different way than the natural context means?" Good question. It depends on the following factors. Are we using that verse or phrase as if it has divine authority, or just voicing our own opinion? Do we do this once in a while or almost every single time we get a chance to quote scripture? Have we been educated on what a scripture really means before we use it? Are we using this interpretation to push a doctrine that the whole of scripture knows nothing of?

The problem with Paul is that almost every time he quotes scripture, he takes it out of context and gives it a meaning that must conform to his own agenda, ignoring the message of scripture as a whole. His convictions about Jesus and the Hebrew Bible are paramount and have the highest authority, even against other apostles, even against Jewish teachers who obviously had and have a better grasp on the teachings of the Hebrew Bible than he did. To go against him means a curse on your head! To have a different interpretation of who Jesus was is to be cut off! To view the writings of the man as a whole, to see his general usage of scripture, where he just cuts out a verse and uses it how he wishes, leads to the conclusion that he is not simply voicing an opinion, but what he considers to be THE truth. And that forceful character of his helps lead to the conclusion that he is forcefully distorting scripture, i.e., twisting it, to conform to his agenda.

Galatians

Chapter 1

verses 11-20

Paul gives us some of his history.

> *(11) And, I make known to you, brothers, the gospel, the one preached by me, that it is not according to man. (12) For I did not receive it from man, nor was I taught, except by a revelation of Jesus Christ. (13) For you heard my former way of life in Judaism, that in [the] extreme, I persecuted the assembly of the God, and ravaged it. (14) And I progressed in Judaism beyond many contemporaries in my race, being much more a zealot of the traditions of my fathers. (15) But when it pleased God, who set me apart from my mother's womb, and having called me by His grace, (16) to reveal His son in me so that I might proclaim the good news of him among the nations, immediately I did not take counsel with flesh and blood; (17) nor did I go up to Jerusalem to those apostles before me, but I went into Arabia and returned again to Damascus. (18) Then after three years I went up to Jerusalem to see Peter, and stayed with him fifteen days. (19) But I saw no other of the apostles, except James the Lord's brother. (20) And what I write to you, behold, before the God, I do not lie. Galatians 1:11-20 (Green's Modern King James Version)*

Now compare this account with Acts 9, especially from verse 1 to 29. This describes Paul upon his conversion to christianity as described by another writer, believed to be Luke. There is no mention of a 3 year time span. Shortly after Paul's conversion, he spent certain days with the disciples in Damascus and immediately began preaching Jesus in the synagogues there. In order to escape the Jews there, he fled over the wall, with help from the disciples there, and Barnabas took him and brought him to the apostles. He was with them, coming in and going out of Jerusalem. Read this for yourself to confirm my words.

There is an obvious contradiction between what Paul says in Galatians and what the writer of Acts says.

Chapter 2

verses 6-9

(6) But from those who seemed to be something (what kind they were then does not matter to me; God does not accept the face of man), for those seeming [to be something] conferred nothing to me. (7) But on the contrary, seeing that I have been entrusted with the good news of the uncircumcision, as Peter [had the good news] of the circumcision; (8) for He working in Peter to the mission of the circumcision also worked in me to the nations. (9) and knowing the grace given to me, James, and Cephas, and John, who seemed to be pillars, gave right hands of fellowship to Barnabas and me, that we [are] for the nations, but they for the circumcision. (Galatians 2:6-9)

Take note of the backhanded comments Paul uses about the true apostles. They only "seemed to be" or were "reputed to be" pillars. In fact, he may have been talking about the apostles as a whole from verse 6, as those who "seemed to be something". In Paul's eyes, it doesn't matter who they are or what importance they had. Note, that that is not the way to speak respectfully of people, especially those who were supposed to have walked and talked with Jesus. These people mattered little to Paul.

What humility! Paul says that the apostles added nothing to him, meaning that he knew or had enough already so he didn't need anything further from the men who actually walked with and learnt from the living Jesus! How humble! *sarcasm*

verse 16

Paul continues his thoughts in a manner that is similar to that of the book of Romans. He says:

Therefore, seeing that a man is not made righteous by works of law, except through the faith of Jesus Christ, and we, we have believed in Christ Jesus so that we may be made righteous by the faith of Christ, and not by works of law, because no flesh may be made righteous by works of law. (Galatians 2:16)

Now, we aren't going to go into any weird exegesis here, looking for ways to see Paul as respecting the Law of Moses, as some "messianic" Jews (i.e., Jews who have abandoned their heritage to become christians) and other christians try to do. Reading the whole book of Galatians, one can see that Paul is speaking of nothing other than the Law of Moses in this verse. He is saying that doing the deeds, the works, that the law commands doesn't make a person righteous. Others use the word "justify", but that just means "to make just, to make righteous".

It should be clear, at least logically or realistically, that Paul makes no sense with his statements. From the side of real life and real experience, how do you know if a person is good or not? Is it if they have wonderful thoughts and great convictions alone? No! It is because they do good and moral actions, actions that line up with a proper code of ethics and honourable lifestyle. If a person can show self control in their actions, that actually shows that they are righteous, as opposed to someone's invisible and internal beliefs.

But what makes Paul's situation worse is that the Jewish Bible as a whole contradicts and undermines his whole "by-faith-alone" theory. How and where does the Jewish Bible do this?

(24) And the Lord commanded us to do all these statutes, to fear the Lord our God; that it would be well for us at all times, and that he might preserve us alive, as it is this day. (25) And it shall be righteousness to us, if we observe to do all this commandment before the Lord our God, as he commanded us. (Deuteronomy 6:24-25)

It is clear here that the Jews get righteousness by doing what God commands in his Law. And it makes sense: if you obey the laws of the Lord, then you are doing what is right, and you are righteous, you characterize, you embody, the God-given standards of the morality and justice.

Now an acquaintance, Prescott Johnson, says this: if a carrot can do what the Lord says, that is, to grow and be edible, then it is absolute foolishness to think that it is impossible for us to. Remember that Paul's fallacy is the notion that righteousness only happens to you if you are absolutely perfect in your obedience of the Law of Moses. His followers may even point to the "all" in Deuteronomy 6:25 in order to say that righteousness would come to those who kept all the commands of God. But again, scripture contradicts their idea.

For a man, there is no righteous one in the earth, who does good and doesn't sin. (Ecclesiastes 7:20)

Now this verse is used by christians to say that there is no righteous person at all. But that isn't what the verse says. It does not say "there is none righteous". It says that there is no one righteous who doesn't make any mistake at all. That means that there are righteous people (see Ecclesiastes 7:15; 8:14), but they don't live in an absolutely perfect way. Another way of saying this is that everyone makes mistakes. But it is essential that you see that even though they make mistakes, scripture still calls them righteous!

This tells us something we should already know in our day-to-day experiences: God knows our frame, our limitations; and thus we know that a general and earnest directed effort to conform to God's law makes one righteous. This is shown in another passage that refutes Paul's doctrine, which I have mentioned before, Ezekiel 18:5-8. This passage clearly shows that if a man does certain deeds, then the Lord declares that that person is righteous! Thus flesh can be and is justified, declared righteous, seen to be just, by works of law, by deeds that line up with the Law of the Lord.

To make the statement clear, let me quote Paul's words and then paraphrase.

Paul: No flesh can be justified by works of law.
Paraphrase: no one can be righteous by obeying the Lord.

The "works of law" are things that the Almighty says and commands to humanity and/or Israel. Therefore, to keep these laws is simply obeying the Lord Almighty. So, you can see that Paul's words make no sense. In fact, scripture teaches that you can be righteous by obeying the Lord, or by keeping his law.

So Paul is just dead wrong.

verse 21

> *I do not neutralize the grace of the Deity; for if righteousness is through law, then Christ died for nothing. (Galatians 2:21)*

So based on what I've already shown from scripture, and scripture's willingness to call people righteous, if we go with Paul's theological statement in this verse, if righteousness comes through law-keeping, then Jesus died for nothing. And we can confirm that with a big YES!. Since righteousness does come through law keeping or by obeying what God commands, then, based on Paul's words, Jesus did die for nothing.

But it is important to know that if we are talking about the law of the Lord, true obedience to it is not a dry affair, with no aspect of a real relationship behind it between a man and his God. The law itself says to "love God with your all" (Deuteronomy 6:5) and to "love your neighbour like yourself" (Leviticus 19:18). It advocates the real worship of God, not some hypocritical routine existence. So when we speak of "works of law" or "deeds of law", it includes the divine and human love by default. Thus, keeping the law properly as a whole must breed a righteousness and a righteous people/person.

Chapter 3

verse 6

Even as Abraham believed the Deity and it was reckoned to him to be righteousness [Genesis 15:6]. (Galatians 3:6)

Paul here quotes Genesis 15:6. This has already been dealt with, so please refer to <u>my comments on Romans 4:3</u>.

verse 7

For you know that the ones [that are] of faith, those are the sons of Abraham. (Galatians 3:7)

Paul says that those of faith are children of Abraham. First let's deal with the extremes.

Paul cannot and must not mean this literally to speak of any faith whatsoever, i.e., he is not saying that anyone that has any sort of faith is a child of Abraham, regardless of whether they have faith in Zeus or Vishna or any god. In his writings, Paul uses "faith" to speak specifically and concretely of "faith in Jesus as the sacrificial christ".

But if we actually look at Abraham's life, the other extreme of interpreting Paul's words, we encounter a problem: this is not the faith of Abraham who only believed in the one true Deity and in obeying His voice, keeping His commandments and laws (Genesis 26:5, see context). At best, the faith of Abraham means God promising him something and then him trusting God to fulfil that promise, as Genesis 15 shows. But this faith of Abraham had nothing to do believing that a man would die as a sacrifice. There is no textual evidence of that. And there is no overt and clear evidence in scripture, in the Jewish Bible, that such a thing was promised. I've looked.

So if we take "faith" too generally, Paul's words are meaningless and confusing. But if we focus on the faith of Abraham, it is not the same as Paul's faith. So once again, this is all about Paul's agenda, and his using biblical words and events and twisting them into his own image for his own purposes.

verse 8

Paul here quotes Genesis 12:3.

And the scripture, that the Deity making the nations righteous, gave the good news beforehand to Abraham that "all the nations shall be blessed in you. [Genesis 12:3]". (Galatians 3:8)

Let's take note of the difference between exegesis, deriving meaning from the scripture, and eisegesis, reading meaning into the scripture that isn't there. Genesis 12:3 and similar verses only say that Abraham would bring a blessing to the world. It is a very general blessing that is not defined by the verse itself. But Paul manages to squeeze a whole doctrine of the nations, the gentiles, being made righteous by believing in Jesus, into a verse and context that says absolutely nothing about such a notion.

If we notice the role of the priestly nation of Israel, or the fact that all the major monotheistic worldviews descend from Abraham, other possible understandings of the verse in Genesis 12, then it is difficult, if not impossible, to say which of these interpretations is meant by Genesis 12:3 when taken in isolation. And even in context, Paul's "interpretation" is nowhere to be found.

verse 10

Paul quotes Deuteronomy 27:26. We'll compare his version with the Septuagint and the original Hebrew version.

PAUL:

οσοι γαρ εξ εργων νομου εισιν υπο καταραν εργων γεγραπται γαρ επικαταρατος πας ος ουκ εμμενει εν πασιν τοις γεγραμμενοις εν τω βιβλιω του νομου του ποιησαι αυτα

TRANSLATION: For as many as are of works of law are under a curse, for it has been written, "For cursed [be] all who do not remain/persevere in all of what is written in the book of the law to do it".

LXX:

επικαταρατος πας ανθρωπος ος ουκ εμμενει εν πασιν τοις λογοις του νομου τουτου του ποιησαι αυτους ...

TRANSLATION: Cursed [be] every person who doesn't remain/persevere in all the words of this law to do them.

HEBREW BIBLE:

אָרוּר אֲשֶׁ֣ר לֹֽא־יָקִ֛ים אֶת־דִּבְרֵ֥י הַתּוֹרָֽה־הַזֹּ֖את לַעֲשׂ֣וֹת אוֹתָ֑ם

TRANSLATION: Cursed be one who doesn't affirm the words of this Torah/Law to do them.

As you can see, Paul doesn't exactly quote either the Hebrew Bible, or the Septuagint. He feels the need to change the words "the words of this Law" to "all of what is written in the book of the Law". Paul's words have a much stricter sense to them than the words of the Hebrew Bible, more strict than even the Septuagint. But let's get to the meat of the matter.

It is very easy to say that εμμενω emmen-o, is not a good translation of the Hebrew word קום quwm. The Greek word emmen-o has the root meaning of "to stay in a place or thing". It has implications of remaining constant or fixed, holding true to something, to stand fast. Here, in Deuteronomy 27:26, it is in its active sense. So with the negative attached to it, it means "he does not continue in or hold true to". The Hebrew word quwm properly means to rise, but has the extension of standing and being erect. Here it is in causative form, so it means "to cause to rise, or cause to stand". So the Greek is saying something slightly different to the Hebrew.

Now despite this difference in meaning, the way each word is used in context doesn't really help Paul's case. But what is Paul's case? Let's see what the classical commentators say. John Gill says when commenting on Paul's words in this verse,

> ... and [the Law] requires perfect obedience, an observance of all things contained in it, which can never be performed by fallen man.
> ... moreover, the law requires constant perfect obedience; not only that a man should do all things commanded in it, but that he should continue to do them from his infancy, to the day of his death; and in failure hereof, it pronounces every man cursed, without any respect to persons, or any regard to pleas, taken from the infirmity of human nature, the sincerity of the heart, or repentance for transgressions.

Adam Clarke, in his commentary of this verse, says:

> All that seek salvation by the performance of the works of the law are under the curse, because it is impossible for them to come up to the spiritual meaning and intent of the law; and the law pronounces them cursed that continue not in all things which are written in the

book of the law to do them. Hence, every Jew is necessarily under the curse of God's broken law; and every sinner is under the same curse, though he be not a Jew, who does not take refuge in the salvation provided for him by the Gospel. It is worthy of remark that no printed copy of the Hebrew Bible preserves the word ... "All" in Deuteronomy 27:26, which answers to the apostle's word "all", here. St. Jerome says that the Jews suppressed it, lest it should appear that they were bound to perform all things that are written in the book of the law.

This commentator goes as far as to accuse the Jews of manipulating their own most holiest portion of scripture. It has to be said that this accusation is ridiculous when you actually take note of the way that the Jews treated their scripture, washing themselves when they wrote every single letter, because they believed that every single letter was given by God. And christians know this!!! Plus they had a nationwide tradition, and multiple copies of the law, all of which buttressed the version that was historically stowed away in the Temple. Everything about the actions of the Jews and their written and oral tradition worked to preserve and protect the letter of the law. The root of such comments can only come from christian arrogance, believing themselves and their teachers to be the truth. Anyone, even the Jews, who contradicts them must be wrong and have covered up the truth! I know that Adam Clarke uses Targums and the Septuagint to prove his point, but his essential problem is the same: all the Hebrew originals have no "all", and only some translations have it.

But his point is the same as Gill's: no one can keep the law because "they are bound to perform all things that are written in the book of the law" and thus "the law pronounces them cursed".

Let's also see what John Calvin says about this verse of Paul:

The sentence of the law is, that all who have transgressed any part of the law are cursed. Let us now see if there be any living man who fulfils the law. But no such person, it is evident, has been, or ever can be found. All to a man are here condemned. The minor and the conclusion are wanting, for the entire syllogism would run thus: "Whoever has come short in any part of the law is cursed; all are held chargeable with this guilt; therefore all are cursed."

And so he concludes boldly that all are cursed, because all have been commanded to keep the law perfectly; which implies that in the present corruption of our nature the power of keeping it perfectly is wanting. Hence we conclude that the curse which the law pronounces, though, in the phrase of logicians, it is accidental, is here perpetual and inseparable from its nature. The blessing which it offers to us is excluded by our depravity, so that the curse alone remains.

Again, all are guilty because everyone, every human, has to keep the law perfectly and no one can. Therefore, there are no real blessings in the law, "the curse alone remains".

John Wesley is very brief in his comment on the verse:

Who continueth not in all the things - So it requires what no man can perform, namely, perfect, uninterrupted, and perpetual obedience.

Matthew Henry's Commentary of the Whole Bible adds its voice:

"for it is written, Cursed is every one that continueth not in all things which are written in the book of the law, to do them," v. 10, and Deut. xxvii. 26. The condition of life, by the law, is perfect, personal, and perpetual, obedience; the language of it is, Do this and live; or, as v. 12, The man that doeth them shall live in them: and for every failure herein the law denounces a curse. Unless our obedience be universal, continuing in all things that are written in the book of the law, and unless it be perpetual too (if in any instance at any time we fail and come short), we fall under the curse of the law. The curse is wrath revealed, and ruin threatened: it is a separation unto all evil, and this is in full force, power, and virtue, against all sinners, and

therefore against all men; for all have sinned and become guilty before God: and if, as transgressors of the law, we are under the curse of it, it must be a vain thing to look for justification by it.

Again, you must have perfect obedience to the law. And it covers every single human in existence.

Let's quote, finally, Martin Luther.

We must bear in mind that to do the works of the Law does not mean only to live up to the superficial requirements of the Law, but to obey the spirit of the Law to perfection. But where will you find the person who can do that? Let him step forward and we will praise him.

Hence, the statement of Moses, "Cursed is every one that continueth not in all things which are written in the book of the law to do them," is not contrary to Paul. Moses requires perfect doers of the Law. But where will you find them? Nowhere. Moses himself confessed that he was not a perfect doer of the Law.

I could continue quoting more commentators, but there is no point. The message is generally the same. It was important that I quote the older commentators. The commentators I quoted span from the 15th to the 19th century. The reason why I chose the older commentators is because I didn't want any of the modern twisted attempts by people such as messianic "Jews" (i.e., christians who used to be Jews but forsook Judaism) to make it appear as if Paul respected the Law. After reading Paul from start to finish, the word for their attempts is simply that: twisted. Looking at the christian church historically, there is no sign that there was ever a different understanding of what Paul meant in this verse: humanity is cursed because it cannot keep the law perfectly, and the law demands perfection.

Let's leave Paul for a while and go back to the actual Law that Paul is quoting from. Something very significant can be gained from just reading the words of Moses as opposed to those of Paul. The

Hebrew word quwm and its context does not mean "perfection". As I said before, it means to cause something to stand. In this case, it means to cause the words of the law to stand in order to do it. To make a little more sense, it means to "affirm" or "uphold" for the purpose of doing it. Now this excludes some possible translations such as "perform". The verse cannot be saying "Cursed be the one who doesn't perform the words of the law to do it". That makes no sense. Why? Because what does the word "perform" mean? It means to actually do something. So that would make the verse actually say "Cursed is the one who doesn't do the law in order to do it". That is nonsense. And, since the Hebrew word doesn't mean "perfection", the verse doesn't mean "Cursed is he who doesn't do the law perfectly to do it". Again, total foolishness.

So what does it mean to cause the law to stand, or to uphold and affirm it? Well, to uphold or affirm something, e.g., a principle, doesn't necessarily mean to do it perfectly. It actually means to see and accept the truth of a thing. As one ancient rabbi, Nachmanides, otherwise known as Ramban, says in his commentary on the verse in Deuteronomy,

> *Every Jew must accept the Torah's validity in full, and must not claim that even one of the commandments is no longer relevant. This curse however, is not pronounced upon one who merely commits a sin, rather, on one who denies that a part of the Torah is G-d given or applicable. This curse also applies to one who can have a positive influence on others but remains unconcerned with their spiritual welfare and fails to assist them.*

So everyone who acknowledges the God of Israel and his Law must "cause it to stand" or affirm its truth, relevance and importance, in order that they do it.

I mean, let's be reasonable here! When the wise Creator commands something, it must be possible to be done! And the scriptures clearly say that he knows our frame, that we are dust, and do fail (see Psalm 103:13-14). If the Lord is all-knowing, as the scripture describes him to be, then he would not demand from humans that which is not in their power to do. And it would follow from this, that this curse that is given in Deuteronomy 27 cannot be placed on someone who makes a mistake, and doesn't keep the law in utter and total perfection, because even christians admit that it is not possible for a human to keep the law perfectly and God does not command the impossible. So it should be clear that this curse is not a bad state of affairs that follows anything less than perfection. It realistically speaks of the person who doesn't uphold or affirm the truth and validity of the words of the Torah in order to do them. Therefore, a person can make a mistake in action, i.e., break a law inadvertently, yet still affirm that all of the Torah is true and valid.

A small additional point is that even the Greek word emmen-o does not speak of total perfection but rather to hold fast to, to remain in a place or state. Thus it just means remaining in the Law. So it is not speaking of the occasions where someone knows the Law and respects God but makes a mistake, but rather a purposeful and serious walking out of Torah. It is the difference between understanding that the Law rules a person's life, and thus when a mistake is made, the proper, lawful, action is done to make up for that mistake; and rejecting the sovereignty of God and his Law just living as one pleases. The person who rejects the truth of God's law can still do the things in it - they can refrain from murder and theft and love their parents - but essentially it means nothing in this context because they have rejected the source of the Law and its relevance for their life, just living on what their own intelligence thinks is best.

[ASIDE: It is important to note that it does make this world a better place on some levels when a person does good deeds even from a purely intellectual basis with no belief in God. That's why when I said that doing good on an intellectual basis alone means nothing, I limited it by saying "in this context". But make no mistake: there are dangers in doing good only based on logic or rationale or just because it feels good rather than being based on something truly objective, God's law, the regulations of the Creator of all.]

So even the Greek version of the Hebrew Bible doesn't give Paul and his followers justification for their conclusions.

You see, Paul's mistake is his mindset. He believes that righteousness is only achieved through perfect obedience to every single thing the Lord says at all times, a conclusion that is not backed up by the Hebrew Bible. As I have shown before, true repentance, where a way of life is transformed, can change a wicked man into a righteous one, and a righteous man can make a mistake and still be righteous. Thus, with this twisted and unrealistic mindset, Paul commits two crimes against scripture and the Deity of those scriptures:

He makes God an unfair, seemingly sadistic, tyrant who demands from people that which they cannot give, and then punishes them when they don't give what they don't have. This is seen in his giving a set of laws that he knows they cannot keep perfectly, but then demanding perfection. And then when they fail to keep the law perfectly, he punishes them with brutal death, exile, torture, loss, fear, heartbreak, plague, defeat, etc;

Paul also condemns those that God, through his scriptures, calls righteous, and labels them all as wicked and cursed because no one is perfect. Therefore since the righteous people make mistakes and Paul says that any mistake makes a person wicked, he calls all humanity wicked, including those who God himself calls righteous. This makes his arrogance stick out like a sore thumb.

Just to expand on the first point: imagine that a father commands his son who is paralysed from the neck down to run in the daily able-bodied 100-metre dash (or sprint) and win and break a world record, and gives the warning that if that son should fail, the father will punch the son's face in until it is black and blue. Not only this, but for most of his life, from the time he is 6 years old until he is 50 years old, the father would consistently put his son forward for the race with the same warning, and knowing he will never be able to succeed. Then, when he is 51, this father tells him that he always knew the son couldn't do it, but that he put him through that just to show him that he could never do it!!! What is worse, since the father is a world-class Olympic athlete himself, the father will run the race for the paralytic son, win, and give him the medal. Let's put the icing on the cake. If the now 51 year old paralytic son doesn't trust his father, then the father decides to give the medal he, the father, won to someone else.

If someone reads that and calls it kindness and that the son should be grateful, then that person is sick to his deepest core. That is called cruelty and that father should be punished for the rest of his life. But that is what christianity fundamentally believes about God!!! He knows the Jews and humanity can't keep the law perfectly, yet he gives it demanding perfection. Then he knowingly "punishes" them with horrible afflictions, massacres, invasions, rapes and pillaging, and exiles for thousands of years since the creation of humanity, until he throws in the towel, and says that he will keep the law perfectly himself and give them "freedom from the law" and "salvation". Then, because the Jews, who he particularly gave the law to, don't accept what he's supposed to have done because it doesn't match with what he's said before (i.e., that the law gives righteousness and that it can be done [Deut 6:25; 30:9-14; Ezek 18, 33]), he gives those gifts mainly to the Gentiles, the other nations. And someone in their right mind would consider that fair!?! I guess that shows the power of indoctrinating the ignorant, since Paul went to the Gentiles who didn't know the law to spread his "gospel".

So, to summarize:

* The proper interpretation of Deuteronomy 27:26 based on the language and scriptural context of the verse does not mean what Paul says. It doesn't mean perfect observance of the law which is impossible, but rather the affirming of the truth of the Law of the Lord as given through Moses. So Paul again has twisted scripture for his own agenda;

* Paul's forced interpretation makes himself an abomination by distorting the truth of Deity's existence and condemning the righteous as wicked and vice versa (Proverbs 17:15).

It is more than obvious by their commentaries that Paul's followers throughout history have made the very same mistakes.

See also Isaak Troki's analysis of this verse which can be found in his book called Hizzuk Emunah or "Faith Strengthened", an English copy of which is online.

verse 11

> *But that [it is] clear in law no one shall be righteous with God because the righteous, by his faith, shall live [Habakkuk 2:4].*
> *(Galatians 3:11)*

Paul quotes Habakkuk 2:4 to prove that because righteous people live by their faith, there is no way of being made righteous by law. He sets up a false dichotomy, a false sense that there are two entities that are opposed to each other: faith and law.

It has already been shown that people are declared righteous by obedience to God, i.e., doing what he commands, keeping his laws. I have shown this in my analysis of Romans 3:20a, and I've already gone through Paul's misusage of Habakkuk 2:4 in my analysis of Romans 1:17. The fact is that Habakkuk 2:4 does not exclude the law simply because it uses the word "faith". In fact, the Hebrew word translated "faith" does not mean simply a belief or a mental, internal conviction, but rather it refers to a holistic faithfulness, steadfastness, steadiness, i.e., a reliable steadfastness in Torah and the Deity of Torah. It is shown by both a real trust in God's word and a consistent keeping of the Law that he has given.

But even if we take the Hebrew word to mean a simple "belief" or "faith", i.e., only the internal conviction, it still does not negate or exclude the law of the Lord. Why? Because it is just a part of a righteous person's life which also includes law keeping. It is only Paul's creation of some artificial separation and opposition between law and faith that excludes the law from Habakkuk 2:4, not the text itself.

verse 12

But the law is not of faith, but rather, the man doing them [i.e, the laws] shall live in them [Leviticus 18:5]. (Galatians 3:12)

Paul here attempts to contrast Leviticus 18:5 with Habakkuk 2:4 in the following way: the righteous lives by faith, but a law keeper only performs the laws of the Torah, and therefore lives by the law as opposed to by faith. So, in a simpler form: the righteous lives by faith, and the doomed law keeper lives by the laws he keeps.

But again, Paul has ripped a verse out of context. Can we actually look at Leviticus 18:5 in context?

(1) And the Lord spoke to Moshe saying, (2) Speak to the children of Israel and say to them, I am the Lord your God. (3) You shall not emulate the deeds of the land of Egypt in which you dwelt, and you shall not emulate the deeds of land of Canaan into which I am bringing you. And you shall not walk in their statutes. (4) My judgments you shall do and my statutes you shall guard to walk in them. I am the Lord your God. (5) And you shall guard my statutes and my judgments which a man shall do and live by them. I am the Lord. (Leviticus 18:1-5)

Leviticus 18 starts with the Lord telling Moses to command the people not to obey the laws and statutes of other nations, but rather they should keep His laws because the man who performs his laws shall live by them as opposed to performing the laws of the nations and dying because by keeping their laws, the man rejects the Lord. So the context has nothing to do with living according to law as opposed to faith as Paul would have us believe. Leviticus 18 is promoting the fact that the Israelites should keep the Law of the Lord and not keep the laws of the other nations.

It should be plain that the Lord is not saying "don't have faith/trust". In fact, there is an important point to repeat here even though I've said it before. Paul has used Habakkuk 2:4 to say that the righteous live by "faith". Now when Habakkuk says "faith", he uses the Hebrew word 'emunah. So remember, for Paul to be consistent, he is saying that the righteous live by 'emunah, as Habakkuk says. But the psalmist David himself says the following:

> *All Your commandments are 'emunah. (Psalm 119:86)*

> *You have commanded Your testimonies in righteousness and 'emunah exceedingly. (Psalm 119:138)*

So 'emunah is an essential part of the commandments, of the Law.

Now some will complain and say something like, "My bible doesn't translate that word as "faith" in Psalm 119." And I would say, if the original Hebrew is going to use the same word to speak of the commandments of the Lord and the quality that gives life, there must be a link, a similarity. Thus, there is strong evidence that says that the law and faith/'emunah isn't as separate and different as Paul would have us believe.

verse 13

> *Christ has ransomed us from the curse of the law becoming a curse instead of us, for it has been written, Cursed is any one who hangs on a tree [Deuteronomy 21:23].(Galatians 3:13)*

Now Paul's logic in this verse is, at best, peculiar. According to Paul, to redeem those under the curse that the Law brings, Jesus becomes accursed by hanging from a tree.

Even before we look into Paul's strange way of thinking and his manipulation of scripture, lets just stop and think!

Imagine a group of men guilty of a crime, let's say, murder. They are guilty, having actually committed the crime of murder. They have been sentenced to death! Then a guy who hasn't committed any crimes comes along and receives the punishment the murderers should get. Would that make the murderers any less guilty? Nope! What if they realised and fully understood that the other guy was totally innocent and showed remorse, would their sentence be revoked? Nope! What if the person who died was the son of the person who created the legal system? Would that change the fact that the murderers are guilty and have been sentenced to death? Nope! And this is all according to the law of the Lord: if a person commits premeditated murder and there are the right sort of witnesses to the crime, then the murderer is put to death. So according to the Law, even according to our own legal system, does it make any difference if an innocent person got executed? Would that ensure that the murderers get off scott free? Absolutely not! Why? Because there is nothing, nothing at all, in the Law of the Lord which has this get out clause: human sacrifice/slaughter in the place of guilty humans. This is totally absent from the law. In fact, the total opposite is stated: no one dies for another person; everyone is responsible for their own crime (Deuteronomy 24:16, cf. Ezekiel 18:4,20).

In fact, for an innocent person to die in the place of the guilty is not mercy but rather injustice! Let me say that again. For an innocent person to be punished and executed for the crimes of the guilty is not the establishment of justice; it is a perversion of justice.

[ASIDE: This reasoning wouldn't usually show a christian, a Pauline christian, his error because they do not reason according to the Law of the Lord, or according to the Hebrew Scriptures, but rather the teachings of Paul and the new testament. Thus animal sacrifices, to them, points "spiritually" or "typically" (using the language of types and metaphorical figures) to a human sacrifice. But for those who read the words of the Jewish Bible, and are open to letting those scriptures speak for themselves as much as possible, it is much more likely they will see the baselessness of Pauline christianity's distortion of scripture).]

Thus Paul's logic is really pointless because the law itself doesn't give any basis for his theory of human substitution and slaughter/sacrifice.

Anyway, let's get back ot the scripture that Paul uses. He says that Jesus became a curse to redeem man from a curse. How? By being hung on a tree!

Oh!

Ooooh!

On so many levels this reasoning is deplorable. Why?

The first reason is seen when you simply read the passage in Deuteronomy in context.

> *(22) And when there shall be on a man a crime with a judgment of death, then he has been put to death, and then you hang him on a tree; (23) his corpse shall not stay overnight upon the tree, but you'll definitely bury him on that date; because the one hung is belittling/slighting of Deity, and you shall not pollute the ground/land, an inheritance, which HaShem your God is giving to you. (Deuteronomy 21:22-23)*

Please, just look at the first words, "when there be on a man a crime with the judgment of death ..." This means that the man has committed a crime worthy of death, i.e., he is guilty. Then the next words apply. But first the man must be guilty.

Now take a simple look at what christians believe about Jesus. They say that he was never guilty, he was guilty of no crime. But wait! The verse in Deuteronomy is talking about a guilty man. Jesus is not a guilty man. So the rest of the passage doesn't apply to him. So this passage can't be used to say that Jesus became a curse if he doesn't even fulfil the first part of the passage!

The second problem with Paul's logic comes from the words of the verses that he uses. He first says that everyone is under a curse, and uses a verse from Deuteronomy 27:26. Then he says that Jesus rescues people from the curse by becoming a curse based on Deuteronomy 21:23. Now thanks to both the translations and versions of translations in ancient Greek and in English, we get the impression that there is some sort of equal trade here, i.e., a curse for a curse.

But if a Jew, one intimately knowledgeable of the Hebrew Bible, i.e., the original language of the scripture, looked at these two verses (Deut 21:23 and Deut 27:26), then he would have difficulty seeing Paul's point. Why? Because two different Hebrew words are used in these verses. It's just that because of translation, these facts are, for better or worse, covered over. And the two different words have, logically, two different meanings. The word that is used in Deuteronomy 21:23 is קְלָלָה, qelalah, which comes from a verb meaning to make light, to slight, diminish. The word that is used in Deuteronomy 21:23 is אָרוּר, 'aruwr, which comes from a verb meaning to isolate and bring ruin; to weaken incrementally. But both words overlap with the English word "curse", but they still have different connotations.

Now because we're actually dealing with two different concepts, or at least two words, we aren't dealing with an equal measure, curse for a curse, thing here. Thus Paul doesn't have a strong case here at all. In fact, it puts some questions on the very idea that Paul really understood the Hebrew language. It also puts some of his other claims about himself into question, but that is for another time.

Based on all this, there is no real equality between the two passages of Deuteronomy, so there can be no real substitution one for the other, as Paul tries to do.

Thirdly, I just want you to think about something. Leviticus 17:11 says that blood atones for sins. Does this mean any blood whatsoever? Can I use pig's blood to atone for sin? Can I cut my finger, draw blood, and use that to atone for my sin? No! The context makes it plain that it is the life blood of an animal used in the temple/tabernacle context that atones for sin. So basically, blood can be used to atone for sin, but only in a specific way. Even ancient Jewish tradition tells us this. But the whole thing must be understood in a Jewish/Israelite environment. The biblical law shouldn't be understood in a pagan context, or a modern American culture. It doesn't really make sense there. It must be understood in its original context first and then proper understanding can be drawn from it.

Now, let's ask a similar question: what did it mean for a man to be hung in ancient Israel? Could he just be hung in any way? Should he be hung in the same way that criminals are hung in different countries today where they are alive before they are hung, but the hanging is a form of execution that actually puts the criminal to death? Extremely doubtful! But let's, at least, look at the Israelite/Jewish tradition of hanging and see what information we get.

First, look at the text of Deuteronomy 21:22a.

And when there shall be on a man a crime with a judgment of death, and then he has been put to death, and then you hang him on a tree
...

A better translation of the text is "he has been put to death", the past tense, something that has happened already. It is not "he is to be put to death" as the King James version has it. It is not "he is put to death by hanging" as the Bible in Basic English has it. The sequence of the verse is: 1) the person is judged as guilty; 2) then he is put to death; and 3) and THEN he is hung. So he is not killed by being hung. He is dead beforehand, and then he is hung, as if to display him to those around.

Well, someone may say, as is common in our Western civilisation, "but that's just your interpretation; where's the proof?" And I could put forward the same Septuagint (the LXX, the ancient Greek translation of the Hebrew Bible) that many christians love and revere, which has the same structure as the Hebrew.

LXX:
> *εαν δε γενηται εν τινι αμαρτια κριμα θανατου και αποθανη και κρεμασητε αυτον επι ξυλου*
> TRANSLATION: *But if it happens, in a certain one [is] a sin of the judgment of death, and he die and you hang him on a tree ...*

So according to this version, like the Hebrew, a man is judged as guilty, killed, and then hung on a tree.

I could put forward the fact that a 2nd century translation by a person who converted to Judaism called Onkelos translates the passage the same way:

> *And when in a man there is guilt with a judgment of death, and he has been put to death, and you have hanged him on a pole ...*

I could even add the ancient tradition of the Targums codified in the early centuries CE which say very much the same thing. Here is what the Targum Pseudo-Jonathan says along with the Jerusalem Targum.

When a man hath become guilty of the judgment of death, and is condemned to be stoned, and they afterwards hang him on a beam, [JERUSALEM. And you hang him on a beam,]

What about Rashi and the ancient rabbis?

"... you shall [then] hang him on a pole": Our Rabbis said: All who are stoned [by the court] must [afterwards] be hanged, for the verse (23) says, a hanging [human corpse] is a blasphemy of God. [Thus, we find that the sin of blasphemy is connected with hanging,] and a blasphemer is punished by stoning. [Consequently, our Rabbis taught that all those stoned must be hanged.]- [Babylonian Talmud Tractate Sanhedrin. 45b]

Here Rashi quotes the ancient tradition that was codified in the Talmud but was in existence before then since it was written in the Mishnah centuries before that (Mishnah, Sanhedrin 6.4). In fact, it is the oldest records and traditions of the Jews that is the most telling piece of evidence. They are the ones to whom the law was given, so they would know how executions were done and where hanging would take place

What is even more astounding is that we have christian commentators who love Jesus and Paul and accept the new testament as God's word admitting that the ancient Hebrews understood this as talking about the hanging of someone already dead!

The Hebrews understand this not of putting to death by hanging, but of hanging a man up after he was stoned to death; which was done more ignominiously of some heinous malefactors. We have the examples of Rechab and Baanah, who, for murdering Ish-bosheth, were slain by David's commandment, their hand and feet cut off, and then hanged up. (Treasury of Scriptural Knowledge commenting on Deuteronomy 21:22)

The hanging of them by the neck till the body was dead was not used at all among the Jews, as with us; but of such as were stoned to death, if it were for blasphemy, or some other very execrable crime, it was usual, by order of the judges, to hang up the dead bodies upon a post for some time, as a spectacle to the world, to express the ignominy of the crime, and to strike the greater terror upon others, that they might not only hear and fear, but see and fear. (Matthew Henry's Commentary of the Whole Bible commenting on Deuteronomy 21:22)

So it is widely known that this was the method of Jewish execution, i.e., stoning to death and then hanging. We can also look to the oral law code of Judaism and see that the Jews only used four methods of execution, putting to death, and no more: stoning, burning, strangulation, and decapitation (Mishnah Sanhedrin 7:1). Thus crucifixion is not a biblical or Israelite form of execution. This can even be seen in the written law itself which only overtly talks of stoning. Now understand that the Mishnah was not invented only around the first few centuries CE. It is the composition of traditions that had been held by the Israelites for centuries, going back to Moses. And even for those who doubt this, it is unlikely, nay impossible, that laws in the Mishnah only existed in those first centuries. They must have had a history beyond that. There is no evidence that the Jews made up those laws out of thin air just for that time.

Thus, based on all this, crucifixion-hanging is historically, biblically, and culturally totally outside the context of the Torah. In fact, it may even be forbidden!

So, putting this all together, crucifixion is not what is meant in the text of Deuteronomy 21:22-23. Just because the text mentions hanging, it doesn't necessarily mean that any sort of hanging will do. The text and the historical interpretation of it points solely to a man who is already dead being hung, not a man hanging until he is dead. And the text says that the man must be guilty to be a "curse" or slighting/belittling of God. Jesus was not guilty so this text doesn't apply to him. Therefore, Paul's interpretation is again totally without biblical basis.

Also note that Paul is using his distorted interpretation of these verses to prove what is in Galatians 3:14, that the blessings of Abraham will be possessed by the nations because of or through Jesus' taking the curse in some substitutionary way. Yet it is clear that Paul's usage of these verses is incorrect, and thus his conclusion has no basis in scripture and therefore has no power or divine backing.

verse 15

> *Brothers, I speak according to man, yet still, a covenant of man having been ratified, no one shall make it void or add to it.*
> *(Galatians 3:15)*

Taking this verse on its own, it can be seen that Paul's thinking is purely self-serving. Why? Because, according to him, even in human terms, a covenant that is confirmed cannot be made void or added to. Yet passages like 2 Corinthians 3 and Ephesians 2 and Hebrews 7-10 show the law covenant vanishing away and being made void! For "believers" the law has no effect on them since they are dead to it (Romans 7:1-6). Thus, when Paul wants it to be, a covenant cannot be made void. And when Paul doesn't want another covenant around, its "glory" is being rendered idle and void, and a veil is over people's eyes so that they cannot see that it is done away with (2 Corinthians 3:14).

So here we see Paul's double standard: there is an "old" covenant given by God himself which is done away with, and a new one which takes its place; yet with man, when a covenant is confirmed, no one can make it void or supplement it!

verse 16

But the promises were uttered to Abraham, and to his seed. He doesn't say "and to [his] seeds" as upon many, but rather as upon one, "and to your seed", which is Christ. (Galatians 3:16)

Hmmmm....

Paul makes himself an easy target by interpreting scripture in the most extraordinary and alien way. He notes that Deity makes a promise to Abraham's seed. Paul says that this is a single "seed" and not plural, or many, "seeds", and thus it refers to one man: Christ.

The problem with this interpretation is obvious if one reads the story of Abraham. A knowledge of Hebrew is an advantage, but not necessary to see Paul's mistake. But the fact that Paul makes this mistake throws doubt upon his knowledge of Hebrew and thus his claims about being a Pharisee.

Let's start with the Hebrew.

The Hebrew word that bibles translate as "seed" is a word very much similar to our English word "sheep". Our word "sheep" can refer to one sheep or to many sheep. You'll notice that we don't say "many sheeps." It just doesn't make sense in our language. The same is true for the Hebrew language and the word for "seed" or "offspring". There is "a seed" and "many seed", but in there language, there is not "many seeds".

You want examples. Well I'll give you some examples from .... errr ... let's use some examples from Abraham, for instance. It happens to be the same place from which Paul gets his quote, so it just fits to see how the word is used there. Now remember, Paul's contention is that "to your seed" means "to one person", and that person is "christ". Now please excuse the list that follows, but it's needed when dealing with some.

(14) And the Lord said unto Abram, after Lot was separated from him, Lift up now your eyes, and look from the place where you are, northward, and southward, and eastward, and westward; (15) For all the land which you see, to you will I give it, and to your seed forever. (16) And I will make your seed as the dust of the earth; so that if a man can number the dust of the earth, then shall your seed also be numbered. (Genesis 13:14-16 - "seed" is numerous as the sand)

(13) And he said unto Abram, Know with certainty that your seed shall be a stranger in a land which is not theirs, and they will make them serve, and they will afflict them four hundred years. (14) And also that nation whom they shall serve, will I judge; and afterward shall they go out with great substance. (Genesis 15:13-14 - "seed" held captive in Egypt and is referred to by "them" and "they")

(10) And the angel of the Lord said unto her, I will multiply your seed exceedingly, that it shall not be numbered for multitude. (Genesis 16:10 - "seed" will be too many to be numbered)

(7) And I will establish My covenant between Me and you and your seed after you throughout their generations for an everlasting covenant, to be a God to you and to your seed after you. (8) And I will give to you, and to your seed after you, the land of your sojournings, all the land of Canaan, for an everlasting possession; and I will be their God.' (Genesis 17:7-8 - "seed" is referred to in the plural when it says "I will be their God")

(12) And God said unto Abraham: 'Don't let it be grievous in your sight because of the lad, and because of your bondwoman; in all that Sarah has said to you, hearken unto her voice; for in Isaac shall seed be called yours. (13) And also of the son of the bondwoman will I make a nation, because he is your seed.' (Genesis 21:13 - Isaac's seed/descendants has been linked to Abraham and Ishmael is Abraham's seed)

(15) And the angel of HaShem called unto Abraham a second time out of heaven, (16) and said: 'I've sworn by myself, declares HaShem, because you have done this thing, and have not withheld your son, your only son, (17) that blessing I will bless you, and multiplying I will multiply your seed as the stars of the heaven, and as the sand which is upon the seashore; and your seed shall possess the gate of his enemies; (18) and in your seed shall all the nations of the earth be blessed; because you have hearkened to My voice.' (Genesis 22:15-18 - the seed is many like stars and sand, but still referred to collectively as "his", as the nation Israel is called many times, e.g., Exodus 4:22)

(7) HaShem, the God of heaven, who took me from my father's house, and from the land of my nativity, and who spoke unto me, and who swore unto me, saying: To your seed will I give this land; He will send His angel before you, and you shall take a wife for my son from there. (Genesis 24:7 - Abraham refers to the earlier blessing in Genesis 17 which refers to plural "seed", to "them" getting the land.)

So Paul tells us that "seed" refers to one person: christ. But look at the eight passages I quoted! Every single passage attached to the promise, which is seven of them, all refer to multiple offspring, many seed, not just one person. Whenever it says "to your seed", it is always speaking of many people. There is only one clear occasion that it refers to one person, and that is Ishmael: it has nothing to do with the promise to Abraham; and it doesn't say "to your seed". And in every single case, there is no mention of a "messiah", a "christ", or an "anointed one"!

Summary: In Genesis, the seed to inherit the promise is always many, not one; and "christ" is nowhere mentioned!

So again [how many times have I said or will I say "again" - Paul is a repeat-offender when it comes to the misuse and abuse of the Hebrew Bible], we see Paul putting into a passage of holy scripture something that was never there.

(17) But this I say: a covenant having been ratified before by the Deity to Christ, the law, coming into being 430 years after, couldn't de-ratify [it], in order to render void the promise. (18) For if the heirship/inheritance was of law, [it is] no longer of promise. But the Deity bestowed [it] to Abraham by means of a promise. (Galatians 3:17-18)

Now Paul is still going on about the covenant/promise which was given to Abraham. In his eyes, the law of Moses couldn't take away the authority of that covenant; it couldn't get rid of that promise. The promise came before the law, and according to Paul, even in human terms, you can't invalidate a covenant that has been ratified and authorised. So the promise to Abraham stands, in spite of the coming of the Law. In Paul's eyes, the law contradicts such a promise, or it makes the promise of no effect because the law with only grant the promise if the law is kept perfectly. No one can keep the law so no one can get the promise. But Paul is saying that since the believer is redeemed from the law, he can still get the promise. So now an enmity is set up between law and promise.

Now, it has already been shown that the notion that the law demands perfection and cuts off anyone who does less, such a notion is foolishness. So we can scrunch that theory, like used paper, in the palm of our hands, and throw it in the garbage.

But I would just ask you to read the promise given to Abraham. It is repeated a number of times to Abraham in Genesis 12, 13, 15, 17, 18, and 22, and even after that. It was not simply that "the nations would possess his blessings" (Galatians 3:14). The Lord is going to give that childless man a nation of descendants through a promised son, that being Isaac. And those descendants will be given the land of promise, Canaan. The Almighty knew that Abraham would teach his children righteousness (not simply a belief, but a whole active lifestyle) so he maintained a close relationship with him, Abraham, and his descendants, and those descendants would be a blessing to others.

Now if a person reads the history as written in the Bible from Abraham to Joshua, through Moses, then they would see something that kicks Paul's theory in the teeth: the law and covenant of Moses is actually part of the fulfilment of the promise to Abraham and not a hindrance to it! For example, see Exodus 3:16-17; 6:6-8; 33:1-2; Leviticus 26:39-42; Deuteronomy 1:8; 6:10-18; 29:9-14; 30:19-20; 34:4. In fact, the promise is part of the law, and the law is part of the fulfilment of the promise. It is by being part of that covenant, the covenant of Moses, that allows a person, a Jew, to have a part in that promise!

So Paul makes no sense here, and shows an ignorance in what the books and the law of Moses has to say.

verse 19

This verse needs to be quoted as a whole because everything in it is important.

Then why the law? It was added because of violation/transgression - until the seed should come to whom it [the blessing of Abraham] was promised - being instituted by angels in the hand of a go-between.

There's not much you can say about such a statement, huh? Well, there is something that could be said. Like, for example, the fact that scripture doesn't say this. Scripture doesn't say that the Law was given simply because of sin. And, just to follow Paul's logic and rule, the law gives sin strength (1 Corinthians 15:56). So Paul adds more disgrace upon God by claiming essentially that God saw that sin was on the earth, and therefore gave sin more strength by giving humanity a law it could not keep, and then inflicted humanity with curse and punishment for breaking that law for thousands of years!!! What's worse is that God himself said that the law itself was the cure when he said that it brings righteousness and blessing, but instead it could only bring curse and more sin, according to good old "saint" Paul. And God would have done all this knowingly! There's no point in using the "doctor" analogy of sometimes adding to the illness in order to cure it. For a doctor to lie to a patient and then to subject the patient to torture when the patient's body responds naturally would consign that doctor to prison for malpractice.

God says why the law was given. It was given to set Israel apart as his chosen possession (Exodus 19:5-6). The law was given for good, righteousness, and life (Deuteronomy 4:1,5; 6:24-25; 10:11-12; 11:8-9; 30:19-20) and a lot more. The Jewish Bible gives no overt sign that the law was "added" simply because of transgression but rather to bless Israel and the world, since Israel would be that light to the nations.

And what if the law was given because of transgression? It is very apparent that it was the cure, not an added burden to carry until someone else could come to carry the load. There was evil, so God gave the instrument for good in showing people, showing the whole world, how to act properly and showing his rulership by means of his people, his priests, Israel!

I just need to caution the reader that there are christians and christian commentators who will say that the law that was added was the so-called "ceremonial" law, the law of sacrifices and rituals. But Paul makes no reference to this section of the law in this letter to the Galatians; he speaks of the whole institution of God which was given through Moses. This can be seen in the fact that Paul quotes non-ceremonial sections of the Law, such as Deuteronomy 21:23 (hanging from a tree), chapter 27:26 (curse to those who don't uphold the law), and Leviticus 18 (living in the law), all of which are not in ceremonial sections of the law. These christians and commentators also make an artificial separation in the law between moral laws and ceremonial laws where as the law gives the same importance to honouring one's parents as respecting the Sabbath (Leviticus 19:3), and has, in the same locality, sections concerning sacrifice, the law of priests, and loving one's neighbour as themselves. Also, it has the law against blasphemy slap bang next to the law concerning holy days and how priests should take care of the bread in the tabernacle (Leviticus 23-24). Such an artificial cutting and editing and labelling of the law isn't really natural to the message of law, at least in the way these sorts of christians use it.

And what about the statement: "being instituted by angels in the hands of a go-between"? The Torah outright conflicts with this baseless notion and shows Paul to be either a liar or giving a false message to people who know no better where it concerns the source of the Law. Rather than using angels, the Almighty gave part of the law to the whole nation of Israel face-to-face and then gave the rest to Moses face-to-face!!! See Numbers 14:14; Numbers 12:7-8; Deuteronomy 5:4; Deuteronomy 34:10.

And this nonsense coming from a supposed student of the great rabbi Gamaliel (Acts 22:3)? Something's definitely not right about this Paul character and his claims!!!

verse 21

The law, then, is against the promise of God? May it not be so! For if a law which had the power to give life had been given, then certainly righteousness would be of the law.

Paul says that neither life nor righteousness can come from the law. All it takes is a little comparison with what the Hebrew Bible says to show the fallacy in this statement.

Without quoting the whole passage, Deuteronomy 30:11-20 shows that the law can be kept and that life comes by accepting Deity and following the commandments and death comes by rejecting Deity and forsaking the commands. Therefore, life comes through the law.

And also, the same law Paul has quoted a number of times also contradicts   Paul. Leviticus 18:5 says,

And you should keep my statutes and ordinances which a man shall do and live by them.

Again, as evidence, King David says,

I shall not ever forget your precepts, for in them you have given me life. (Psalm 119:93)

So what does the Hebrew Bible say? The law says that it gives life, and a person who followed the law - despite sinning at times and making mistakes - says that it gives him life, it quickens him. And I've already shown before that the Hebrew Bible says that those who keep the law are righteous and that there are such people on the earth (e.g., Deuteronomy 6:24-25; Ezekiel 18). There is a whole psalm dedicated to righteous people (Psalm 112).

So Paul says that law doesn't give life or righteousness. The Hebrew Bible, and those in it that lived by the law, says that obedience to the law - which is possible - gives life and righteousness. So, surprise surprise, Paul's words once again contradict the Jewish Bible making his claims full of falsehood.

verses 22-23

(22) But the scripture hath concluded all under sin, that the promise by faith of Jesus Christ might be given to them that believe. (23) But before faith came, we were kept under the law, shut up unto the faith which should afterwards be revealed. (Galatians 3:22-23 - King James Version (1769))

Now it's important to quote the King James Version here because of the mistake that can be easily made in reading it. You see, a modern reader of this version wouldn't see much in the word "concluded". Our modern understanding of "conclude" would weaken the message that Paul is trying to give. The typical christian would easily get the idea that Paul is just saying the following: "the Old Testament has given us the conclusion that everyone is under the power of sin". But someone who read this over a hundred years ago would get a different understanding of this verse. Someone who knew the Greek would also see some editing, some unbalanced treatment, in the way the translators of the King James did their job.

You see, the Greek word translated "concluded" is used in another place in the passage quoted above. And with our common understanding of the word "conclude", the normal reader would be hard pressed to uncover where that other usage is. Let me make it easy for you! The Greek word translated "concluded" in verse 22 is translated as "shut up" in the next verse! It is the word συγκλειω sugklei-o. It means "to shut up together", "to lock down in a common place". The commentator, John Wesley, compares it to being shut up in a prison. In fact, the Old English meaning of "conclude" is "to shut up, enclose, restrict, confine". So a better modern translation would be:

(22) But the scripture has imprisoned all under sin so that the promise may be given to the believers out of [the] faith of Jesus Christ. (23) But before the faith came, we were kept under guard under the law, having been imprisoned for the expected faith to be revealed.

Paul appears to still be speaking of the law when he mentions "scripture". So, basically, because of the law, all are under subjection to, are ruled by, are dominated and trapped by sin and law.

I don't need to nor am I going to re-quote the same old scriptures in the Jewish Bible to show the falsehood of Paul's words. I've referred to them over and over throughout this series. But I will add the following:

I shall run the way of your commandments, you have enlarged my heart.

And I shall walk around in liberty for I have sought your precepts. (Psalm 119:32,45)

These verses just show how the law is linked with and gives a person such liberty.

As I've shown before, and the true holy Bible shows us, there is no contradiction between law and faith (or, more properly, faithfulness); being in one does not exclude the other.

verses 24-25

(24) Therefore the law has become our paidagogos to christ so that, by faith, we may be justified, (25) but when faith comes we are no longer under the paidagogos.

Now if Paul's words have been baseless so far, then these verses about the law being some "tutor" or "paidagogos" that you graduate from means little to nothing!

But there is something interesting about these verses, and that is the Greek word translated "schoolmaster" or "tutor" in various translations. According to Greek dictionaries and the christian publication, the International Standard Bible Encyclopedia, the Greek word translated "schoolmaster" or "tutor", παιδαγωγος, paidagogos, does not mean a simple teacher or headteacher. The word literally means "child-leader", i.e., someone who leads a child! That basic meaning should at least make you question a translation that emphasizes instruction or being in charge of the teaching and discipline in a school, namely "schoolmaster" or "tutor". Yes, I'm saying that those English words don't reflect the meaning or thought behind the Greek words.

Generally, christian commentators interpret this word as a slave who is put in charge of a child; he takes the child to school and back home; and he watches over the child, restraining him/her from evil and temptation.

According to the International Standard Bible Encyclopedia and Easton's Bible Encyclopedia, it had negative tones of strictness and sternness, something that young boys did not enjoy. Although the more educated "paidagogues" may have helped the child with some lessons, the essence of the role was not instruction, but control and strict limitation, literally leading the child.

Now let's look at the context! Paul is talking about the law of Moses confining, basically trapping everyone under sin's domination. This "paidagogue" (not the English distortion "pedagogue") would confine and restrain a child and lead them to school, i.e., the "christ". But note what happens! Once the child reaches its destination, whether that mean school or maturity, the "paidagogue" is no longer needed, thus it goes away. So what does this mean for the law of Moses, which is supposed to be the paidagogue? Well, when the destination has been reached, i.e., Jesus the "christ", then it has no more function, and is done away with. In other words, Jesus is the final destination of the law as a means of becoming righteous for anyone who believes in Jesus (Romans 10:4).

It's necessary for you to know and see that there is no hint or sign in the Hebrew Scriptures, the supposed "old testament," that the law of Moses had some temporary role, especially the paidagogue role imposed upon it by Paul. Just read the law of Moses, and see the many times where it says that laws are forever, or everlasting, or perpetual, or "for [all] your generations", or "in all your dwellings". When the prophets spoke of the end of time, they are overtly filled with laws and sacrifices, Levites, priests, and Torah festivals, such as Sukkoth, the feast of booths/huts/tabernacles, as seen in Leviticus 23. Just see passages like Ezekiel 40-47, which speaks of a future temple; Jeremiah 33 which speaks of not only a special descendant of David who will be king, but also the perpetuity of the priesthood descended from Levi, which cannot apply to Jesus since he was not a descendant of Levi according to all his genealogies in the "new testament!" In fact, the "new testament book" of Hebrews uses Jesus to contradict the statements of Jeremiah by having Jesus end and abolish the Levitical priesthood (see more about this when I deal with the book of Hebrews).

One has to consider this: with the Law of Moses, the spoken word of Deity, given through a prophet of much more authority, credibility, and divine connection than Paul, speaking in such perpetual terminology, it is obvious that Paul is contradicting its message. In light of this, when it comes to the acknowledged direct word of the Almighty versus the "commentary" of Paul, the facts would tell anyone to run from the words of man and cling to the words of the Creator.

If that isn't clear enough, then let me be as plain as possible: Paul's words are baseless, fundamentally flawed deceptions which should be rejected when seen in the clear light of God's words, the Law of Moses!

Chapter 4

verse 8-10

(8) But then, when you didn't know God, you were slaves to those things which by nature are not gods. (9) But now, having known God, and more precisely being known by God, how shall you revert again to the weak and beggarly elements, to which you wish again to be in bondage anew? (10) You painstakingly observe days, and months, and times, and years. (11) I am afraid of you, that perhaps I have pointlessly put work into you. (Galatians 4:8-10)

I want to make a specific point here. When I was a christian and learning about the Law of Moses, I came across people who were also christian but also believed that Paul has some positive overall view of law. When anti-law christians would use verses like these (Galatians 4:8-10) to say something negative about the law, the pro-law christians would say that these verses are only referring to, not the law, but to Gentile ways and practices, namely that it was about people who were Gentile by birth and upbringing going back to Gentile ways of idolatry.

But as I've been reading through Galatians, I find this view - the view that says that the Gentiles believers were going back to Gentile ways - to be contextually out of place and inaccurate. Why? Because, up 'til now, Paul has consistently been talking about the Jewish law and way of life (chapters 2 and 3). The text afterwards again focuses on the law covenant (Galatians 4:21-5:15). Added to the fact that Paul says very little about their Gentile origins, the problem he is facing is people preaching the law as can be seen by his referring to the apostles who obviously taught and lived by the law of Moses (chapter 2). Chapter 3 again refers to the law and apparently seems to be a response against those who teach that a man can be justified, made righteous, by the law. So this Gentiles-going-back-to-Gentile-ways point of view doesn't really make sense in terms of the context.

The pro-law people then make the claim that Paul's argument was actually against a sect mixing that early "christianity" with Judaism and philosophy. But again, reading through Galatians, there is not enough textual evidence for this notion. It's clear that Paul's issue is thus the law, and the point he is making is that the law is no better than the ancient idolatrous ways of the Gentiles, since the law is supposedly weak and mediocre, like the old ways of the Gentiles, unable to justify a person, and beggarly when contrasted to Paul's view of what belief in Jesus can do. In other words, Paul is saying to the Galatian christian group, "why revert to a system that is just as useless as your old ways?"

This begins to shed light on Paul's view of law and the reason why people, especially Jews, should avoid Paul and his followers like the plague, since his teachings make void and insult the law. A Jew should learn the law that God gave through Moses and what it says first! Even a Gentile should do this! Even just reading the written law on its own is an advantage. Because once it is read and learned in completion, in context, then Paul's deceptions become transparent, and you can be inoculated, protected against his falsehood, being able to see how he distorts its message. Reading the rest of the Hebrew Scriptures will further strengthen and educate a person enough to see that the natural voice of those writings refutes Paul's words.

Please note that this method may not work for indoctrinated christians since their main aim or their conditioning will generally not allow scriptures to speak, but rather they wish to see Jesus in, or read Jesus into, the Tanakh (another name for the Jewish Bible), or they wish to make sure there is agreement between Paul and the Tanakh. This is either done by saying that Paul's words must be divinely inspired and thus the "old testament" must be read in light of his words; or they essentially silence the Tanakh: whenever the Hebrew Scriptures appear to contradict the message of the "new testament", it will always, always, be the voice of the NT that wins out. In that latter view, the "new testament" is the "true" and "clear" meaning whereas the Jewish Bible is "dark", full of hidden meanings that were only correctly perceived by Jesus and his followers/apostles, chief of whom is the untimely arriving Paul.

Let's hope that at least a few choose to hear the voice of Deity in the Hebrew Scriptures before they automatically assume that Paul and the christian scriptures must be true.

verses 21-31: The Sinai-Hagar Analogy

As it's important that you actually read what Paul is saying, I'm gonna quote all the verses.

(21) Tell me, those wishing to be under law, don't you hear the law?
(22) For it has been written, that Abraham had two sons, the one by

a maidservant, and one by a free-woman. (23) But he who was of the maidservant was born after the flesh; but he of the free-woman was by promise, (24) which things are an allegory: for these are the two covenants; the one from the mount Sinai leading to slavery, which is [Hagar]. (25) For this [Hagar] is mount Sinai in Arabia, and it corresponds with the present Jerusalem, and is a slave with her children. (26) But the higher Jerusalem is free, which is the mother of us all. (27) For it has been written, Rejoice, barren one that didn't bear offspring; break forth and shout, the one who didn't experience birth-pangs: for many are the children of the lonely one, more than the one who has the husband [Isaiah 54:1]. (28) And we, brothers, accordant with Isaac, are the children of promise. (29) But as then he that was born after the flesh persecuted him that was [born] after the Spirit, even so it is now. (30) Nevertheless what does the scripture say? Throw out the maidservant and her son [Genesis 21:10]; for the son of the maidservant shall not be heir with the son of the free-woman. (31) So then, brothers, we are not children of the bondwoman, but of the free. (Galatians 4:21-31)

It is important to see the picture that Paul has painted about the essence of the law, the Law of Moses. According to him, it breeds slavery and bondage and is a covenant that needs to be thrown out and dispensed with. He even misquotes Isaiah 54:1 to make his point, which I'll deal with soon.

So moving past another of Paul's distortions, it has already been shown in this book and verses have been given showing that the law never brought bondage but was a way of life for a people freed from bondage (Exodus 20:2). But just to note: how counter-intuitive, how self-defeating is it for the Almighty to deliver his people from bondage to Egypt just to deliver them into another bondage??? That approach makes no sense and is not good at all.

Some may say that Paul is only attacking these Gentiles' view of Law, holding a wrong view that it could justify, that was bondage. But, again, look at Paul's analogy. He is not describing how a person views Torah/Law; he is dealing with the covenant itself. He is not saying that people's view of Law brings bondage; he is saying that the selfsame covenant of Moses given at Sinai brings bondage and slavery. So he is contradicting the very essence of the Law of God given to a redeemed people!

So for all those who think that Paul is pro-Law, this passage refutes them. For Paul, the law and its covenant only breeds slavery (Galatians 4:24)! I don't need to repeat myself concerning Paul's error.

verse 27

(25) For this [Hagar] is mount Sinai in Arabia, and it corresponds with the present Jerusalem, and is a slave with her children. (26) But the higher Jerusalem is free, which is the mother of us all. (27) For it has been written, Rejoice, barren one that didn't bear offspring; break forth and shout, the one who didn't experience birth-pangs: for many are the children of the lonely one, more than the one who has the husband [Isaiah 54:1]. (Galatians 4:25-27)

Paul quotes Isaiah 54:1 to show the difference between the law covenant and the christian new covenant, the Jerusalem below and a Jerusalem that is supposed to be above. But again, we face a problem.

The context of Isaiah 54 speaks of a wife who was forsaken for a while but who was welcomed back by the husband, i.e., the Lord punishing Israel who he had a covenant relationship with but was allowing the nation to return to him. Pay close attention: there is no new marriage or marriage agreement, just the loving reunion of a husband (the Almighty) and his wife (Israel). So Isaiah 54:1 simply means to refer to Jerusalem (Israel) which was empty and thus "barren", due to punishment, its inhabitants being in captivity and exile, and that it would soon be filled once again with inhabitants and descendants.

There is a possible allusion to Sarah, but it has nothing to do with a "new covenant" or faith in a dead and supposedly resurrected messiah.

Now there may be those, mainly christians, who would feel somewhat confused, thinking that their special "Isaiah 53" passage, the supposedly great messianic text is just before this verse. In their minds, it's logical that the next verse, Isaiah 54:1, must speak of something related to it, i.e., the higher Jerusalem for believers in their messiah figure. I'm not going to go into the christian misunderstanding of Isaiah 53. I'll just summarize with the following: whenever Isaiah identifies the servant of the Lord from chapter 41 onwards, he speaks of Israel the nation; the only time an anointed one is spoken of, it is the Gentile king, Cyrus; Isaiah 53 speaks of the servant of the Lord, and the only candidate in the text is the nation of Israel. With this in mind, Isaiah 53, speaking figuratively of Israel, rolls naturally into Isaiah 54 which speaks of Jerusalem figuratively.

So Paul, once again, takes a verse out of context and gives it his own meaning.

verse 30

> *(28) And we, brothers, accordant with Isaac, are the children of promise. (29) But as then he that was born after the flesh persecuted him that was [born] after the Spirit, even so it is now. (30) Nevertheless what does the scripture say? Throw out the maidservant and her son; for the son of the maidservant shall not be heir with the son of the free-woman [Genesis 21:10]. (31) So then, brothers, we are not children of the bondwoman, but of the free. (Galatians 4:28-31)*

As with the last verse Paul took out of context, I don't need to go through different translations. All that is needed is context.

The context of Genesis 21 is as follows. Abraham was promised by God a son and Sarah's servant, Hagar, bore a child for Abraham and Sarah, that child being Ishmael. But God later clarifies that it was Sarah to have a son, and then gives her one, and he is named Isaac. Sometime later, after signs of dissent and disrespect from both Ishmael and Hagar, Sarah says "Drive out this maidservant and her son; for the son of this maidservant shall not inherit with my son, with Isaac".

Sarah was not prophesying. And therefore Paul is not seeking to give us understanding of what the text actually means and says. He is giving his own message and ripping a piece of scripture out to help him. And Paul's message? "Cast out the law covenant and those who live by it, for it has no part in the Pauline covenant!" Again, there is no clear voice in the Hebrew Bible that agrees with Paul. In fact, there is no agreement between the message of the Hebrew Bible and the preaching of Paul on this point and many others.

And also remember what Paul said about the covenants of men (Gal 3:15)! He said that when a man's covenant is confirmed, no one can abolish it. Yet, here, Paul feels his own authority to annul a covenant given by God himself!!! He is only contradicting himself.

Chapter 6

verses 12-13

(12) As many as desire to make a display in flesh, they compel you to be circumcised, only so that they should not be persecuted for the cross of Christ. (13) For neither they themselves who are circumcised keep the law; but they wish to have you circumcised, that they may boast in your flesh. (Galatians 6:12-13)

Paul here is saying that those who want others to be circumcised do so to escape hardship. They want the easy life. They can't even keep the law themselves but they just want others to be circumcised to boast.

This shows the spirit of condemnation which Paul exemplifies to his followers. He, who isn't even present, feels himself righteous and powerful enough, having psychic powers to read people's minds and motives, and judge another's level of righteousness. It is obvious that he would condemn anyone who claims to keep the law because he thinks a person must keep it absolutely perfect in order to be righteous, a thought that is shown in the Jewish Bible to be totally wrong. And unbeknownst to Paul, people might preach the law for sincere reasons of real conviction, and not merely the pride he imposes on his enemies.

Who knows? Maybe Paul sees in others what is really in himself and doesn't even know it.

verse 16

(15) For in Christ Jesus neither is circumcision worth any thing, nor uncircumcision, but a new creature. (16) And as many as walk according to this rule, peace be on them, and mercy, and upon the Israel of God. (Galatians 6:15-16)

Unfortunately, many take this small and slightly ambiguous phrase to say that it refers to "spiritual Israel", i.e., the believers in Jesus, regardless of links to national Israel, which means it includes Gentiles.

Now just to show that I'm not just making unfounded claims, let me just quote a few christian commentators who say the same thing.

The "Israel of God", or as the Arabic version reads it, "Israel the propriety of God"; which he has a right unto, and a claim upon; who are chosen by him, Israel his elect; who are redeemed by him, out of every kindred, tongue, people, and nation; who are called by his grace, and are styled Israel his called; who are justified in his Son, and by his righteousness; and for whose sake he is exalted as a Prince and a Saviour, to give them repentance and remission of sin; and who are, or will be saved by him, with an everlasting salvation; and is a name that includes all God's elect, whether Jews or Gentiles ... (John Gill's Exposition of the Whole Bible)

And upon the Israel of God [101] This is an indirect ridicule of the vain boasting of the false apostles, who vaunted of being the descendants of Abraham according to the flesh. There are two classes who bear this name, a pretended Israel, which appears to be so in the sight of men, -- and the Israel of God. Circumcision was a disguise before men, but regeneration is a truth before God. In a word, he gives the appellation of the Israel of God to those whom he formerly denominated the children of Abraham by faith, (Galatians 3:29,) and thus includes all believers, whether Jews or Gentiles, who were united into one church. (John Calvin's commentary of Galatians 6:16)

And upon the Israel of God: The true church of God; all who are his true worshippers. See Barnes "Romans 2:28"; See Barnes "Romans 2:29"; See Barnes "Romans 9:6". (Barnes' Notes on the New Testament)

I'm not going to quote any more sources, even though I easily could because of the amount of christian commentators who parrot the same belief.

A lot of theology has to be read into the phrase in order to come to the conclusion that "Israel of God" refers to a group of people made up of both Israelites and non-Israelites who just have the same belief system. But, unfortunately, it may be very possible that Paul is referring to Gentiles as "Israelites". A twisted view like this cannot be fixed with a simple comment, although I wish it could be. Verses like this and in parts of Romans are the source of the views like that of the Jehovah Witnesses and the "replacement-theology" christians claim to be the real Israel, who gets the fullness of all the blessings originally given in the Jewish Bible. But I'll try to summarize the facts that contradict this theology. I'll deal with this in two ways.

APPROACH 1: Who do the scriptures belong to?

In a certain sense - and I say again, in a certain sense - the scriptures do not belong to christians. They don't belong to righteous gentiles or Noahides. They don't belong to Muslims or Americans, or any other people group ... apart from the nation of Israel.

The Scriptures, the Jewish Bible, grew and thrived amongst the Israelites, who kept it as national law given by their Deity, the Creator of heaven and earth. The words in the Hebrew Scriptures were mostly written down by Israelites mainly for an Israelite audience. All the great prophets, Isaiah, Jeremiah, and Ezekiel were Hebrews, speaking to Hebrews. As universalistic the message of scripture may be and is, it was planted and grown in Israelite soil, not Gentile soil.

It was not written with a note saying "to the future christians" or "to the future Gentile believers in Jesus". There was no cover letter saying "to the future Muslims who will reject it as tainted and distorted". It was and is Israeli national history and heritage, although parts of it include the history of the whole human race and the world and universe as a whole.

So with all this in mind, an Israelite prophet talks or writes to an Israelite audience and prophesies about the main kingdoms of Israel, i.e., Israel and Judah, or at least using words in Israeli culture and terminology, using terms like "Israel", "Judah", and "temple", and "law". Now, thinking simply, the plainest understanding of such prophecies and messages is that they are talking about the natural audience, namely, the Israelites, unless there is something clear, something that distinctly says otherwise.

It's a bit like the American president speaking to his people saying "my fellow Americans, Michigan is now going to become the financial centre of Detroit". It would seem alien and abhorrent for a person living in China, who has been born and raised in China, to think that the American president is somehow talking about Chinese people living in Shanghai. It would be even more ridiculous if this Chinese person started claiming that his people were the true "spiritual" Americans, and that Michigan and Detroit were some how codewords for Chinese places or groups of people. If that happened in our day and age, we would call such a person crazy or totally misguided.

Yet, christians do this on a daily basis when they take words from the Jewish Bible and apply it to themselves, when they call themselves Israel, when they have taken that word from a person totally unrelated to them, living in a land totally unrelated to theirs, speaking to his own people.

The point is that the scriptures were given to and belong to the Israelites and their modern day descendants, the Jews and clearly speaks of their land and people groups.

This can go some way to refuting some of the strange interpretations and conflicts christians find themselves in. For instance, they say that Isaiah 53 refers to "the servant of the Lord" as guiltless in some way; but since Israel has done something, anything wrong, then Isaiah 53 can't refer to the nation Israel or to a righteous remnant amongst them. This is despite the fact that numerous times from Isaiah 41 to Isaiah 52, the Israelite prophet, Isaiah, speaking or writing to the Israelite people, calls Israel God's servant (remember the American president analogy given above)!

So, to reiterate, looking at the source and development of the Jewish Bible, it would seem highly unlikely that the scriptures were really meant for another set of people who would adopt the name "Israel". If you have an Israelite speaker, communicating to Israelites, about matters concerning the land of Israel, using the Israelite language of

Hebrew and using Israelite terms, then it is more than reasonable to suspect he may be speaking of natural Israel about the people of Israel, and not some distantly removed (both in time, lineage, and space) group of strangers.

APPROACH 2: Reading scripture for what it says, not what we want it to say.

For those who at least try to allow scripture to speak for itself as much as possible, those who don't have the approach that Jesus must be read into everything, or the words of Paul are of greater validity or strength than the so-called "old testament", and who believe that the Almighty can communicate clearly enough for his words to be understood by looking at their normal, natural meaning; for those people, I want you to think about what I say next! (I go through all this introduction because there is no point in even attempting to speak to those who are stuck in their ways, and it's better to point them out right now)

According to the first book of the Bible, Abraham was given a promise and a special covenant which was passed down to Isaac, which was then passed down to Jacob, who was renamed Israel. Jacob's descendants bore that name "Israel" as a nation. Israel was then saved from Egypt and given a law for their land and for their lives which contain the way of righteousness and holiness (i.e., which set them apart in a special way). They, the nation of Israel, then came to occupy the land of promise, given by the Creator to their ancestor, Abraham. They had forged a history and a culture. None of what I told you before is shown in scripture to be figurative or spiritual. Israel was a literal nation. The prophecies given to Abraham about his biological descendants being in Egypt in Genesis 15:13-16 wasn't about spiritual or figurative descendants who were not his physical offspring! The prophecy was about a real, literal seed/offspring. No other nation could claim that prophecy and usurp the name of the descendants of Abraham. That prophecy didn't have a spiritual meaning which would have meant that the descendants of Abraham wouldn't literally leave the literal country of Egypt, the people oppressing them in real life. The prophecy is full of literal meaning.

Jacob's and Moses' prophecies about the tribes of Israel (see Genesis 49 and Deuteronomy 33), although very picturesque, still refers to the literal tribes of Israel, not some other people group, or a mixture of some who are and some who are not descended from Jacob, yet who all claim to be a spiritual tribe claiming the name. The texts refer to the literal tribes.

And the pattern continues in scripture of prophecies about Israel and Judah, or Ephraim (another name for Israel). Looking at this general pattern, what gives Paul, or anyone, the right to usurp the name "Israel" or "Judah" and give it to people who are not the literal descendants of Israel (Jacob) and have not properly, legally, naturalised to become a full part of the covenant nation, in essence stealing the fullness of their blessings? There is something terribly wrong with this act! Whether Paul really did it or not, his disciples took and spread it! It is just like identity fraud and theft!

I implore you to pray for a listening heart and a discerning, seeing eye, and just read Psalms like Psalm 78, 81, 105, and 115. I hope that you will see a distinct nation of people with a history that includes rescue from a literal Egypt, with a literal Aaronic priesthood. They had their share of sin and punishment, praise and worship. How can any other nation or people take the prophecies and promises that are so linked to Israel's history? Or how can anyone "spiritualise" or make into allegory such a divinely given, well-journeyed and hard-fought heritage and claim it for themselves? The exiles, the captivities, the warnings, and encouragements given through the Lord's prophets; could the gracious Creator and God really allow such things to happen to a nation only for the everlasting blessings promised to their literal offspring (e.g., Isaiah 54:3; 59:20; Deuteronomy 10:15; 30:6) to be given to another people who didn't go through such trials, like the Jehovah Witnesses or Gentile christianity???

May it never be so!

Some may say that the history of Israel is an allegory for the present "spiritual Israel", the vast majority of which are non-Israelites. Or that the prophecies pointed only allegorically to "spiritual Israel", the church. But although allegory may teach and can edify in moral lessons, it is no means of proving real identity; it cannot prove anything! If the prophecies are truly allegorical, then they have no meaning and are no source of hope. Why? The nature of allegory is to use one thing to describe another, and a person has to figure out what the real meaning is. Because of this, you can use it to prove anything using similar characteristics or traits. Why? Because with enough thought, any allegory can have a multitude of possible meanings to the point that even your enemies can get meanings to encourage their cause! And since allegories can be used to prove anything (even contradictory things), then they prove nothing! No meaning is certain because there are so many others.

Paul and his gentile disciples have built a castle of soft sand, or, more properly, sinking sand. Allegory can only teach, not prove!

So for anyone to take Israel's names and blessings for themselves, that act can only be understood as a horrible, disgusting lie, the most insidious form of identity theft, and more reason to hate the fruits of the teachings of Paul!

Let's move on, shall we?

Ephesians

Chapter 2

verses 11-12

Paul makes the following case:

(11) Therefore, remember that you, in times past Gentiles in the flesh, called "uncircumcision" by that which is called circumcision in the flesh handmade, (12) that, in that time, you were estranged from the state of Israel and strangers from the covenants of promise, having no hope and without God in the world. (Ephesians 2:11-12)

Now, contextually, there's not much to comment on in this passage. But, unfortunately, some derive from this that all Gentiles, non-Jews, are naturally hopeless, without God, having no relationship with him. In fact, some state that it was impossible for non-Jews to have any relationship with God without becoming a Jew! And it's not hard to see how such a conclusion could be reached with Paul's words describing these Gentiles has having no hope and being without God in the world, linking this state to being estranged from Israel and from the covenants.

In addition, there is nothing overt in the text to come to a firm conclusion that the Gentiles Paul was writing to were somehow different from other non-Jews in the world. Therefore in the same way these Gentiles were in such a deplorable state of hopelessness and Godlessness, all Gentiles would be in the same state.

But here's the question: Is this conclusion consistent with the message of the Hebrew Bible? Whether this opinion just comes from Paul or was constructed by his followers, does it comport with what the Jewish Bible has to say?

Did the Law of Moses consign Gentiles to the abyss of Godlessness? In Leviticus 22, God through Moses tells the people of Israel and the sojourners in their midst not to offer animals that have blemishes or injuries. He continues,

> *Neither from the hand of a foreigner shall you offer the bread of your God of any of these [blemished animals], because their corruption [or, disfigurement] is in them, there is a blemish in them; they shall not be accepted for you. (Leviticus 22:25)*

So here God not speaking about Israelites or the non-Jewish sojourners but rather total outsiders, foreigners. When these foreigners would offer animals for sacrifice, those animals were not to have disfigurements.

But wait! If non-Jews, if Gentiles, were without hope and without God, then this statement would make no sense. How could foreigners without hope and God in the world bring any sacrifice to the one true God? Remember, God was known before Sinai by others, such as Melchitzedek. In fact he was known by Ishmael and Esau. Remember, these Gentiles would not be part of the state of Israel and would have no part in the covenants of promise. Yet there is a law about such foreigners offering sacrifices.

Let me get to some other evidence.

Was the world without God except for Israel according to the Jewish Bible?

When Solomon dedicated the temple, he said the following in 1 Kings 8:41-43.

And also, concerning the foreigner which is not from your people Israel, when he shall come from a far country because of Your name - for they shall hear [of] Your great name, and Your mighty hand, and Your outstretched arm, and shall come and pray towards this house - May You, Yourself hear [in] the heavens, Your dwelling place, and do according to all that the foreigner calls to You [for], so that all peoples of the earth may know Your name, to fear You as Your people, Israel, and to know that your name is called upon this house which I have built.

So Solomon is distinctly referring to a foreigner, a non-Jew, who is not from Israel, living in a far away country and therefore not part of the state or commonwealth of Israel and having no part of the covenants of promise. Yet this Gentile prays to God and fears God. That's odd behaviour according to Paul and/or his followers, but expected behaviour according to Solomon. This Gentile doesn't seem to be without hope.

What about the Gentile city of Nineveh? Regardless of its ultimate fate, God saw fit to send the prophet Jonah to it in order to warn of its impending doom in 40 days. Yet this people with no hope, having no part in the covenants of promise, repented and the doom was averted and didn't happen.

Just think of Psalm 117 verse 1. Think how odd it sounds if the nations are without God and without hope.

Praise the Lord, all nations: praise him, all people.

Be warned – because the ideas I'm about to bring up may be thrown around amongst christians circles! There is nothing in the text that says that this Psalm is only for the future or for some time when God's kingdom and rule is restored on the whole earth. The text clearly points to the nations of the world and encourages them to praise God. Does that really make sense if the rest of the world is without God and without hope? No, of course not! Such an idea makes no sense.

Shall I mention Naaman the Syrian who, without becoming a citizen of Israel, accepted the God of Israel? There's no point in bringing up the fact that before Israel even existed, a human being, any human being could walk with God, as shown by Enoch and Noah. There is no evidence that with the coming of Israel, all of a sudden the rest of the world is cut off by God.

In fact the very opposite message is given. Israel would show God to the rest of the nations, not so the nations would become Israelites, but so that they would be amazed at the wisdom of God. Just look at Deuteronomy 4. Israel wasn't chosen to cut God off from the rest of the world, but rather in order to be a nation of ministers, teachers and examples for the rest of the world, so that the nations could see the hand of God in the world.

So rather than God abandoning the world at large, leaving the nations without hope, he is still available in the world, not only through the miracle of nature, but also through the witness of the covenant nation of Israel.

So Paul's idea of the Gentiles being without God and without hope is baseless, having no real foundation in the Jewish Bible. As the Jewish Bible teaches loud and clear:

You open your hand, and satisfy the desire of every living thing. God is righteous in all his ways, and kind in all his works. The Lord is near for all those who call him, for all who call him in truth. The desire of those who fear him will he fulfill, and their cry for help will he hear, and save them. The Lord watches over all those who love him ... (Psalm 145:16-20)

God satisfies the desire of every living thing. Do you think that leaves out Gentiles? Don't be silly! He is there for anyone who calls him with truth. The fact that this song says it means that it is possible.

For a very brief response, I'll just say that the Hebrew Bible again contradicts such thinking, showing that non-Jews can have a relationship with Deity without becoming Jews.

verses 13-16

Paul continues to press his point:

(13) But now in Christ Jesus you who before were far off become near by the blood of Christ. (14) For he is our peace, who has made both one, and has broken down the middle wall of division; (15) Having nullified in his flesh the enmity: the law of commandments in regulations, in order to create in himself of the two one new man, [thereby] making peace; (16) And that he might reconcile both to God in one body by the cross, having slain the enmity thereby (Ephesians 2:13-16)

So, according to Paul, in order establish peace between Jew and gentile, Jesus did the following with his blood (sacrifice, or death):

τον νομον των εντολων εν δογμασιν καταργησας
TRANSLATION: ... having made void/rendered idle/nullified/abolishing the law of the commandments in regulations
...

Now, is Paul talking about the law of Moses? Why even ask the question since that's all that Paul has been attacking so far? Well, there are some who would say that Paul is not talking about the law of Moses! They would say that the Greek word translated "regulations" (other translate it as "ordinances", but that's not a commonly understood term) refers everywhere else in the "new testament" to authoritative decrees made by man (Acts 16:4; 17:7; Luke 2:1). Therefore, according to their logic, the word cannot refer to the word of God, the law He gave to Moses. So the "regulations" refer to the decrees made by man, that they are either our sins (Colossians 2:14), or the oral law of the Pharisees (Ephesians 2:15), which they believe to be man-made.

But the problem with this thinking is that the Greek word is only used 5 times. There are 3 clear occurrences that refer to man-made decrees. But that, in itself, is not enough to dictate the meaning of the other two occurrences. If we were dealing with a word that occurred many, many times, like 50 times, and they all had a certain meaning, and there were 4 uncertain occurrences, we'd have a good idea about the meaning of the 4 uncertain ones. But if we have 60 certain occurrences but 40 uncertain ones, then it is not so easy to state, for certain, what the other 40 mean because the amount of certain one is not a big enough proportion to dictate the others.

The same is true for having 3 occurrences that have one certain connotation, and 2 that have some uncertainty or possibly a slightly different meaning. Three is just not enough to dictate two.

Add to this, the fact that there is nothing in the Greek word for "regulations", δογμα, dogma, that stops it from referring to a decree or regulation from God. In fact, a writer around the time of Paul, called Josephus, referred to God's Law as the regulations, δογματα, dogmata, of God (Josephus, Contra Apionem 1.42 – I searched on the internet and there is another version currently at http://www.earlyjewishwritings.com/josephus.html where the phrase is at book 1 section 8).

It is clear in practice how we approach our own writings. Although such a time is long now passed, no one has dared to add, to take away, or to alter anything; it is innate in every Judean, right from birth, to regards them as decrees from God. (taken from page 31 of "Flavius Josephus: Translation and Commentary, Volume 10: Against Apion" by Flavius Josephe, edited by Steve Mason, translation and commentary by John M.G. Barclay, published by BRILL)

Throughout the Pauline writings, Paul consistently has a problem with regulations, laws, and decrees: the Law of God given through Moses. So, seeing Paul's track record with attacking the Law, there is no real sound argument for not taking Paul's words to their obvious meaning: The Law of Moses is the enmity which was nullified by Jesus. It is the Moses' divinely given law that is supposed to make a separation between Jew and non-Jew, a separation Paul takes as a dividing wall, a hostility between Jew and Gentile.

Let's just take this interpretation which mainstream christianity takes as true, namely, that Paul is talking about the abolition of the law of Moses as a whole, or laws within the Mosaic law. One notable thing that has to be taken into account is one of the verses Paul quotes in his book, in Galatians 3, i.e., Deuteronomy 27:26. It's interesting that Paul refers to laws being abolished and nullified, contradicting its validity. Paul is doing exactly what Deuteronomy 27:26 speaks against.

Going back to Paul's words, we must ask if they accurately depict the purpose of God's law, or even a result of it. You see, the true intent of God's law that is outwardly spoken of and written about in the Hebrew Bible was never segregation with hostility. It is only Paul and his followers who try to link the Law with segregation and hostility. But, on the other hand, the law sets apart a people in order to purify and disseminate. Remember that! The law sets apart a people in order to purify and disseminate!

The law sets apart the people of Israel as chosen for a purpose. The law purifies those people, that nation, for a purpose. And then an important part of that purpose is for Israel to spread, or disseminate, the truth of God by being a light to the nations (Exodus 19:3-6; Deuteronomy 4:5-8; 7:6; 14:2). As a royal priesthood, the nation of Israel does not segregate to the point of total isolation from the world, but, by maintaining a high standard, they minister to the world and shine the light of the truth of Deity for all to see. Thus, there must be some interaction with the world in order to truly minister to it. But there also must be some separation - the set-apart nature of Israel - not for hostility, but rather that the message and messengers can remain pure, not getting mixed up with foreign elements.

What is overlooked by Paul's interpretation of the role of the law is the fact that it encourages and commands love for God and for mankind. That doesn't really tally with Paul's law-hostility doctrine.

A way to understand the relationship between Israel and the world is to look at the relationship between the Levitical priests and the rest of Israel. The Levites, who were a tribe of Israel, were "segregated" from the rest of Israel in a way, but not completely, by their special laws. Yet, according to that law, they were an integral part of Israel, always aimed at working with and for the rest of the nation as a whole as a loving and cohesive unit. In the same way, the priestly nation of Israel, though segregated in a way (not completely), should, according to that law, be working for and with the world until the knowledge of God fills the earth as the waters cover the sea.

So, the notion that the law, the true observance of it, produces hostility is wrong! It is through the law and the example of living it that real love is promoted in the whole world. It is not the case that Jews are in one corner with God and a covenant, a relationship, and laws that govern that devoted relationship, whereas the Gentiles are in the other corner without Deity, without covenant, without a relationship with God, and without divine laws. The whole world has a covenant with God, the covenant of Noah. The world has divine laws that they should keep and we are accountable to God for our deeds, as can be seen by God's judgment against the generation of Noah who perished in the flood, God's judgment against Abimelech for taking Abraham's wife for his own, Naaman who accepted that the God of Israel was the only true God although he was Syrian, God's judgment against and mercy towards Nineveh, etc. So everyone can have a relationship with God without being a Jew if they want it. It is evident throughout the books of Moses, the law and history recorded in them and all the pages of the Hebrew Bible, and the historical heritage of the Jews that such laws were preserved throughout history and spread abroad.

So, if it is Paul's contention that the law creates or maintains hostility between Jew and non-Jew, then, once again, the Law itself with the rest of the Jewish Scriptures refute him.

Chapter 4

verse 8

Paul quotes Psalm 68:18 to say that Jesus came down to earth, went back to heaven, and gave gifts (such as apostleship and teaching) to his followers. Let's just look what Paul says and compare it to what the Hebrew Bible says, as well as its ancient Greek translation.

PAUL: ενι δε εκαστω ημων εδοθη η κατα το μετρον της δωρεας του χριστου, διο λεγει αναβας εις υψος ηχμαλωτευσεν αιχμαλωσιαν και εδωκεν δοματα τοις ανθρωποις
TRANSLATION: And to each one of us he gave the grace according to the measure of the gift of the christ. Therefore he said, He ascended into height[s]; he captured captives; and he gave gifts to men.

LXX: αναβης εις υψος ηχμαλωτευσας αιχμαλωσιαν ελαβες δοματα εν ανθρωπω
TRANSLATION: You ascended into height[s]; you captured captives; you took gifts among man.

HEBREW BIBLE:
בָּ אָדָ ם מ תָּ נוֹ ת לָ קַ חְ תָּ שֶׁ בִ י שָׁ בִ יתָ לַ מָּ רוֹ ם עָ לִ יתָ

TRANSLATION: You ascended to the height[s]; you captured captives; you took gifts among man.

Can we be honest with ourselves and the text? OK, let's state the facts: Paul changes the words of scripture! Even the LXX, the questionable Septuagint, does a better job of translating the original Hebrew text than Paul. Paul has reversed the direction and meaning of the word: instead of the proper word "take", Paul uses a word with the opposite meaning and says "give"! So Paul is NOT being faithful to scripture, but, rather, he is again fulfilling his own agenda.

Also note that, contextually, the passage in Psalms has nothing to do with messiah. It is talking about God's action at and around Sinai (see Psalm 68:17).

I would point out that christian commentators try to say that Paul was justified in his translation based on the Jewish ancient Aramaic paraphrase/commentary called the Targum. They say that the Targum of Psalm 68 uses the phrase, "you gave gifts to the sons of man". And they are right! The Targum does use that phrase! But do you want to read the whole passage from the Targum? OK, here goes:

(18) The chariots of God are two myriads of burning fire, two thousand angles guiding them; the presence of the Lord rests on them on the mountain of Sinai in holiness. (19) You ascended to the firmament, O prophet Moses; you captured captives, you taught the words of Torah, you gave gifts to the sons of men, ..." (Psalm 68:18-19 - verse numbering is different in the Hebrew, Greek, and Aramaic versions than in the English versions)

Do you see a problem here? Compare the Targum with an "accurate" translation of the Bible, or, even better, if you know Hebrew, compare it with the original text. You'll see that the Targum adds a lot of phrases and concepts that are not explicitly in the text. Why? Remember, I said that the Targum was a paraphrase/commentary of the text. It is not an attempt at our modern conception of a translation: it doesn't attempt to just convey the meaning of each word in the text. It actually uses Jewish tradition and interpretation and puts it in a translated portion. It doesn't even claim to be a plain translation!

So people who claim that Paul is using the Targum to make a point are already standing on shaky ground, and that's IF he's using the Targumic tradition, which he never claims to. It is the commentators who are putting words in Paul's mouth when we can never know if he really said them.

But the essential problem with people claiming that Paul is quoting from the Targum is right there in its text. Do you see the subject of verse 19 (or verse 18 in christian versions)? It's the prophet, Moses! So it's not talking about Jesus. It's not talking about God. The Targum is only talking about Moses! You may be able to see that this piece of Targumic commentary actually fits the context of the original Hebrew text, i.e., what happened at Sinai, with Moses being the main human player. So, if Paul is using the Targum, then he is not right in using it to make his alien claim.

And one has to wonder why Paul is using this verse at all from Psalm 68. Remember he is talking about Jesus coming down and ascending and then giving gifts. This is what he said in Ephesians 4:7-10.

But grace has been given to every one of us according to the measure of the gift of Christ. Therefore he says, When he ascended up on high, he led captivity captive, and gave gifts to men. (Now that he ascended, what is it but that he also descended first into the lower parts of the earth? He that descended is the same also that ascended up far above all heavens, that he might fill all things.)

Now christian commentators are almost universal in saying that this refers to Jesus.

But, as usual when it comes to Paul, such a message is totally missing from Psalm 68. There is no "messiah." There is no Jesus. Paul's topic is wholly missing from the text of Psalm 68.

So, this is another case of out of context misusage and distortion by Paul.

Chapter 5

verse 14

> *(12) Because it is a shameful to speak of the things which are done by them in concealment. (13) But all things that are exposed are revealed by the light, because everything that reveals is light. (14) Therefore he says, Awake, sleeping one, and get up out from the dead, and the Christ will shine on you. (Galatians 5:12-14)*

Now Paul, in verse 14, seems to be quoting something. How can I make such a claim when all Paul says is, "therefore, he says"? Well, I can make this claim based on two principle places of evidence: firstly, from a good number of christian commentators who say that Paul is either quoting, paraphrasing, or referring to something in the Hebrew Bible; and, secondly, from Paul's own writings, namely that he uses this little phrase here that he used in a previous place where he quoted scripture (Ephesians 4:8), i.e. "διο λεγει", "therefore he/it says". So Paul seems to be referring to something in the Hebrew Bible.

But that's where we hit upon a problem. What exactly is Paul quoting or paraphrasing from the Hebrew Bible? Where is he referring to? There is a difference of opinion here. Some say he is neither quoting or paraphrasing; that these are just his own words (see Wesley's commentary). We'll ignore them for now. We'll focus on christian commentators like Gill, and Jamieson, Faucett, and

Brown. They give two possible sources. That shows the ambiguity we are dealing with in this "quote". But let's look at the options.

Firstly, there's Gill in his Exposition of the Whole Bible, who refers to Isaiah 26:19.

Your dead shall live; my corpses shall arise. Awake and sing, dwellers in the dust, for your dew is as the dew of light, and the earth shall bring to life the shades. (Isaiah 26:19)

But the words and the message of Isaiah 26:19 don't match that of Paul. Paul is speaking of deeds being done in secret being revealed by the light. But Isaiah is speaking about the abundant revival of a nation, a people. The subjects are different. Plus, the words of the Isaiah say nothing about a "christ" or an anointed one. In essence, the subject Paul is talking about has nothing to do with the message of Isaiah. [Some may say that Paul already is expert at ripping verses out of context and giving them his meaning, but there is not a strong link between Paul's words and Isaiah's.]

Secondly, we have both JFB (Jamieson, Faucett, and Brown) and Gill referring to Isaiah 60:1, which is much closer in some ways.

Arise, shine, for your light has come, and the glory of HaShem has shone upon you. (Isaiah 60:1)

But it is still very dissimilar to what Paul is saying. There is nothing about sleep, nothing about resurrection, and nothing about a "christ" or an anointed one. So again, both wording and subject matter are different.

Now, in my original notes of going through this verse of Paul's, I thought that Paul could have possibly done a cut-paste-edit of both verses, both Isaiah 26:19 and 60:1. I mean, there are hints of both in Paul's "rendition". At the very least, it has the light motif from both verses. And there would be no point in complaining that Paul wouldn't do such a thing, because it has already been shown in Romans 9:33 that Paul is not beyond cutting verses from two different portions of a book each in half and sticking them together for his own purposes. So it's not beyond Paul to sink to such levels. Neither is it far from Paul to add words to scripture in Galatians 3:10 where Paul adds the word "all" to help his point. But I didn't really want to push the point here because there is little point in speculating when Paul does more than just split-and-stick verses together: he rewrites it!

Someone may say, "Well, maybe he's not quoting anything." But then we have to make this verse alien to the rest of his writings, and imagine some unwritten identity who said these words, since Paul prefaces the words with "therefore, he says": who is "he"? We can either understand this preface in light of how Paul generally speaks, or, for some arbitrary reason, make an exception. Until, I see basis for the latter approach, I'll just move on and leave it.

In the end, Paul has either distorted scripture [beyond recognition] for his own purposes, or he has made up a scripture that doesn't exist.

Philippians

Chapter 1

verses 15-18

Paul makes the following statements:

> *(14) And many of the brothers in the Lord, being confident by my
> fetters, are more bold to speak the word without fear. (15) Some
> indeed preach even because of envy and strife; and others also
> because of good will. (16) Some preach the Christ out of selfish
> ambition, not with sincerity, thinking to add affliction to my fetters.
> (17) But others out of love, knowing that I am set for the defence of
> the gospel. (18) What then? Notwithstanding, every way, whether
> with pretence, whether with truth, Christ is preached and in this I
> rejoice, but I shall rejoice. (Philippians 1:14-18)*

Just a small note: in different versions of the new testament, verse 16
and 17 are swapped. I don't think anyone has any idea which is the
true version, although I'm sure many have their beliefs and
persuasions. So much for the honourable new testament, well
preserved!

Anyway, after we get through all the methods by which Paul's
"gospel" is proclaimed to all, we get Paul's conclusion: it doesn't
matter how "christ" is proclaimed, whether truthfully, or with
pretence (just an outward show wit no real true core), as long as it's
proclaimed! It don't matter how the job gets done, as long as it gets
done! Is there some significance to this? Paul doesn't mind if fakery
is used to promote his message. At the very least, that puts some

questions in my mind about Paul and his own sincerity. But I won't prolong this one. I won't give my full conclusions.

I'll leave that up to you.

Chapter 2

verses 5-11

Paul says:

(5) Because, let this intent be in you which was also in Jesus Christ, (6) who, being in the form of Deity, did not consider to be like Deity *robbery/a prize to be grasped* [contentious phrase]. (7) But he emptied himself taking the form of a slave being in the likeness of men. (8) And being found externally like a man, he abased himself being obedient to the point of death, and death of the cross. (9) Because of this even the Deity highly exalted him and bestowed [on] him a name, the higher-than-everything name, (10) so that in the name of Jesus every knee shall bend heavenly and earthly and subterranean, (11) and every tongue shall confess that Jesus Christ is Lord to [the] glory of Father God. (Philippians 2:5-11)

One of the most controversial passages in christianity! Parts of it are so ambiguous, such as verse 6b. Is it saying that Jesus thought equality with God was not something to be snatched at or grasped, like the American Standard Version or the World English Bible translates it? Or is it saying that Jesus didn't see anything wrong with being equal to Deity, like the translations of the King James Version and Young's [supposedly] Literal Translation? We can leave that for christians to battle over.

But we do have some facts that we can judge in light of the Jewish Bible.

"Jesus, being in the form of Deity" - What does this mean? Jesus had God's form. The simple understanding of this is that Jesus, before "becoming human", had God's form, namely, his attributes. Christian [generally, trinitarian] commentators generally assume this to mean that Jesus was of a divine nature, not like the angels who are spiritual creatures, but as Deity himself. Knowing that there is a distinction between Jesus (the "son") and his divine Father, we are confronted with a statement of idolatry in the new testament, the writings of Paul, if understood in this light. The Creator of the universe has no equal, someone similar to him, and no superior or father; he exists alone as one (Deuteronomy 4:35,39; 11:14,17; 32:39; Isaiah 43:10-11; 44:6). [And just to clarify for trinitarians who may struggle with what I mean by "one", I do mean absolute one, not a one that can be two or three.] Who can have the form of deity apart from Deity himself? No one! And Deity makes it clear that he doesn't share his attributes/glory with others (Isaiah 42:8).

Just to note: I do know that there are christians that believe that Jesus was not God. They may have a different interpretation of this verse, but the ones I've seen aren't too convincing for me personally. So I deal mainly with the view that accepts Jesus as "God". And I also know that the word "god" had a much wider meaning in ancient times. People nowadays think that there is only God, meaning the creator of the universe, and everything and anything else is not God or a god. In ancient times, kings and amazing people and higher beings were called "god" without being THE God. I'm not bringing that aspect into this monologue.

"at the name of Jesus, all shall bow and confess Jesus' lordship to the Father's glory" - This is more or less the usurping of God's glory when compared with Isaiah 45:21-25 which says:

(21) Make it conspicuous, and bring [them] near; yea, let them take counsel together: Who has caused this to be heard from ancient? told it from then? is it not I, HaShem [The LORD]? and there is no other god except me, a just god and a saviour; there is none beside

me. (22) Turn to me, be helped, all ye ends of the earth; for I am God [Heb. "el" not "elohim"], and there is no one else. (23) I have sworn by myself, a word has gone out of my mouth - righteousness - and it shall not return, that every knee shall bend to me, every tongue shall swear. (24) Only in the Lord, - shall men say of me, - [there are] righteousness and strength. To Him shall come and be ashamed all that are incensed against him. (25) In HaShem [the LORD], all the seed of Israel shall be declared righteous and shall boast.

Just to clarify, here I used the name "HaShem," a Jewish term meaning "the Name," because it is at those places where the special name of God is used, a name I don't want to put in this text. It is the name some people conclude as being "Jehovah" or "Yahweh." But since these are both simply attempts by people to guess the name rather than the one that God actually revealed, I'd rather not put those two attempted names there either. But in this case I believe it is important to highlight the fact that a specific personal name is there that is not spelt J-e-s-u-s.

Now in Isaiah's vision, there is nothing between a worshipper and God, no intermediary. And there is no plurality in God; there is no unified group of three, just one alone. This is clear by the fact that Isaiah uses the singular term "el" to refer to God. Every knee bows and every tongue vows to God alone, straight and simple. But Paul adds a foreign component which Isaiah didn't even include: the man Jesus.

Again, we are not looking at exposition (exposing the meaning from the text) but rather imposition (imposing meaning into the text) from Paul. The prophet had already spoken of the future Davidic king in Isaiah 11. If he wanted to - if the Lord had wanted to - he would have added the Davidic king to this universal acknowledgement of the truth of the Creator. But as the context of Isaiah 45 shows, the emphasis is HaShem, the one true God, alone, and not the messiah, a figure which has no place in this passage or its intention.

Chapter 3

verse 2

> *See the dogs! See the evil works! See the κατατομην [katatomen]!*
> *(Philippians 3:2)*

I've left a certain term untranslated. We'll get back to that.

Here we see the "grace" and "beneficence" in Paul's describing those who believe differently about the role of circumcision. He calls them "dogs", which is a plain insult. I'm surprised how christians either take on Paul's manner or do the exact opposite. How comes? Well, either they are just like him and unafraid to insult and demonize those with a different point of view. So their holistic imitation of Paul is their downfall. Or they take his teachings but not his manner, and thus it seems like a pick-and-mix discipleship, even though Paul himself says "imitate [Paul] as you imitate [Jesus]" (1 Corinthians 11:1).

Anyway, Paul adopts tit-for-tat tactics, lashing out with words as he himself may have been scalded for his beliefs. He calls them "evil-workers". There's little point in arguing with Paul there, since his interpretation of their acts depends on what you think of Paul. No, what really catches the eye is his description of those who adopt the circumcision of Abraham and Moses and Israel. He calls them the κατατομη, katatome, which has a really interesting meaning. A form of this word is used in the Septuagint, the LXX. I'll quote the verses both in Greek and English.

LXX: και φαλακρωμα ου ξυρηθησεσθε την κεφαλην επι νεκρω και την οψιν του πωγωνος ου ξυρησονται &kai;αι επι τας σακρας αυτων ου κατατεμουσιν εντομιδας

TRANSLATION: And you shall not shave your heads for the dead with a bald spot at the top, neither shall they shave off the corners of their beards, neither shall they make gashes on their flesh. (Leviticus 21:5, LXX English Versions)

Can you see the word in question, a form of which Paul makes use of to describe his opponents? Can you see it? No, it's not "shave" or "beard. No, the verbal form of the word κατατομη, katatome, is translated as "they shall not make gashes". This is the notion that comes across from Paul's word. Greek dictionaries translate the word Paul uses as "mutilation". He is saying "Beware the mutilation!" Thus, Paul calls those who choose to get circumcised according to the law "the mutilation", or those that preach that a person should be circumcised. Apparently he has cast off his own circumcision heritage/background, as shall be confirmed with a later verse of his I shall quote.

Just to note, it is clear that Paul is talking about those circumcised because he stresses in the next verse that he and his group of Gentile followers are the real "circumcision".

So what point am I trying to make here? Paul goes too far in his attempt to denounce his opponents by degrading a practice commanded by God himself, the circumcision, the sign of the covenant of Abraham. He takes this sign and tramples it underfoot in order to show himself and his point righteous by calling it "the mutilation".

Please ignore weak "translations" like the World English Bible which glosses over this word with the English phrase "false circumcision" which totally misses Paul's purposeful insult.

Now some may think that Paul is justified making his statements. To them, he is attacking the people who preach what he disagrees with as opposed to the circumcision they have. Now if this was a statement in isolation, where there is no other place where Paul discredits the law and its role and its purpose, then I could give this theory some credit. But, as we've seen so far in Paul's escapades, he only gives lip service to respecting the law and paints it as if he is drawing horrible two-dimensional caricatures, we'll see later on that he is ok with putting forward the righteousness in God's law as trash. So let's not put it too far from Paul to regard circumcision of the flesh as mutilation. If he didn't see it as useful as a badge in front of other Jews who opposed him, one wonders if he would have had an operation to reverse the circumcision that he claimed was in his own flesh.

verse 3

Paul continues:

For we are the circumcision, the ones worshipping God spiritually and boast in Jesus Chrsit, and have no confidence in flesh.
(Philippians 3:3)

What confusion Paul creates! Seeing that Paul was speaking of his Gentile Philippians, he only causes a mess-up in what was divinely ordered. In Paul's world, the circumcised are uncircumcised (or mutilated) and vice versa. Once everything is spiritualized and allegorized, then black becomes white, and white becomes black; the righteous become sinners, and the sinners are imputed with righteousness.

What a confused and messed-up world!

verses 4-8

And the painful song plays on ...

(4) And, indeed, I have confidence, even in flesh: if any other [man] thinks that he has confidence in flesh, I more: (5) Circumcised the eighth day, of the stock of Israel, of the tribe of Benjamin, a Hebrew of Hebrews; concerning the law, a Pharisee; (6) Concerning zeal, persecuting the assembly ["church", in some translations];

concerning the righteousness which is in the law, faultless. (7) But what things were gain to me, those I counted loss because of Christ. (8) Yea doubtless, and I count all things but loss for the excellency of the knowledge of Jesus Christ my lord: because of whom I have experienced loss of all things, and deem them as dung, that I may win Christ ...

Paul is willing to count everything as loss to gain Jesus; he regards them as "dung". What connotations does the Greek word translated "dung" have? It has meanings of excrement, faeces (the sort you flush in the toilet), and refuse (what you would throw out to the wild dogs). Amongst those things that he would regard in this scummy position, as the most vile garbage is the "righteousness of the law". It's important to understand the implications of what Paul says. Moses, the greatest prophet, a man who God actually spoke to, said:

And it shall be righteousness for his when we are careful to do all this commandment before the LORD our God, as He commanded us. (Deuteronomy 6:25)

The righteousness of the law that God commanded Israel is what Paul sees as the vilest piece of garbage to throw to wild dogs!!! And some christians would have the nerve to say that Paul was pro-law???

The interesting thing is that although no one can keep the law perfectly, it seems that one person has managed to escape the condemnation and blame the law is supposed to give: Paul himself! He considers himself blameless, faultless, and irreproachable with regards to its righteousness. What humility!

To some, I may seem a bit harsh. They may think that it is possible that Paul is just saying that he was highly respected and led a publicly decent life. But Paul didn't simply say "decent." He said blameless, meaning that in public, he was, more or less, perfect. Thinking about the implications of Paul's words, it's difficult to imagine he only had general decency in mind, especially when we see he is willing to call circumcision, "mutilation"!

What is clear is that Paul's respect for God's law is terribly low, if not non-existent!

Colossians

Chapter 1

verse 15

Paul makes the following statements:

(13) [God] Who has rescued us from the power of darkness, and has carried us away into the kingdom of his beloved son; (14) in whom we have redemption through his blood, even the forgiveness of sins; (15) who is the image of the invisible God, the firstborn of every creature: (16) For in him were all things created, that are in heaven, and that are in earth, visible and invisible, whether they be thrones, or dominions, or governments, or authorities: all things were created through him, and for him: (17) And he is before all things, and in him all things are held together. (Colossians 1:13-17)

Jesus, according to Paul is "the image of the invisible God". The second part of verse 15, about him being "firstborn," doesn't have a clear and singular meaning, since it can speak simply of a pre-eminence or superiority above all others, not simply the fact that a person was born, with regards to time, before his siblings. This is seen in places in the ancient Greek translation of the Jewish Bible where, for example, Israel is called God's firstborn in Exodus 4:22. The exact same connotation is used and it doesn't mean that it was literally begotten from God, God is not Israel's biological father. But it did have a special status, a chosen status, above all other nations.

But the phrase "image of the invisible God" needs some thought. What is Paul actually saying? Paul doesn't seem to be using the word "image" in the same way that humans are made in the image of God (Genesis 1:26; 5:1-3) because Paul is listing aspects of this special "son" of God that make Jesus distinct and different from everyone else. And yet Jesus, this "son", is a separate and different entity to God Himself since the Creator of the universe has never been and can never be called "firstborn" in scripture.

In case you're wondering how "firstborn" can speak of a superiority yet not apply to God the Creator, the reason is fairly clear: the very word "firstborn" implies an honour of someone who was first brought into being, i.e. born first. Although the honour can be put upon other people, like how Jacob took Esau's birthright [literally, "firstbornship" in Hebrew], it still implies an honour of someone who was born or brought into being first and the word is linked to that concept. The God of the Jewish Bible was never born or brought into being so the word "firstborn" in any form cannot apply to him at all. And the word would become useless if applied to him since he has no use for the honour of one born or brought into being first. God's superiority is essentially different to any concept of "firstbornship."

But back to the matter at hand: so we have this special "image of God" which is not God, as can be seen by Paul's wording. The only thing that comes to mind is a form, a visible image or shape, that either contains the qualities or attributes (i.e. the powers) of God and represents him, or just someone who shows God's character, personality, and morality.

Now if we are talking about the second meaning, i.e., character and personality of God, then this is not strictly idolatry, since it just describes a good person who is in touch with God's words, laws, and spirit. That could be a prophet. It may just be that Jesus, in Paul's eyes, better reflected God in that way than anyone else. Again, this isn't idolatry. It may be, and is, dead wrong, but it isn't idolatry, worshipping someone in the place of God or believing that a human being has all of God's abilities and powers and attributes. Therefore there is no real need to comment on Colossians 2:8-9 since it may not be idolatry inherently. Being full of θεοτητος theotaytos may simply refer to being full of Deity's characteristics and personality, as opposed to the very essence of who God is being in a human body which is impossible (1 Kings 8:27), or someone else having his attributes as discussed in my treatment of Philippians 2.

If Paul meant anything more by his words, then the Hebrew Scriptures already cited show his foolishness.

verse 16

And Paul continues:

(13) [God] Who has rescued us from the power of darkness, and has carried us away into the kingdom of his beloved son; (14) in whom we have redemption through his blood, even the forgiveness of sins; (15) who is the image of the invisible God, the firstborn of every creature: (16) For in him were all things created, that are in heaven, and that are in earth, visible and invisible, whether they be thrones, or dominions, or governments, or authorities: all things were created through him, and for him: (17) And he is before all things, and in him all things are held together.(Colossians 1:13-17)

Paul says that everything was made εν αυτω, "en auto", i.e. "in him [Jesus]". What does this mean? Based on the Hebrew Scriptures, it cannot mean everything was made "by Jesus", as if Jesus created everything, because scripture proclaims that God (his special name represented as "HaShem") alone created everything (Isaiah 44:24; Nehemiah 9:6), and the descriptions of Jesus and God (HaShem) don't match (i.e., the being born, the dying, the sleeping, the bodily form). If Paul is preaching that Jesus did create everything, then he is contradicting the truths of God as revealed in the Jewish Bible.

But if it means "in Jesus", as meaning in a pre-existing "form" of Jesus, we are again left in ambiguity. Why? Because according to some, in Jewish thought, if something existed in God's mind, and it was always in his plan, then it is said to have pre-existed (though, obviously, not literally). And thus, if Paul says "things were made in Jesus", it may simply mean that everything was formed with Jesus in mind, meaning that God had Jesus as part of the plan when he created everything, or Jesus' coming into existence was the framework in which everything was made. Again, this second possibility is not idolatry per se. It may be (and is) dead wrong, but it isn't idolatry.

Because these statements contain this ambiguity, and the following statements in Colossians can be understood in each light, either Jesus being God himself or Jesus just being a superior representative of God, then there is little point in making hard and fast comments or condemnations of Paul here at least. If Paul is saying that Jesus is God (having the Divine nature can mean the same thing), then I've already cited the Jewish Bible here and elsewhere to show that Paul would be creating an idol-worshipping religion and that he is wrong. If Paul is not saying that Jesus is God, but some elevated person, then he is just wrong, but not an idolator nor a creator of some form of idolatry.

Chapter 2

verses 13b-14

(13b) having forgiven us all our trespasses, (14) blotting out the handwriting in ordinances which was against us; and he has taken it out of the way, nailing it to the cross (Colossians 2:13b-14)

Paul remains master of ambiguity. Why? Because we are left wondering what the "handwriting in ordinances" is. And here we have a choice. Paul could simply be reflecting the phrase in the latter part of verse 13, and the "handwriting in ordinances" is really the bill of our sins, and it is these sins that were nailed to the cross. Or Paul is saying that the only way to forgive sin was to blot out the handwriting, which is the law of Moses itself, which was written by hand and which was, in Paul's eyes, against humanity.

Knowing Paul's tendencies from the letters I've looked at before, either option could be true! But here in the book of Colossians, Paul doesn't really deal with Law, i.e. the Law of Moses. This book doesn't contain his usual anti-law tirades. And, with regards to Jesus nailing anything to the cross, that has been discussed in my analysis of Paul's previous epistles, and will be dealt with when I handle the book of Hebrews.

So since this passage is ambiguous, and the possible topics have been and will be dealt with, then I'll just leave this one.

verses 16-17

(16) Therefore, don't let anyone judge you in drinking or in eating or in respect of festivals or sabbaths, (17) which are shadows of things to come, but the body of Christ. (Colossians 2:16-17)

Just a small note on this one. It just says, "let no one judge". It doesn't say "let no one keep the festivals or dietary laws or practices.

How many times, when I was a christian, and even when I had left christianity but was still doing what I thought was respectful concerning the holiness of the seventh day, how many times did some poor christian come to me quoting this verse which says very little about whether it is right or wrong to keep these practices? Too many to count! And this was when I hadn't said a thing about their non-observance of these practices. Yet they have to stick their judgment (and ignorance) on me? How weird some christians are!

1 Thessalonians

Chapter 2

verses 14-16

Paul says:

> *(14) For you, brothers, became followers of the assemblies of God which in Judaea are in Christ Jesus: for you also have suffered like things from your own countrymen, even as they have from the Jews: (15) Who both killed the Lord Jesus, and their own prophets, and have persecuted us; and they please not God, and are contrary to all men: (16) Forbidding us to speak to the Gentiles that they might be saved, to fill up their sins always: for the wrath has come upon them to the uttermost. (1 Thessalonians 2:14-16)*

These verses are one of the main sources of pain and trouble against the Jews. The words are loaded with contention and condemnation, a blanket statement against the majority of Jewish nation and their descendants, not only as "christ-killers", but also as being antagonistic, against, contrary with all people. There is also a clear message that Jews are enemies of God as well as Paul charges them with killing the prophets, who are God's messengers.

But does Paul's accusations hold any water?

Let's ask a few questions based on the Jewish Bible, as many christians these days claim to follow the Jewish Bible.

Who killed Moses, the first "official" prophet of the Jews? Did the Jews kill Moses? No! What about Joshua? No! Did the Jews kill Samuel or Elijah or Elisha or Jeremiah? There are many prophets in the Bible. Did the Jews kill the majority of them? The answer is no! So where does Paul get off accusing the Jews of killing the prophets. Also it is a biblical principle that everyone is guilty for their own crimes. So who exactly killed the prophets? Which individuals? Does Paul have any real justification to give a blanket condemnation against "the Jews" for killing their own prophets? Was it the Jews of his own age or Jews for all ages?

The fact is that reading the Jewish Bible, there is no real basis for the accusation against the Jews. And christians don't tend to accept Jewish tradition. So there is no strong evidence against the Jews, none presented by Paul and none presented by the Jewish Bible.

Paul then says wrath and condemnation has fallen upon them. And with Paul's anti-Jewish message, and thus assistance, the Jews surely did get their "condemnation" and "trouble". And what a sorry story that was! Years, decades, centuries of persecution, torture, and death from Paul's spiritual descendants, the christian church, protestant and catholic alike. The hatred pasted on the words of Martin Luther, John Calvin, and John Gill, amongst others, basing their beliefs about the Jews on the words of Paul and the "new testament" only shows the fruits of the labours of Paul and his ilk.

So much for Paul's teaching of love!

1 Timothy

Chapter 1

verses 3-4

(3) As I implored you to stay further at Ephesus, when I travelled into Macedonia, that you may charge some not to teach error. (4) Neither to pay attention to tales and endless [or inconclusive] genealogies which cause questions/disputes rather than edifying stewardship to God which is in faith. (1 Timothy 1:3-4)

Paul warns his followers not to listen to certain teachers who include something about genealogies in their teachings. The "new testament" itself bears witness to this teaching when it includes two contradictory genealogies of Jesus, both of which textually only speaks of Joseph's lineage and says absolutely nothing about either one being the lineage of Mary [NB. It's only christian tradition, not the actual text of the new testament, that say that the genealogy of Jesus in Luke leads to Mary].

In light of this, I can definitely understand why Paul wouldn't want people hearing about genealogies.

verses 8-10

And we know that the law is good if a person uses it lawfully. Knowing this, that the law is not made for a righteous man, but for the lawless and disobedient, impious and sinners, unholy and impure, father-killers and mother-killers, murderers, sexually-loose, homosexuals, kidnappers, liars, perjurers, and if there be any other thing that is contrary to sound doctrine. (1 Timothy 1:8-10)

So understand what Paul is saying. The law was not made for righteous people, for good people; it was made for wicked people. How odd! Again, Paul shows his one-dimensional view of law which ignores what the Jewish Bible says about it and what the law says about itself.

But again, read Psalm 19 and 119, which praises the law as a blessing even for righteous men. Psalm 1 says that a man is blessed, prosperous, and happy who spends his days studying the law. Was King David a wicked man in the eyes of God? No! And let's not be naive enough to mistake a wicked deed for a wicked person, as is inherent in christian doctrine. The law, the Law of God, is for everyone, not just for wicked people.

The Law of God also contains the stipulations of a very special pact and covenant between Deity and Israel, the terms to maintain the special relationship, not just to punish evildoers! Honestly, without revelation from the Almighty, how can anyone know for sure how to do what He requires? Since God doesn't have our mind and He is a totally transcendent, totally different kind of being, and we can't grasp anything about his nature, then the only way God's way is for Him to tell us. And that is the job of Israel and its laws, to spread that divine law and knowledge (Exodus 19:5-6; Deuteronomy 4:6).

The problem is that if Paul meant better than this, he should have said better than this. But looking at his track record with regards to the Law of God, looking through his writings so far, then it would appear that Paul doesn't mean any better than an overly narrow view of a much richer Law and Torah.

Since Paul doesn't do any better, I should not expect any better.

Chapter 2

verses 11-15

I'll just quote this straight from the King James Versions.

(11) Let the woman learn in silence with all subjection. (12) But I don't permit a woman to teach, nor to usurp authority over the man, but to be in silence. (13) For Adam was first formed, then Eve. (14) And Adam was not deceived, but the woman being deceived was in the transgression. (15) Notwithstanding she shall be saved in childbearing, if they continue in faith and charity and holiness with sobriety. (1 Timothy 2:11-15)

I do not need to change a thing that the KJV translates from Paul's words!

Paul's view of women ... hmmmmm .... So because Eve was deceived, women should learn in silence??? Because one women, the first woman, got it wrong, that means that no woman can teach??? How silly! How stupid!

Just two examples are needed to show that the Jewish Bible does not share the same view of women: Deborah, a judge (something like a ruler) of Israel (Judges 4); and Huldah, the prophetess (2 Kings 22:14). You see, in Judaism and in the Hebrew Bible, there are a good amount of female prominent figures. It definitely does not have such a foolish and insulting view of women. The mistake of Eve is not pasted on all womankind, as Paul would have it. And their salvation doesn't come through child-bearing, although both men and women wanted to have children to make the nation and godliness prosper.

No place in scripture gives any real basis to Paul's "teaching".

2 Timothy

Chapter 1

verse 15

Paul describes his plight.

This you know, that all of them which are in Asia have turned away from me, of whom are Phygellus and Hermogenes. (2 Timothy 1:15)

Now some may ask, why would I even comment on these words when they have nothing to do with the Hebrew Bible? Well, along my journey of life, I've come across some interesting views of Paul. One of those views that I saw involved his claim to apostleship and those he wanted to claim as his own in Asia.

You see, there was only one person explicitly endorsing Paul's apostleship in the pages of the new testament, one person explicitly calling him an apostle: Paul. As can be seen in other parts of Paul's writings, people challenged that claim to apostleship. And these words in 2 Timothy may be evidence that Jesus' disciples didn't accept him as an apostle either.

"How so?", I hear some ask. As I go through the following theory, remember that only Paul explicitly, in plain words, claims his own apostleship.

In the new testament book of Revelation, John, one of the disciples of Jesus, claims to have had a vision of Jesus giving a message to seven christian assemblies in Asia. One such group was in Ephesus, the assembly of the Ephesians. This is what the message to the Ephesians was.

I know your works, your labor, and your patience, and that you cannot bear those who are evil. And you have tested those who say they are apostles and are not, and have found them [to be] liars. (Revelation 2:2)

The question is, do we have any record of someone claiming to be an apostle and the people of Asia or Ephesus rejecting them? And the answer is yes! We know for certain that Paul claimed to be an apostle in the first verse of the book of Ephesians where he says "Paul, an apostle of Jesus by the will of God" (Ephesians 1:1). According to Paul's follower, Luke, in his book "Acts of the Apostles", which focuses on Paul more than anyone else, Luke says that Paul was in Asia, including Ephesus, and preached to many, some not accepting his words (Acts 19). So everything seems nice and sweet for a while there. But some time later, in Acts 21, when Paul returns to Jerusalem, he meets with James, the leader of the Jerusalem, who tells Paul that he's heard rumours of Paul teaching to reject the Law. In order to prove this wrong, James advises Paul to take part in a practice that involves sacrifices. But who should turn up and oppose Paul?

(27) And when the seven days [of the sacrificial rite] were almost ended, the Jews which were from Asia, when they say [Paul] in the temple, stirred up all the people, and laid hands on him, (28) crying out, men of Israel, help! This is the man that teaches everyone everywhere against the people and the law and this place. And further, he brought Greeks also into the temple and has polluted this holy place. (Acts 21:27-28)

Do you see the link? Do you see why 2 Timothy 1:15 could be seen as evidence against Paul's apostleship? And why there may even be signs that Jesus' disciples may not have even accepted him? Let me at least make it plain for you.

Paul's claims of being an apostle generally came from himself, or at best his follower. No disciple of Jesus who became apostles ever called Paul an apostle, and there is no one else that affirms Paul's claims of being an apostle. There are parts of his writings that shows that there were some that challenged his claims. And as I've shown previously, whilst going through Galatians, Paul appeared not to respect the apostles, namely Peter, James and John, always calling them those who "would seem to be pillars", as if they really weren't (Galatians 2:9). But on the other hand, we have John and the people of Asia. John congratulates the Ephesians, who are from Asia, for rejecting false apostles.

In Acts, we see people from Asia showing clear signs of rejecting Paul's apostleship by laying hands on him and accusing him of false teaching. And Paul himself says in 2 Timothy 1:15 that all of Asia has turned away from him. Notice that he never accused them of turning away from Jesus, but simply turning away from him. In other words, the people of Asia had rejected Paul. And it is also taught in christian history that ancient sects of christianity, like the Ebionites, rejected the teachings of Paul and Paul himself.

So there are signs that at least John saw Paul as a false apostle and that Paul's claim of being apostle is not as certain as his modern day followers would have us believe.

Now what I've described in this section is, at the very least, a theory with evidence. I'm not pushing the notion that this must be the only truth. I'm sure the Paul-loving christians of today will have their explanations for the evidences that I've given. But at the very least, I want to show you the doubt that has always hung over the person and apostleship of Paul from the time he even claimed to follow Jesus, and this is without going into the oddities in his history and conversion story.

So Paul raises questions about his own authority.

Chapter 3

verse 16

Paul says:

(16) All scripture is God-breathed, and is profitable for doctrine, for reproof, for correction, for instruction in righteousness (2 Timothy 3:16)

I only quote this verse to say that the "scripture" that Paul refers to is only the Jewish Bible, the Hebrew Scriptures. The "new testament" wasn't around during Paul's day, and if a portion of it was, it is very unlikely that it was already considered "scripture". This fact is an indictment and accusation against so much of modern day christianity which is so hooked on the new testament and so ignorant of the Jewish Bible that they make a mockery of the words of the "apostle" they revere so highly.

Titus

Chapter 1

verses 10-11

(10) For there are many unruly, empty-talkers, and deceivers, most of all those of the circumcision, (11) whose mouths must be stopped/silenced, who destroy whole households, teaching things that they must not, for the sake of dishonest gain. (Titus 1:10-11)

I just want you to note what Paul is saying here. Here he speaks evil of the Jews, the circumcised ones. They should be shut up, according to his "unbiased" opinion. It is the fact that Paul singles out the Jews that makes his point so anti-Semitic. In the past, especially before I went through this study, I never really understood why Jews thought the new testament said things against them. Now I've seen the evidence, I must say that they have a valid point.

But just take note of the fact that Paul here speaks evil of the Jews, i.e. he insults them, especially as we compare this to Titus 2:2 where he says "speak evil of no man". After reading what Paul has just called the Jews, someone would be excuses for shouting "WHAT?!?" when they see Paul admonishing Titus to speak evil of no man. After all the things Paul says about Jews, the disciples of Jesus that were still alive, and all who disagree with him, it is incredible that he would then say these words. I guess this is just another case of Paul's two-facedness or unequal standards: "Don't do this and that, but it's ok for me, Paul, to do it!"

Now that's a man you can trust .... or maybe not.

Hebrews

Introduction

Now I do know that the author of Hebrews is anonymous: he doesn't reveal his identity. That fact in itself makes it doubtful as to whether Paul wrote it. In the epistles of Paul, it is all about him and his gospel and it is difficult to leave his writings without knowing that it has to be him. But this book, this letter to the Hebrews, isn't so selfish. Its focus is much more about the identity of Jesus and the temple rites of the Jews, which were not Paul's focus in his writings.

But regardless of the uncertainty about its authorship - which is a bit of a joke when someone tries to claim that it's the infallible word of God [How do you know it is inspired of God if you don't know who the author was???] - the fact is that its philosophy reflects Paul's way of thinking: spiritualizing scriptures to get rid of the law and its ceremonies, making everything point to Jesus and his death. So I'm going to deal with this book too.

Now just to warn you, since the author is unknown and I don't really want to assert that it is Paul, and also because he shows a lot of Greek thinking (called Hellenistic thinking), I'll be sometimes calling him "the Hellenist" or "the Hellenist author" rather than always calling him "the author of Hebrews" or calling him something weird like "the Hebrew author".

And just another small note. The name "Melchizedec" can be written in a number of ways, and throughout this book of Hebrews, I don't really settle on one. So if you see the different spellings, I am still referring to the same person. Someone may ask why I didn't just stick to the traditional form or just stick to one version all the way through. And that would be fantastic question. I just didn't feel any compulsion to follow the English convention.

OK, let me get this started.

Chapter 1

verse 5a

Let's begin.

> *(4) Being made so much better than the angels, as he [Jesus] has obtained a more excellent name than they through inheritance. (5) For to which of the angels has He [God] said, You are my son; this day I have fathered you? ... (Hebrews 1:4-5a quoting Psalm 2:7)*

The writer is quoting Psalm 2:7 as something that the Deity said to his "son", i.e., to Jesus and not to any angel. The King James Version kindly helps lead us towards the "divinity" of this entity by adding a capital letter to the word "son" to make it say "Thou art my Son". I'm sure many other christian versions follow its trinitarian tradition.

But the problems with using this verse to refer to Jesus can be seen in the context of Psalm 2. The person spoken of in Psalm 2 has been set up as king in Zion, a specific place in Jerusalem where David reigned (see Psalm 2 verse 6). No such thing happened to Jesus! He was never set up as king of Israel at Zion.

Understand two tactics of christians and the Hellenist writer of Hebrews: one tactic is to take scriptures out of context and reinterpret them; and the other tactic is to spiritualise words and prophecies or make them metaphorical/figurative if the actual textual concepts don't match their pre-existing beliefs. But note that it is not the text that supports them in their belief, but rather their belief which forms their understanding of a text taken out of context.

In this case, whether the Psalm is a prophecy or, as its wording seems to suggest, something that has already happened, or if it is just a song about any already existing king, it doesn't point to Jesus.

verse 5b

Now the Hellenist quotes 2 Samuel 7:14 in the following way.

(4) [Jesus was] made so much better than the angels, as he has by inheritance obtained a more excellent name than they. (5) For to which of the angels has he said at any time, You are my son, this day have I fathered you? And again, "I will be to him a Father, and he shall be to me a Son?" (Hebrews 1:4-5)

So the writer would have us believe that 2 Samuel 7:14 refers to Jesus, but, again, reading the Hebrew Scriptures shows that to be a faulty interpretation.

Firstly, this is what 2 Samuel 7:12-16 says.

(12) When your days have been fulfilled and you lay with your fathers, I will set up your seed after you which shall come out from your own bowels, and I will establish his kingdom. (13) He himself shall build a house for my name, and I will establish his kingdom forever. (14) I will be to him a father and he will be to me a son in that when he commits iniquity, I will chastise him with the rod of men and with the afflictions of the children of man. (15) And my kindness shall not depart from him as I removed it from Saul who I removed from before you. (16) And your house and your kingdom shall be made sure for ever before you. Your throne shall be established for ever. (2 Samuel 7:12-16)

Now you should already see a difference between what the author is telling us and what the book of Samuel is telling us. The writer of Hebrews, the Hellenist, is telling us that this refers to Jesus. But when you look at Samuel, it says that this son would be literally descended from David and would actually reign as David reign, i.e., he would rule over Israel as David ruled over Israel. It should be obvious to all that Jesus has never ruled Israel as David ruled Israel (so there is no point referring to "spiritual" Israel, since David never ruled over that imaginary entity).

The passage in Samuel also says that this son will build a house for God's name. Jesus never really did that. There is no evidence in the "new testament" that Jesus built any house for anyone, and nothing in the christian bible refers to the believers being a house for God's name. I know that some will try to use some long logical path to draw a person to that conclusion, but dealing with the plain words of scripture and what the "new testament" says, there is no conclusive evidence that Jesus did that.

Also Samuel shows that this son of David could sin, as it says "when he commits iniquity ..." Just to warn readers of some translations, the translation is "when he commits iniquity ...", not "if he commits iniquity ..." But it is obvious from the same book of Hebrews that Jesus committed no sin. The very fact that the words in Samuel include this part about committing iniquity shows that the person it refers to would commit iniquity. It would be defunct and unnecessary to add this part if the person it refers to wouldn't or couldn't sin!

So before we even discuss the rest of the Hebrew Bible, the Hellenist has already showed his weakness in using the Hebrew Bible in that he has distorted its natural meaning.

But to add the killer blow, the Jewish Bible itself gives the proper interpretation: Solomon is the son that 2 Samuel 7:14 speaks of! See 1 Kings 8:15-21; 1 Chronicles 17:11-14; 22:7-11; 2 Chronicles 6:4-

11,15. Let me just quote one of them to show how clearly the Hebrew Scriptures tells us that Solomon was the son of God.

(7) And David said to Solomon, My son, as for me, it was in my mind to build a house to the name of the LORD my God; (8) But there came concerning me the word of the Lord, saying, You have shed blood in abundance, and you have made great wars: you shall not build a house to my name, because you have shed much blood upon the earth before me. (9) See, a son will be born to you; he shall be a man of rest; and I will give him rest from all his enemies on every side; for Solomon shall be his name, and I shall bestow rest and quietness on Israel in his days. (10) He himself shall build a house to my name; and he shall be unto me as a son, and I will be unto him as a father; and I will establish the throne of his kingdom over Israel for ever. (11) Now, my son, may the LORD be with you, that you may prosper, and build the house of the LORD your God, as he has spoken concerning you.(1 Chronicles 22:7-11)

That should silence the matter: scripture itself has interpreted scripture and we shouldn't need the writer of Hebrews to add meaning that isn't in the text.

verse 6

And the Hellenist continues:

And again, when he brings in the firstborn [Jesus] into the world, he says, "And let all the angels of God worship him."

Now a good many christian study bibles will point their masses to Deuteronomy 32:43 and say that the writer of Hebrews is quoting that. And then the normal bible reader would go to that verse in, let's say, the King James Version, or their New International Version, and they'll see something like the following.

O nations, acclaim his people!

For He shall avenge the blood of his servants,
And He'll return vengeance on his adversaries,
And He'll atone for His land, His people! (Deuteronomy 32:43)

Now I must make it clear that I'm talking about people who read attempts at translations, like the KJV and, at a stretch, the NIV. I'm not talking about paraphrases and bibles that are more like a christian's attempt at rewriting the words to fit their beliefs, like "The Message" and "The English Standard Version" and "The New Living Translation". The people I mentioned first (those who read somewhat "literal" translations) will read their translations and note that something is missing: the words "quoted" by the Hellenist. That is to say that the words that the Hellenist quotes are not in the standard text that the "old testament" is translated from. There are no words that say "Let all God's angels worship him!" In fact, no such words appears throughout the whole Hebrew Bible!!! So it would seem like the writer of Hebrews is making up verses.

But then a lot of christian bibles - and this is exclusive to christians bibles for some "strange" and "unknown" reason (*sarcasm*) - add an informative footnote. Now this does not occur for Jewish Bibles, but only for christian bibles. I'll give you some examples of the footnote.

NEW KING JAMES VERSION: * A Dead Sea Scroll fragment adds And let all the gods (angels) worship Him (compare Septuagint and Hebrews 1:6).
NEW INTERNATIONAL VERSION: Dead Sea Scrolls (see also Septuagint): people, / and let all the angels worship him

You'll also find, if you look, that some translations actually put those words in the main body of the biblical text and put as a footnote that that the standard Masoretic text used to translate the Bible leaves it out. How helpful!

But what we have is these christian versions telling us that the words are not in the standard text that they translate from, but rather from sources like the Dead Sea Scrolls and the Septuagint. So we are pointed to two texts not accepted to have any authority by the Jews or Judaism: the Septuagint, the ancient Greek translation of the Torah, which is in an uncertain state because its history is dark and obscure and is by no means free of alteration, i.e., people would change the translation just as people have made changes to the English translations throughout the centuries; and the Dead Sea Scrolls, which was found in an out-of-the-way cave, belonging to an uncertain sect of Judaism with clear signs in the spelling of Hebrew words that it was written at a later period than the original Masoretic text and with little certainty about how they treated the text. By that, I mean it is well known how much sanctity and seriousness was put upon the standard traditional Masoretic biblical text of Judaism, so much so that so much was done to treat the text as carefully as possible, making textual error and addition nigh-impossible. But nothing certain is known about how these Dead Sea texts were treated.

I could go through all the arguments in the world about the doubt surrounding texts other than the Masoretic, which is the standard text used to translate christian bibles, but I think it better to deal with the facts that we have, which I'll tell you now.

All the Jewish Bibles and the vast majority of others (i.e., christian) rely on the Masoretic text. If we were to look at Deuteronomy 32:43, or any other part of the Hebrew Bible (the "old testament"), we would only see what I've shown before: the "quote" of the Hellenist author doesn't exist! The writer of Hebrews has chosen a different standard which leaves him without a leg to stand on when it comes to all those who accept the authority of the traditional Hebrew text. So for all those people, the rest of this critique isn't too important: the Hellenist writer is just making up verses or using texts that have no authority.

For anyone else, let's just do what we normally normally do. Let's look at the Septuagint (also known as the LXX) and see who is being talked about in context. Now despite the mixed up state of the Septuagint (or LXX), since the first part of verse 43 has a different order in different versions of the Septuagint (or LXX), it is still possible to see who the text refers to. If you have an English version of the Septuagint, read all of Deuteronomy 32, and if you understand ancient Greek, take a look at the Greek version.

It is clear from the whole chapter that there are only three parties involved: Israel, the nations, and Deity. No one else gets airtime. There is no messiah. When the passage speaks of "His people", the "His" refers to the Almighty (e.g., Deuteronomy 32:9,36) of the LXX). So when we come to verse 43 using the LXX extended "amplified" version, we are not wondering who is being spoken of. It is not Israel or the nations, the only other parties in the chapter: it is speaking of the Almighty. There is no one else who will fit, contextually speaking. So when it says in the LXX, "Rejoice, you heavens, with Him, and let all the angels of God worship Him, rejoice, you gentiles, with His people ... "it is clearly referring to Deity himself. Whenever "son" is mentioned, it is as "sons", i.e., more than one son. The same version of the LXX says "for He will avenge the blood of His sons ..." which refers to Israel being God's children (see Deuteronomy 14:1). There is no messiah son or divine son. There is no messiah in the text at all.

So even the LXX version of the Hebrew Scriptures doesn't help the writer of Hebrews! Amazing! Again, it makes me wonder how christian/messianic the LXX is if it even trips up the "new testament".

But either way, it doesn't matter how you take this subject, whether you respect the Masoretic text, or see the Dead Sea scrolls or Septuagint as having any importance, no text, when read in context, helps the writer of Hebrews at all.

verse 7

The Hellenist adds to his list of "quotes".

And of the angels he says, "Who makes his angels spirits, and his ministers a flame of fire." (Hebrews 1:7 quoting Psalm 104:4)

Now although there may be some difference in translation, contextually speaking, this is one of the few accurate quotations in the book of Hebrews. Not much more to add about that.

verses 8-9

(8) But unto the Son he saith, Thy throne, O God, is for ever and ever: a sceptre of righteousness is the sceptre of thy kingdom. (9) Thou hast loved righteousness, and hated iniquity; therefore God, even thy God, hath anointed thee with the oil of gladness above thy fellows. (Hebrews 1:8-9, King James Version)

The Hellenist quotes Psalm 45:6,7 and here we face problems galore for christians. I'll focus on the two main issues.

The main problem has to be the question of who Psalm 45 really refers to. We also have a more specific question: does the chapter refer to the Messiah specifically? Does it refer to Jesus specifically? Or is it a song that can be used for any anointed king of Israel?

Here I'll deal with the sub-problems within the questions I asked, i.e., who exactly the Psalm refers to.

Let's be blunt and to the point! We are dealing with a song here. Psalm 45 is a song! It isn't primarily a prophecy, and it is not a narrative. It's a song! It's in a book of songs. The very title of the psalm says that it is literally a love song, or a song of loves. There would need to be a distinctive sign to say that it was meant to be a prophecy. And, reading throughout the whole song, Psalm 45, attempting to let the words speak for themselves, there is not overt sign that it is a prophecy. Some may say that the Jews applied it to the Messiah. I'll deal with that issue later. But for now the main point is this: we're dealing with a song, not necessarily a prophecy.

Unfortunately, we are dealing with christian theologies here, and, in this modern time, that means dealing with doctrines that state that the messiah (or, more concretely, Jesus) had to be Deity, Divine: he had to be God himself. And the verses quoted by the Hellenist author here play right into the hands of that idolatrous and fundamentally unbiblical belief. The problem is with the word "God" in translations such as the Septuagint (θεος theos), KJV, Geneva, WEB, YLT, MYLT, ASV, BBE, Rotherham, etc, i.e., mainly christian translations. In those kinds of translations, the reader sees the word "God", goes with the common definition of the word, i.e., "Almighty Creator of heaven and earth" and/or "a divine supernatural being", and thus thinks that "God" has a throne, and is anointed, and has a "God" above him, by reading these two verses.

Now I'm not going to deal with the trinitarian absurdity with the Hebrew word translated "God" here at this time. But something needs to be said about it here.

I've already said that the hebrew words sounds like "elohim". It is used in various ways in scripture. But it is a Hebrew word, not an English one! So if it is a Hebrew word, the question must follow: what is its natural Hebrew meaning? The English word "God" means something in the English mind. But what would the word "elohim" bring up in the Hebrew mind?

The word "elohim" comes from the root concept of strength, mastery, authority, and power (check out the meaning of the root verbs אלה, spelt "alef-lamed-heh" איל spelt "alef-yodh-lamed" and the word אֵל, spelt "alef-lamed," Strongs number 410). That's why, in Hebrew, the word can refer to entities that are worshipped due to their mastery over different aspects of nature, i.e., "gods" and "deities". And the word can also refer to the Mighty Authority, the

Deity of heaven and earth, a "God". But it can also refer to angels, being powerful beings, deputies of the Almighty, and also human authorities, i.e., the judges of Israel (e.g., Psalm 82). That's why, in certain parts of Exodus, some Jewish translations will translate the word as "judges" where christians would translate it as "God" (Exodus 21:6; 22:8). That's why Moses was an "elohim" to Pharaoh, which is what the Hebrew literally says in Exodus 4:16 and 7:1, although some christian translations have distorted the meaning.

With this in mind, it can never be said that the first part of Psalm 45:6, where it says "your throne, O God [elohim], ..." must be referring to The God of heaven and earth, as can be seen in the commentary of the Jewish scholar, Rashi, who translates the beginning of verse 6 as "Your throne, O judge, [will exist] forever and ever." It can refer to a human king (elohim can mean authority) which the whole Psalm is about.

There is no point in complaining in the following fashion: how can the word "elohim" refer to two different people in the space of a verse, i.e., Psalm 45:6 referring to a human king and Psalm 45:7 speaking about God? There is no point in doing this because the writer of Hebrews already does it! It is understood that the first "elohim" or "theos" (in Greek) refers to Jesus and the second "elohim" or "theos" refers to his Father. So that's not an issue. But also, look at Psalm 82! In the first verse, you have two mentions of "elohim" referring to different people, the first being God Almighty and the second being powerful beings, most likely judges and earthly authorities looking at the rest of the Psalm/song.

Let me just note one other problem with Psalm 45:6-7. I may have referred to numerous translations that agree with the LXX (Septuagint) rendition, like the NKJV, NIV, NASB, a good amount of christian translations, but there are other translations that don't agree with the Septuagint, e.g., JPS, NJPS, Leeser, Targum, RSV, NEB, GNB, the Message, footnote of the NLT, etc. None of these have the potentially idolatrous connotations of the other christian versions. For example, the JPS renders the verse as "Your throne given of God is for ever" and the other translations are similar.

All of this is just to show that the verses quoted by the Hellenist author does not point to some supernatural messiah or a "God".

But let's get back to the original question. Reading Psalm 45, is it a specific prophecy? And does it specifically speak of Jesus alone? Or it can describe any king of Israel?

What we have in Psalm 45 is a love song about a great king, prepared for battle (verse 5), who is getting married. It actually seems to be describing King Solomon and one of his marriages. But the identity of this king is not specified. None of the text really speaks of the end times overtly. So at least the plain message of this chapter doesn't seem to specifically be talking about one king. In fact, that very observation that it is an unspecific song, not distinctly naming or pointing out a certain king, is the reason why Jews can apply it to "messiah". Why? Because it can fit almost any anointed king of Israel. But nothing that Jesus did on this earth and nothing he did visibly that can be verified by sight or experience fits its description. He did nothing battle-worthy and he married no one.

The only way christians can fit this into their image of Jesus is if they "spiritualize" all of it so there's nothing really literal about it, i.e., the way to "fulfil" the so-called "prophecy" is to make its "fulfilment" invisible so you need the eyes of "faith" to "see" it. So Jesus wasn't a political king but was only a "spiritual" king who had a "spiritual" kingdom. Jesus didn't marry a bride you can see, but marries a "spiritual" bride, namely, some invisible "church." But since its fulfilment is invisible then it really proves nothing at all.

To summarize, there is no sign that Psalm 45 is anything other than what it says it is: a song about love that can be sung about many Israelite kings since it has no specific subject. It is not a "prophecy" per se and it doesn't speak of a supernatural divine son of Deity.

verses 10-12

(10) And, You, Lord, in the beginning have laid the foundation of the earth; and the heavens are the works of your hands. (11) They shall perish, but you remain; and they all shall get old like a garment; (12) and like a cloak you shall fold them up and they shall be changed; but you are the same and your years don't fail. (Hebrews 1:10-12 quoting Psalm 102:25-27)

An important question to ask, even before we deal with writer of Hebrews, is what Psalm 102:25-27 is really talking about. When read in context, it is plain that the verses in Psalms refers to the Almighty Creator alone. The is no messiah, no "divine son" mentioned in the Psalm at all. Just read the psalm with the intent to let it speak for itself and you will see that there is not one single mention of messiah or a supernatural thing that becomes man and becomes divine again, i.e., a changing being. The verses quoted by the Hellenist writer speak of God and God alone, the Unchanging Being.

So we have yet another example of the Hellenist author ripping verses out context and giving them an alien meaning.

verse 13

But to which of the angels did he say at any time, Sit at my right hand until I make your enemies your footstool?(Hebrews 1:13 quoting Psalm 110:1)

Based on the Hellenist's current track record so far with concerns about his butchering of the Hebrew Scriptures, it is necessary to ask what Psalm 110 actually says. I'll just quote the first verse according to the Hebrew version.

A declaration of HASHEM (God) to my master, Sit at my right hand until I set your enemies [as] a stool for your feet. (Psalm 110:1)

It is best to just summarize the actual passage in Psalm 110 to compare it with the words of the Hellenist author.

So, in short, what does Psalm 110 speak about? Basically it is about a king ruling from Jerusalem (Zion) for whom God will subjugate his enemies (verse 2), in whose day there will be much death and slaughter as he conquers nations and their kings (verse 6). This king appears to have some priestly power and would command the respect and reverence of many (verses 3-4).

It can already be seen that Jesus didn't fulfil any of this and it is even questionable if the passage speaks about him or a particular king of Israel since the identity is not made clear. Jewish traditions assigns it to Abraham or David or just a king of Israel.

The foundation of the whole matter is that this is a song and not necessarily a prophecy. Beware of christian commentaries that attempt to say who wrote the chapter and for whom. This psalm as well as the rest of the Hebrew Bible was in the possession of the Israelites/Jews originally and it's that authority that can be seen as authentic as opposed the alien, centuries-later-appearing, gentile christianity that now exists, cut off and degraded from its roots.

Regardless of what authority this passage belongs to, the clear words of Psalm 110 cannot refer to Jesus who never ruled from Jerusalem or the Zion that the writer of the psalm speaks of. The Zion of the Hebrew Scriptures was never the heavenly one created later by christians but was the real-life place in Jerusalem from which the Davidic kings reigned.

So in the end, the Hellenist author of Hebrew continues in the manner of taking scripture out of context and giving it alien meanings.

Chapter 2

verse 6b-8a

(6) But someone earnestly attested in a certain place, saying, "What is man, that you have him in mind? or the son of man, that you visit him? (7) You did set him a little lower than the angels; you crowned him with glory and honour, and appointed him over the works of your hands: (8) You put all things in subjection under his feet." For in that he put all in subjection under him, he left not one thing to him that is insubordinate. But now we don't yet see all things put under him. (9) But we see Jesus, who was made a little lower than the angels for the suffering of death, crowned with glory and honour; that he by the grace of God should taste death for every man.
(Hebrews 2:6-9 quoting Psalm 8:4-6)

The Hellenist quotes Psalm 8:4-6 as a basis to say that not all things are under the feet of, or obedient to, man as the psalm says since it is observed that there are still things not under man's dominion. But, the author continues, either it is possible for this to happen through Jesus, or Jesus perfectly fulfilled the verse of the psalm as a man.

There is a problem with this reasoning: it takes a song too literally. Not only that, it flat out contradicts the Psalmist. When David write the psalm, the song, he wasn't writing a wish or a hope, something that man didn't have yet but was expecting some day. He was stating what man experienced in his time. The "all" which the Lord put under man's feet is described in the following verses of Psalm 8, which speaks of sheep, oxen, beast of the field, birds of the air, and the fish of the sea. That chapter of Psalm is just a confirmation of what was said in the very first chapter of the whole bible, in Genesis 1:26-28 which says that man was given dominion and control of all the animals, birds, and fish, and the earth as well. This doesn't mean that everything is life is easy as some things do need to conquered, but man at least as the right to conquer it.

So in essence, what has the writer of Hebrews really done? He has taken the word "all" to unrealistic levels. He has taken a verse and twisted its meaning in such a way that it contradicts the original intent of the song. By that, I mean to say that it is a fact that man has been given dominion over creation, but the writer of Hebrew says that man doesn't really, Jesus does!

Basically, the Hellenist creates a straw man and says that Jesus is better than the straw man.

The writer of Hebrew has to push the meaning of Psalm 8 beyond its realistic meaning for it to help his cause. But in the end, the words of the Psalm just end up contradicting the Hellenist.

verse 12

(11) For both he who makes holy and those who are made holy are all from one: for which cause he is not ashamed to call them brothers, (12) Saying, "I will declare Your name unto my brothers, in the midst of the assembly I'll sing praise unto you." (Hebrews 2:11-12 quoting Psalm 22:22)

The Hellenist writer puts Psalm 22:22 in the mouth of Jesus. To christians, Psalm 22 is a crucifixion song describing the death of their "messiah", especially with their mistranslation of renumbered verse 16 ("they pierce my hands and feet", a mistranslation of the Hebrew). But to those who actually read the psalm, without reading into it new testament ideas, it is only a song!!! This is a song of David describing someone's experiences, mostly like David's own painful and humbling experiences. There is no overt sign in the psalm that it was written for a specific person. This song appears to be at the disposal of any and everyone that struggles in a way that goes with it's theme of feeling small before God, feeling abandoned and surrounded by hostility, yet, in the end, ready to give praises to the Most High.

So looking at the context of the Psalm, if anyone is speaking, it is David or the writer, and not Jesus. And its words can apply to anyone going through struggles, not just Jesus in particular.

verse 13

(11)For both he who makes holy and those who are made holy are all from one: for which cause he is not ashamed to call them brothers, (12) Saying, "I will declare Your name unto my brothers, in the midst of the assembly I'll sing praise unto you." (13) And again, "I will put my trust in Him." [quoting Isaiah 8:17b] And again, "Behold, me and the children that God gave me."[quoting Isaiah 8:18a] (Heb 2:11-13)

The Hellenist writer puts more words of Scripture into Jesus' mouth quoting, according to christian commentators, the last part of Isaiah 8 verse 17 and the first part of Isaiah 8 verse 18. And he still refuses to just take the Hebrew Bible for what it says. Who is speaking in Isaiah 8? Who is the "I" and "me" in Isaiah 8:18? Let me quote the christian KJV rendition of Isaiah 8:1-3 taking note that Isaiah is the writer of the prophecy.

(1) Moreover the LORD said unto me, Take thee a great roll, and write in it with a man's pen concerning Maher-shalal-hash-baz. (2) And I took unto me faithful witnesses to record, Uriah the priest, and Zechariah the son of Jeberechiah. (3) And I went unto the prophetess; and she conceived, and bare a son. Then said the LORD to me, Call his name Maher-shalal-hash-baz. (4) For before the child shall have knowledge to cry, My father, and my mother, the riches of Damascus and the spoil of Samaria shall be taken away before the king of Assyria. (5) The LORD spake also unto me again, saying ... (17) And I will wait upon the LORD, that hideth his face from the house of Jacob, and I will look for him. (18) Behold, I and the children whom the LORD hath given me are for signs and for

wonders in Israel from the LORD of hosts, which dwelleth in mount
Zion. (Isaiah 8:1-5, 17-18)

Just to say, I'm going to overlook the difference in meaning between
what Isaiah 8:17b says and the Hellenist's depiction of it. I don't
think it significantly impacts the point to be made.

Now christians don't believe that Jesus had sex with a woman and
had a child. But Isaiah did do all those things! These verses speak of
Isaiah's experience. There is no one else in the context of Isaiah 8
who could be speaking when it says, "I will look for Him," and
"Look, I and the children whom the Lord has given me are for signs
and for wonders in Israel" (Isaiah 8:18). So it is Isaiah who said
those words. Jesus has no place in this chapter or the verses quoted
by the Hellenist. But the Hellenist author stole these words from
their context, edited them so as to chop of the end of Isaiah 8:18, and
then pretended Jesus said them.

It's another case of taking scriptures out of context and distorting
their meaning!

Chapter 3

verses 7-11

The Hellenist writer continues.

(7) Because of this, (as the Holy Spirit says, Today if you listen to his
voice, (8) don't harden your hearts as in the provocation, in the day
of testing in the wilderness; (9) when your fathers scrutinized me,
tested me, and saw my deeds forty years. (10) Because of this, I was
vexed with that generation and said, They always go astray in their
heart and have not known my ways. (11) So I swore in my wrath that

they shall not enter my rest.) (Hebrews 3:7-11 quoting Psalm 95:7-11)

The Hellenist writer quotes Psalm 95:7-11 as if to say that one must not harden one's heart to belief in Jesus.

But the passage is from a song acknowledging God, the Creator, as having everything in His hand and that it is Him, God the Creator, whom we must hear and trust according to the Psalm. It has no messianic message in it whatsoever. Just look!

O come, let us sing unto the Lord: let us shout joyfully to the rock of our salvation. Let us come before his presence with thanksgiving, and shout joyfully unto him with psalms. For the Lord is a great God, and a great King above all gods; In whose hand are the deep places of the earth; and whose are the heights of mountains; Whose is the sea, and he made it; and whose hands have formed the dry land. Oh come, let us prostrate ourselves and bow down: let us kneel before the Lord our Maker. For he is our God; and we are the people of his pasture, and the flock of his hand: yea, this day, if ye will listen to his voice, don't harden your heart as at Meribah, as on the day of temptation in the wilderness. (Psa 95:1-8)

As is evident by the words, it is just a song of praise to God. There is nothing messianic – meaning about an anointed Davidic king – in it whatsoever. It's not even prophetic.

But we can take this point: since the Psalm admonishes a person to listen to Deity and know His ways, it is imperative for us to learn his ways as written in the Law of Moses, the Torah; and by doing this we can properly test the claims of Jesus and Paul and see them if they really agree with Torah as christians and the new testament claim. We would see whether Jesus was the promised Davidic king or some supernatural being.

To focus on the writer's use of Psalm 95, if one just reads the Psalm, it would be seen that it has nothing to do with any message promoting Jesus or the writer's claims. So it is another occasion of the writer taking a verse out of context.

Chapter 4

verses 3-11

(3) For we which have believed enter into rest, as he said, As I have sworn in my wrath, if they shall enter into my rest: although the works were finished from the foundation of the world. (4) For he spoke in a certain place of the seventh day in this way, And God rested the seventh day from all his works. (5) And in this place again, If they shall enter into my rest. (6) Seeing therefore it remains that some must enter into it, and they to whom it was first preached didn't get in because of unbelief; (7) Again, he limits a certain day, saying in David, Today, after so long a time; as it is said, Today if you listen to his voice, don't harden your hearts. (8) For if Joshua had given them rest, then he wouldn't afterwards have spoken of another day. (9) There remains therefore a rest to the people of God. (10) For he that has entered into his rest, he also has ceased from his own works, as God did from his. (11) Let us labour therefore to enter into that rest, lest any man fall after the same example of unbelief. (Hebrews 4:3-11 quoting Genesis 2:2 and Psalm 95:11)

The writer of Hebrews interprets the "rest" mentioned in Psalm 95:11 as the "rest" mentioned in Genesis 2:2. He says that Deity had rested from the time of creation but David still speaks of a "rest" to come which Israel supposedly never entered; and thus this "rest" has yet to be entered. This "rest" is for those that believe in Jesus. He does this also by redefining the "rest" mentioned in Psalm 95:11 as a "rest from work".

Now this amazing re-interpretation of the Jewish Bible has fundamental problems. One such problem is the fact that the "rest" mentioned in Psalm 95 is the Hebrew word מְנוּחָה, menuchah, and the "rest" spoken of in Genesis 2 is שָׁבַת, shavath or shabath. This difference at the very least should make a person pause: there is not textual link or word-link between Psalm 95 and Genesis 2 in the Hebrew text. But the same verb is used in the Greek translation, the Septuagint, in both places. So the only way the Hellenist author could make this mistake would be if he was relying on a Greek translation of the Jewish Bible which uses the same verbal form (the stem καταπαυ-, katapau- which means "to cause to cease" or "to rest") in both passages, and he didn't have the sense to check the original.

Not only is there no textual link between the two passages, there is no contextual link between the "rest" in Genesis and the one in Psalms: they are each talking about different subjects. For example, there is a strong contextual link between the sabbath command in Exodus 20:8-11 and Genesis 2:1-3. One is very much based on the other. But what is Psalm 95 talking about?

Psalm 95 is talking about the trek of Israel the nation once they escaped from Egypt, through the desert for 40 years, a trek in which all of the original Israelites died—apart from Joshua and Caleb—while their children went on to claim the land of promise. The reason why all the originals died is because of their disobedience. The mention of Meribah refers to the historical disobedience of Israel is the wilderness (Exodus 17). And the disobedience that sealed them out of the promised land happened in Numbers 13-14 where Israel chose to listen to the spies who gave an evil report of Canaan just as they were about to enter it, and they chose to ignore Joshua and Caleb and Moses and Aaron, which you can go and read for yourself.

But what is the rest mentioned in Psalm 95:11? Is there some bible passage that tells us? Yes there is! Numbers 14:20-24, 28-35 tells us how the Lord punished the people who disobeyed, but it says that they would not enter Canaan, the promised land. So is the promised land of Canaan the "rest", the מ נוח ה, menuchah, of Psalm 95:11? See Deuteronomy 12:8-10 which shows that the "rest" is meant to be the land of promise and that the "rest" is not a rest from work, but rather rest from all the enemies round about (and possible rest from the nomadic lifestyle of travelling from place to place as opposed to having no fixed home). What buttresses this points is that the word מ נוח ה, menuchah is used in Deuteronomy 12:8-10! See also 1 Kings 8:56 which says very definitely that Israel entered into the rest promised by the Lord. The same Hebrew word, menuchah, is used there as well.

So this exclusion from the "rest" only applied to those Israelites who had sinned in that specific case in the book of Numbers. Since then, the rest had already been entered and was occupied by the people of Israel (see also 1 Chronicles 22:9; Exodus 33:14; Deuteronomy 25:17-19). Deuteronomy 3:18-20 is also telling in that it says that Reuben, Gad and Manasseh would help the other tribes enter into their "rest" before the three tribes can occupy a piece of land that they had wanted on the other side of the Jordan river. So the "rest" which David speaks of in Psalm 95 is the land of promise which the original Israelites who left Egypt (except for Joshua and Caleb) missed out on due to their disobedience.

So again we experience distortion by the writer of Hebrews. By re-interpreting David's words in a twisted fashion, he tries to transfer a literal promise given to national Israel to "believers" who had forsaken Israel's law (as we will see later in Hebrews).

Some may say again that the writer if Hebrews is revealing the true "spiritual" meaning of David's words and the "rest" promised. But remember that these "spiritual meanings" claimed by people who use this argument is actually people imposing their own ideas onto the text of scripture as opposed to an honest extraction of information from the text and context. Thus this "spiritual meaning" is not the intent of the writings of scripture, but, more accurately, the intentions of a believer's mind based on a faith already accepted before and in spite of a knowledge of scripture.

verse 14 through to chapter 5 verse 10

The Hellenist author of Hebrews continues by repeatedly calling Jesus "high priest". For example,

Seeing then that we have a great high priest, that has passed into the heavens, Jesus the son of God, let us hold on our profession (Hebrews 4:14)

But it must be noted that in the Jewish Bible, there is only one sort of high or great priest, and that is a Levitical one, one descended from the tribe of Levi and from Aaron, particularly through the father working amongst the tribes of Israel (see Exodus 28:1-3; 29:9,28; Leviticus 21:10; Numbers 35:25-28). That is the only high priesthood established in Israel!

But christianity has already accepted Jesus as a king who is descended from David and from the tribe of Judah; and this king must be descended from David and Judah biologically through the father. Thus they cannot have it both ways. Either he is a Judaean through the father, or a Levite through his father. It can't be both. In fact he is neither due to the christian claims of a virgin birth! But the writer of Hebrews and mainstream christianity try to get around this, as we shall explore further.

But the main thing is that Jesus cannot be both priest and king, because both roles are given to two separate tribes of Israel and Jesus cannot descend from both.

Now I have heard it said Jesus is still a high priest because, like David, he performed priestly duties. And the Hebrew word כֹּהֵן, kohen, meaning priest, can refer to Jesus because David's sons, who were not Levites, we called priests. But we must be very clear on what we are talking about. Based on the Jewish Bible, there is only one high priest, and that man must be descended from Levi and Aaron biologically through the father. He and his biological relatives, the Levites are the only ones noted in law as being allowed to perform certain offerings like the purification offering (also known as the sin-offering), or the guilt offering. Although David's son (and others) were called by the hebrew word "kohen", the word can and does mean "official" in those places. They by no means are able to fulfil the role of Levitical priests.

It should also be seen that the Hellenist author confuses the issue by referring to both Melchizedek and Aaron, but neither of these can point to Jesus because, as shown in other places, Psalm 110 contextually cannot refer to Jesus, and Jesus is not descended from Aaron. So he still has no place in any priesthood.

Chapter 5

verse 5

And in this manner, the christ didn't glorify himself to be high priest but rather the one who having said to him, You are my son, today I have birthed you. (Hebrews 5:5)

I've dealt with this passage earlier, when I dealt with Hebrews 1:5 and showed that it didn't have anything to do with Jesus. So I won't reinvent the wheel here.

verse 5-6

(5) In this manner also the christ didn't glorify himself to be made a high priest, but rather he that said to him, "You are my Son, today have I give birth to you." (6) Even as he says also in another place,

"You are a priest for ever after the order of Melchisedek. (Hebrews 5:5-6, in verse 6 quoting Psalm 110:4)

Hebrews 5:6 quotes Psalm 110:4 in order to say that Jesus is a high priest of the order of Melchitzedek, a person mentioned in Genesis 14:18. But here again we meet with fundamental problems.

As mentioned before, there is no other high priest sanctioned by scripture apart from that of Aaron, i.e., having descended from Aaron through the father. Melchitzedek was not a high priest, only a regular priest (Genesis 14:18). Psalm 110:4 doesn't speak a high priest either, only a regular "priesthood" of some undefined sort, and that's only if we go with that interpretation of the word "priest" and of the verse on a whole (as there are other interpretations of Psalm 110:4 that are equally valid). So the writer of Hebrews is creating a high priest of Malki-tzedeq out of nothing, from thin air, a creation of his own active imagination.

Now with regards to the substance of Psalm 110, the fact is that Jesus has not fulfilled the words of this song; it applies better to other people that it does to Jesus, e.g., David or most other real kings who were righteous. It can even apply to Abraham better than it applies to Jesus.

Also, a central point is that it is a song, not necessarily a prophecy, therefore even if it can be applied to a messiah, its main subject may not be a definite individual. And if it must be said that it applies to an individual, it has either been better fulfilled by someone else and/or it has been unfulfilled by Jesus. Thus this verse cannot apply to him unless, as is the modus operandi of the new testament as a whole, it is taken out of context and its subject distorted.

Just to be very clear, in case I haven't been, the natural voice of Psalm 110 says nothing about Jesus. Verse 2 speaks of the person ruling in the midst of his enemies. There is no evidence that Jesus ruled anything. Jesus was not a priest in a way that reflected either Malki-tzedeq or Aaron according to verse 4. No kings were crushed in his day according to verse 5. He didn't judge the nations or executed anyone according to verse 6. So the major portions of this chapter have nothing to do with Jesus. It is for these reasons that the chapter applies more to David or to a king that actually did do battle rather than "the meek and lowly Jesus. That's why it must be seen as taking verse 4 out of context and changing its meaning to apply it to Jesus when the whole chapter revolts against it.

If the following verses in Hebrews, chapter 5 verses 7 and 8, is in any way linked to the quote from Psalm 110, then the question must be asked if strong prayer and petition and obedience is all that is needed to be a priest of Malki-tzedeq's order. If so, then there must be a great many people who are part of that priesthood as many Jews would have fit that criteria. If the criterion is that the Lord himself must call such a person a priest, then Jesus' claim falls flat since that never happened.

Chapter 7

verses 1-3

(1) Because this Melchisedec, king of Salem, priest of the most high God, who met Abraham returning from the slaughter of the kings, and blessed him; (2) To whom also Abraham gave a tenth part of all; first being by interpretation King of righteousness, and after that also King of Salem, which is, King of peace; (3) Without father, without mother, without descent, having neither beginning of days, nor end of life; but made like unto the Son of God; remains a priest continually. (Hebrews 7:1-3)

Note the strangeness of this passage. Malki-tzedeq remains a priest forever?!? According to Hebrews, he has no father, mother, or genealogy, or beginning or end. Now anyone who reads scripture can see the problem with this. The fact that scripture gives no mention about his family doesn't mean that he never had one any more than the other king mentioned in Genesis 14:1-2.

Then it happened in the days of Amraphel king of Shinar, Ariokh king of Ellasar, Kedarlaomer king of Eylam, and Tidal king of Goyyim made war with Bera king of Sedom [in many translations, "Sodom"], Birsha king of Amorah [in many translations, "Gamorah"), Shinav king of Admah, and Shemever king of Tzevoyyim and the king of Bela (which is Tzoar). (Genesis 14:1,2)

Those kings never had their fathers, mothers or genealogies mentioned. Are their kingships eternal? Are they eternal? Are they still alive because scripture doesn't mention their deaths??? The reasoning of the Hellenist is both ludicrous and arbitrary. There are plenty of people in scripture whose genealogies aren't mentioned.

And even if if this description in Hebrews is figurative, what real meaning could it have? Malki-tzedeq is similar to Jesus in what way? A figurative way? Jesus had a mother and a genealogy. In fact Jesus has two conflicting genealogies. So that messes up any similarity that the Hellenist writer of Hebrews just mentioned. Should christians then be saying that Malki-tzedeq is superior to Jesus??? Or may he's more divine than Jesus?

If the Hellenist is trying to make the point that Jesus is Malki-tzedeq or like him, having an eternal pre-existence, then it has already been shown that this is idolatry since only one being has no beginning or end. To say Jesus has the same attributes, despite what Jesus worshippers would wish, would mean there are two separate gods. Or, despite what oneness doctrine adherents wish, it would mean that the eternal God changed, was limited and died. These characteristics are opposite to the characteristics of God, and therefore there would be an inherent contradiction. God would not be God! There is no such thing.

Since Hebrews plainly says that Malki-tzedeq has these attributes, then maybe there are more gods to the christian godhead than we ever suspected. Or it makes Malki-tzedeq a nonsensical, contradictory and therefore non-existent being.

But to summarize, the writer of Hebrews makes no coherent point with these verses. No matter what level you take his words, they are always inconsistent with the biblical facts.

verses 4-10

> *(4) Now consider how great this man was, to whom even the patriarch Abraham gave the tenth of the spoils. (5) And verily they that are of the sons of Levi, who receive the office of the priesthood, have a commandment to take tithes from the people according to the law, that is, of their brothers, though they come out of the loins of Abraham: (6) But he whose descent is not counted from them received tithes of Abraham, and blessed him that had the promises. (7) And without any despite, the lesser is blessed by the better. (8) And here men that die receive tithes; but there he receives them, of whom it is witnessed that he lives. (9) And as I may so say, Levi also, who receives tithes, paid tithes in Abraham. (10) For he was yet in the loins of his father, when Melchisedec met him. (Hebrews 7:4-10)*

See the reasoning of the Hellenist here! Malki-tzedeq must be a greater man than Abraham. Why? Because Abraham gave Malki-tzedeq tithes and Malki-tzedeq blessed Abraham. In the mind of the Hellenist, the lesser pays tithes to the better, and the greater person blesses the lesser person. The Levitical priests came from the loins of Abraham. So, in a way, they paid tithes to Malki-tzedeq, a man isn't descended from them, whose genealogy has nothing to do with theirs. Therefore, Malki-tzedeq must be both a greater man and have a greater priesthood!

Sounds convincing, right?

Sounds reasonable and plausible too, huh?

But that's before we understand the history and principles of the Hebrew Bible, the erroneously called "old testament."

According to scripture, the righteous deeds of a righteous man are his and his alone (Ezekiel 18:20). They can't be done by one person and somehow conferred (carried across) to another who hasn't done those actions. Everyone is responsible for their own deeds. So Levi and his descendants didn't give tithes to Malki-tzedeq at all. He wasn't in the loins of Abraham. Abraham fathered Isaac, and then Isaac fathered Jacob, and then Jacob fathered Levi. Jacob is Levi's father, not Abraham. Abraham is Levi's great-grandfather.

The Levitical priesthood wasn't even around at the time of Malki-tzedeq, so it was a simple case of Abraham giving his tithes to someone who was around at the time. Levi wasn't born yet, so of course Malki-tzedeq's own genealogy has nothing to do with Levi's. Since Malki-tzedeq and the Levites lived in different time periods, then laws concerning the latter (Levites) can't really apply to the former (Malki-tzedeq).

In other words, the law concerning the giving of tithes to the Levites did not exist before the Levitical priesthood. So if someone gave tithes beforehand, the Levitical law would not apply. So in that sense, the reasoning of Hebrews 7 verses 5 and 6 is severely lacking. If Abraham giving tithes to Malki-tzedeq had happened during the existence of the Levitical law, it may have meant something (although still less than what the writer of Hebrews was gunning for) but since it was before the law, the reasoning of this Hellenist writer is undermined.

Think about it! A descendant can be greater than his ancestor. Moses was greater than many of his ancestors. A person coming after someone else doesn't say anything about their greatness. So if Abraham gave gifts to a priest, does that really say anything about the greatness of the priesthood of his descendants? If this line of reason is scrutinized rationally and biblically, it would follow that there is no compelling evidence to make you draw the Hellenist's conclusion.

Let me also add this! What exactly are the detail of the priesthood of Malki-tzedeq? What does the Jewish Bible explicitly teach about this priesthood? There is an utter dearth of information regarding what exactly it is. With this utter lack of evidence from the source material (the Jewish Bible, the "old testament") then there is no firm means of testing whether it is qualitatively better than that of Aaron or of Levi.

What can be seen is that the priesthood of Malki-tzedeq has no jurisdiction over the Jews after the giving of the Torah at Sinai. No space is given to it in the laws of God given to Moses at Sinai. Offerings and sacrifices for Jews are limited only to Levitical priests. There is not even any overt statement that Malki-tzedeq's priesthood applies to all non-Jews.

With this in mind, what proof is there that Malki-tzedeq's priesthood was any better than Aaron's? Since there was no option for Abraham to give tithes to a Levitical priest, then there is no real proof, just allegory based on figurative meanings, which is the weakest of the weak when it comes to evidence.

verses 11-18

(11) Therefore if perfection came by means of the Levitical priesthood (for under it the people received the Law), what further need was there that another priest should rise after the order of Melchizedek, and not be called after the order of Aaron? (12) For the priesthood being transferred/changed, there is, out of necessity, a transfer/change made in the law also. (13) For He of whom these things are spoken belongs to another tribe, from which no man gave attendance at the altar. (14) For it is evident that our Lord arose out of Judah, of which tribe Moses spoke nothing concerning priesthood. (15) And it is still far more evident, since there arises a different priest after the likeness of Melchisedek, (16) who is made, not

according to the law of a fleshly commandment, but according to the power of an endless life. (17) For He testifies, "You are a priest forever after the order of Melchizedek." (18) For truly there is a cancelling of the commandment which went before, because of the weakness and uselessness of it. (Hebrews 7:11-18)

The writer of Hebrews goes on to say that with the existence of another priesthood, the Levitical priesthood is done away with because of its weakness and uselessness, it's giving no benefit or advantage.

Now I've gotta say something right off the bat. This is to anyone who is actually serious about the Torah, the Law of God through Moses. That is most likely to be the Jews, but there may be some more studious Gentiles around as well. It says in Deuteronomy 4:1-7 (especially verse 2) and 13:1 (or 12:32 in christian bibles) that is absolutely forbidden to add or subtract anything from God's law. Deuteronomy 27:26 says that those who don't confirm or affirm the words of the Torah in order to do them is accursed, which means (and I'll quote from my earlier refutation of Galatians 3:10):

... to see and accept the truth of [the law]. As one ancient rabbi says, it means "that every Jew must accept the Torah's validity in full, and dare not claim that even one of its commandments is not relevant". So everyone who acknowledges the God of Israel and his Law must "cause it to stand" or affirm its truth and importance, in order that they do it.

The test of any prophet in the Hebrew Bible was whether their teaching agreed with or contradicted the Law of Moses, given by God. For you Jews, or more studious Gentiles, once you see someone or some book teaching you that a law that is part of the Torah is change, transferred or cancelled, especially calling it useless and weak, you must understand what it is: a teaching that is forbidden by the law which God gave to his greatest prophet!

The writer of Hebrews is trying to use allegory and an invalid form of reasoning to turn you away from the blunt truth of God's law which I'll get into a little later: he is saying that God's law is cancelled and God's priesthood is abolished! He is saying that God's law and priesthood are useless and weak, worse than irrelevant! So you don't have to read anything more to know what you should do with Hebrews, book and author! "What's that?" I hear some ask. "What should they do with the book of Hebrews?" Here's my blunt response:

KICK IT TO THE KERB!

But let me continue with my response for all and sundry.

Here's a question: The Malki-tzedeq priesthood was first and the Levitical priesthood came second; the Hebrew Bible said nothing about the cancellation of Malki-tzedeq priesthood because of the institution of the Levitical one; so why, if the Malki-tzedeq priesthood always existed, would it abolish the Levitical? They either existed fine together, or one existed without abolishing the other, so there would be no reason why the first one must abolish the latter.

Again, let's look at the plain word of the Hebrew Bible. Please read Jeremiah 33:19-22. I'll quote it for you.

(19) And the word of the LORD came to Jeremiah, saying (20) The LORD has spoken thus, If you shall break my covenant with the day and my covenant with the night, and there be not day or night in their [proper] times; (21) Also my covenant with David my servant shall be broken so that he won't have a son of his to be upon the throne, and the Levitical priests, my ministers. (22) As the hosts of heaven shall not be counted, and the sand of the sea shall not be measured, in like manner I shall increase the offspring of David my servant, and the Levites who minister to me. (Jeremiah 33:19-22)

Please read it again!

What does it say?

To summarize, it is a firm promise to David and the Levitical priests. There will always be a descendent of Levi around who can be a priest!!! Note that the word "Levitical" means "descended from Levi." So that means that there cannot be an abolishing or cancelling of that priesthood, or a change in that commandment. As I quoted before, Aaron and his sons were given a perpetual command and priesthood. That, on its own, stands in the face of the book of Hebrews and directly contradict it. How can you end the endless? Look at Numbers 18:19,23.

(19) All the terumah-offerings of the holy things which the children of Israel shall raise to the LORD, I have given to you [the Levites, see context] and to your sons and your daughters with you for an everlasting statute. It is an everlasting covenant of salt before the LORD for you and for your offspring with you ...

(23) And the Levite, he shall do the service of the tent of meeting and they shall bear their iniquity: an everlasting statute for your generations and in the midst of the children of Israel: they won't inherit an inheritance.

Also see Exodus 29:9:

And you shall gird them with a belt, Aaron and his sons, and you shall bind to them turbans and they shall have a priesthood for an everlasting statute, and you shall consecrate [literally, fill the hand of] Aaron and his sons.

The scriptures show no sign of their ending.

Now again, some may ask: if there is supposed to be an eternal Levitical priesthood, what happened to it with the destruction of the Temple in 70CE? Surely, this must mean that Jesus has now become a spiritual King and High Priest since the Jews have neither king or priest. [Special thanks to the "Treasury of Scriptural Knowledge" for the typical christian response to these points.]

Please put your thinking caps on. What I'm gonna say is not difficult or complex, but it may miss you.

* You do not fulfil a law by abolishing it!
* You do not fulfil a promise to give something to one particular person only for it to be given to someone else!
* To promise something to someone and then give what was promised to someone else without warning or condition is a lie!

Read all the Jewish Bible, and the plain meaning of it will never give the statement that the Levitical priesthood will end forever!

Now let me address my point.

* The Torah, the Law of Moses, says that the Aaronic and Levitical priesthood has everlasting responsibilities and thus has an everlasting existence. This clearly means the priesthood passed down biologically from Aaron and Levi is everlasting. This law cannot be fulfilled by abolishing or cancelling it, i.e., there can't be Levitical priests if there is no more law.
* The Lord, whose promises are true and who never goes back on his word, gave a promise and his word to the priesthood of those descended from Levi. This promise is as sure and firm as the heaven and earth and is everlasting. This promise does not apply to anyone descended from another tribe like Judah, as Jesus was supposed to have been.
* The Lord, whose promises are true and who never goes back on his word, could not take what was promised to the descendants of Aaron and Levi and, without warning or condition, give it to someone descended from Judah. Why? Because doing so would be deceitful, i.e., a lie. And Deity does not lie or go back on his word.

So, to say that God has fulfilled his promises and laws by taking what was promised to a Levitical priest and giving it to someone who the new testament itself says is not from Levi is illogical, ridiculous and incredibly short-sighted. It just ain't right.

Even Jesus never said such a thing!!!

And even if he did say something to this effect (which he didn't), it still would not have mattered because there was no warning or condition of any change in the Torah!

For those who would want to refer to Zechariah 6, please note that it still does not distinctly refer to the end of the Levitical priesthood at all. Again, the typical christian response is both nonsense by making God essentially lie, and blasphemous by insulting and attempting to abolish or cancel a command and promise of the Lord.

OK, with that out of the way, seeing the logically and biblically bankrupt "answer" of christianity, what is the answer?

The fact is that there are still descendants of David and Levi walking around today. Whether it be via genetics or through family records, a good amount of Levites can be found today. So even with no temple, there are still Levitical priests around today.

And then you will say "but they can't do their job without a temple." But just think back with me! There was another time when Israel was evicted from their land and the temple was destroyed. Yes, this event was even in the scriptures. It's when Babylon came and conquered and captured Jerusalem. The temple was destroyed and the people scattered. Yet, surprisingly, during the time of the exile, there was not a single authoritative notion that the commandments were done away with or the promise of David and Levi made void. The fact is that the promise is that there will always be a descendant of David and Levi alive and available with the ability to fulfil the task.

Remember the prophecy in Hoshea 3:4-5 which clearly states that, for a long time, Israel will be without king or sacrifice (i.e., the temple practice), but that the kingship of David's lineage will be re-established. Also reading Ezekiel 37 and 40-46, we see that the temple and its Levites will be re-established. This prophecy doesn't refer to the 2nd temple, the one that was destroyed in 70CE, since it doesn't match the description of these chapters. It refers to a future temple.

So all that is happening is a pause, not a cessation, just like the 70-year Babylonian exile, but longer. Thus the promises will be put into effect, especially with descendants of David and Levi still in existence. The Lord's promise is still what is preserving them.

I just ask you to understand what happened in the Babylonian exile, especially to the descendants of David and Levi still in existence at that time and the state of the Temple, and then to apply those principles to what is going on today, what has been going on since the destruction of the second Temple in 70CE. It makes no sense to follow the reasoning of the writer of Hebrews and much of the christian church which clings to the Hellenist author and his words. The word of the Lord in the Hebrew Scriptures makes much better sense and is a witness that God Almighty does what he has said from the beginning: he means what he says and keeps his word.

Now the writer of Hebrews calls for this abolition of divine law due to his view that it made no one perfect and thus is weak and useless! Noting the fact that such a view, i.e., to call divine law weak and useless (of no benefit) is insulting to the One who gave such a law, and thus is blasphemous, let me deal with this claim of the Hellenist author.

1) God never said that the priesthood would make things perfect! This is most important because the Hellenist author of Hebrews has basically created a straw man, stating something that has never had

any reality, something that God never said, and then calls God's law weak and useless for something that God never said.

2) The fact that it was to have an ongoing and everlasting role in the Israelite/Jewish community means that it can't be said that it was going to make everything perfect. Because, even in the messianic age, a time when the whole world knows Deity and the carnivorous way of animal life would come to an end (Isaiah 11:6-9), the Levites would still have a role and be in existence. So it would seem that even in the face of world renewal, the priesthood remains. So something seems to be missing from the Hellenist author's logic. The very fact that the priesthood's existence continues even into times of greater perfection shows that its purpose was not to make people perfect.

3) If the purpose of the Levitical priesthood was not to make people perfect, then it doesn't matter what Jesus did or didn't do. His actions become irrelevant to the existence of the Levitical priesthood since it continues even in the future divinely restored world.

I would argue that the Levitical priesthood fulfilled its purpose throughout history, i.e., obeying God's commands regarding the priesthood whenever possible, taking care of the sanctuary, receiving and presenting to God the various sorts of offerings of all sorts of people (note: offerings were not only for atonement of sin), teaching the law, judging difficult judicial matters, etc.

In essence, the priest belongs to the Almighty to perform a special role. Now it doesn't matter how perfect the world is, aspects of these roles can have everlasting continuity as long as there is an earth and a heaven and the people of Israel and of the world. Thus the priesthood will always have an existence and a purpose.

Thus, the law is not weak and useless, but it gives a task that humans can do to elevate themselves in divine service. Such a task can never be weak and useless unless you ask of it something it was never meant to do! And that's the Hellenist author's mistake. His deplorable understanding of law causes him to make blasphemous statements which insult God's law.

This is the weakness of many christian encyclopedias because their descriptions of priesthood are based on the understanding of the author of Hebrews, and thus are skewed and distorted.

verses 26-27

> *(26) For such a high priest was suitable for us, who is holy, harmless, undefiled, separate from sinners, and made higher than the heavens; (27) Who doesn't have to (as those high priests) daily offer up sacrifice, first for his own sins, and then for the people's: for this he did once, when he offered up himself. (Hebrews 7:26-27)*

Jesus is supposed to have offered himself as a sacrifice, once and for all people at all times.

Despite all the praises the Hellenist gives to Jesus, one still must stop and think! According to this author, Jesus gave his human body as a sacrifice. But according to whose law?

It's definitely not according to the law of God given through Moses! There is nothing in the revealed law, the Torah, that gives instructions for a "perfect" human sacrifice. The Law of God outlaws, and thus makes illegal, human sacrifice by allowing only animal sacrifice or offerings of plants or flour. The Law of God tells the Jews what altar to use and how Deity wants his offerings.

Remember, it is God that tells us what He requires, and without his revelation we have no clue. And what He has revealed leaves out humans dying on crosses as sacrifices. His servants have told us what he accepts: specific animal or flour sacrifices; repentance; prayer; and obedience to the Torah. But nowhere does it prescribe a human death as atonement for sin. It doesn't even prescribe divine death, if such an abhorrent thing were possible.

So Jesus' death is not in accordance with Torah and is thus an illegal act that would alienate him from any notion of priesthood. His righteousness would not save or help anyone based on Ezekiel 18:20 and Deuteronomy 24:16.

Chapter 8

verses 4-5

(4) For if he [Jesus] were on earth, he would not be a priest, being of those that offer the gifts according to the law, (5) who serve an illustration and shadow of heavenly things, as Moses was admonished of God when he was about to discharge his duty of building the tabernacle: "Therefore see, He said, that you shall make all things according to the pattern showed to you in the mountain." (Hebrews 8:4,5 quoting Exodus 25:40)

Here, the Hellenist author of Hebrews quotes Exodus 25:40 to say that Jesus was not a priest on earth but rather a priest in heaven, namely in the heavenly tabernacle of which Moses could only do a shadowy earthly copy, according to the above quoted scripture.

Let's first deal with the verse quoted. You can read all the context of Exodus 25 that you want, but one thing is for sure: it doesn't say overtly what Moses or was shown at the top of the mountain. All we do know is that Moses saw the form or shape of everything that was meant to be made in the tabernacle, and he was told to make everything as he saw it.

Since he alone saw it, made sure that those who made the parts of the structure made it according to plain, he set it up and arranged the tabernacle, who exactly is the writer of Hebrews to say that it was but a shadowy copy???

If Moses had to obey God, and make things according to what he was shown, then he had to get things just right as he was commanded. With this is mind, there is every chance that Moses simply saw exactly the form of the completed tabernacle! That's the only way it can make sense when it says Exodus 39:32,42,43, and Exodus 40:19,21,27,29,32 that it was all done as the Lord had commanded. The constant repetition of the phrase "just as the Lord commanded ..." in the final chapters of Exodus when it talks about both how people constructed each part of the tabernacle and how Moses set it up shows that Moses reproduced what he saw exactly, as opposed to him just doing some shadowy copy.

So the writer of Hebrews again goes above his station and makes a baseless points he is not qualified to make.

Can we derive from that verse, Exodus 25:40, that there is a tabernacle in heaven? No! Moses sees a pattern, a blueprint (to reflect the Hebrew) in the mountain. That all we get!

But what if this means that the tabernacle is a metaphor for something else? Metaphor can be another word for "shadow" in christian circles. As I said before, allegories are the worst form of evidence since different people get different ideas about the same metaphor or allegory. So there is no strong basis to follow the writer's view yet. Let's see how he does as we carry on.

verses 6-13

(6) But now he has obtained a more excellent ministry, by how much also he is the mediator of a better covenant, which was established upon better promises. (7) For if that first [covenant] had been faultless, then a place would not have been sought for a second [one]. (8) For finding fault with them, he says, Behold, the days come, says the Lord, and I will bring about a new covenant with the house of Israel and with the house of Judah: (9) Not according to the covenant that I made with their fathers in the day when I took their hand to lead them out of the land of Egypt; because they didn't

remain in my covenant, and I disregarded them, says the Lord. (10) Because this is the covenant that I will make with the house of Israel after those days, says the Lord: I will put my laws into their mind, and write them upon their hearts: and I will be to them a God, and they shall be to me a people; (11) And they shall not teach every man his neighbour, and every man his brother, saying, "Know the Lord," because all shall know me, from the least to the greatest. (12) For I will be merciful to their unrighteousness, and I will not remember their sins and iniquities anymore. (13) In that he says, "new," he has made the first old. Now that which is old and aged is close to destruction [or disappearance, meaning removal from sight].
(Hebrews 8:6-13 quoting Jeremiah 31:31-34)

Essentially, the Hellenist author of Hebrews uses a passage from Jeremiah to say that Jesus mediated a new covenant making the old covenant, the covenant of the Law of Moses, obsolete, old, and ready to be put into obscurity (or destroyed).

I will summarize some of this passage and pick up some points on how the writer of Hebrews, the Hellenist, "uses" this scriptural passage.

Point 1: verse 9 - καγω ημελησα αυτων
The above Greek means something like "and I was without concern or care for them" or "and I disregarded them" or "and I neglected them." This is according to the LXX. But it is a mistranslation of the Hebrew which says "and I was a husband to them, " or "and I married them." Since the Septuagint (LXX) has a mistranslation which the writer of Hebrews continues with, then it cannot be said that the book of Hebrews is infallible or the word of God on the same level as the Jewish Bible, or that that the writer had the such a level of God-given spirit which would have not made a mistake. This mistake says the complete opposite to what the words of Jeremiah were, so it cannot be true.

Point 2

God had already given his laws to Moses and Israel in the history recorded in the books of Exodus to Deuternomy, which included the law concerning the priesthood. When God, through Jeremiah, said He would put his law into the hearts of the people of the houses of Israel and Judah, this priestly law would have been included.

Yet the Hellenist tells in this book of Hebrews that divine laws have been done away with and abolished. So the writer has written himself into a contradiction. There's no point in saying that the priestly laws are not "my laws" - God's laws - since they obviously are, according to the Law of Moses written in the Jewish Bible. And the passage in Jeremiah says nothing about God giving new laws. So the writer of Hebrews contradicts himself or he contradicts Scripture, neither of which would be a new thing considering what we've seen before of this writer.

Point 3

Israel and Judah, when the new covenant comes into effect, will no longer have to be taught, "Know the Lord," for all of them shall know Him. As is plainly obvious, this has not happened from Jeremiah's time up until this present time. The need for christian missionaries, like Jews for Jesus, in Israel today shows that this new covenant hasn't happened yet. A lot of Israel is atheist or agnostic today so they don't even know the Lord. Thus, the "better covenant" that Jesus is supposed to have brought in hasn't started in the past 2000 years. So this doesn't add to the Hellenist's claim.

As an aside, it should be noted that the "new covenant" was not for non-Jews according to Jeremiah 31. It was only for the houses of Israel and Judah, names that have nothing to do with the christian church, but has everything to do with the literal nations of Israel and Judah.

Point 4: "making the first obsolete"

According to Jeremiah 31, the terms of the new covenant says nothing about the first one being obsolete. This is just the imagination of the Hellenist. Do you know how many covenants were made in the Jewish Bible? A good few. Did you know that no later covenant ever abolished a former one? Whether it's the covenant of Noah, or that of Abraham, or Moses and Israel, or Phinehas, or David, no latter divine covenant abolished a former one. The covenant of circumcision that Abraham got in Genesis 17 did not abolish the covenant of Noah in Genesis 9. The covenant of Moses and Israel did not make the first covenants - that of Noah and Abraham - obsolete.

So on what basis does the Hellenist author of Hebrew say that the "new" covenant of Jeremiah abolishes or does away with the Mosaic covenant? It's not from the words of Jeremiah 31, that's for sure! The basis of the Hellenist's argument is nowhere in the divinely given scriptures, the Jewish Bible. So basically he doesn't have a leg to stand on.

The Jeremiah covenant actually shows the opposite of Paul's message: in the time of the new covenant, the Law (that of Moses, the only one mentioned in scripture) will be obeyed and known by every Israelite, which stands in total contradiction to the abolition or rendering idle of law which Paul and the writer of Hebrews goes on about.

Thus the "first" covenant is not made obsolete or annulled, but instead is re-affirmed with the people of Israel (as opposed to some gentile church) keeping their law and living safely in their land with the Temple rebuilt (Jeremiah 23 and 31; Ezekiel 37).

Chapter 9

verses 6-15

(6) Now these things having been thus prepared, the priests went always into the first tent, accomplishing the service of God. (7) But the high priest alone [went] into the second once every year, not

without blood, which he offers for himself, and for the mistakes of the people: (8) The Holy Spirit making this plain: that the way into the holies was not yet revealed, while the first tabernacle was still standing: (9) Which was an analogy/symbol/simile for the present time, in which both gifts and sacrifices are being offered, that cannot make the one who did the service perfect with regards to the conscience; (10) only in foods and drinks, and various washings, even fleshy ordinances, imposed on them until the time that things get straightened out. (11) But Christ having come, a high priest of the coming good things through a greater and more perfect tabernacle, not made by hands, that is, not of this creation/building; (12) And not by the blood of goats and calves, but by his own blood he entered in once into the holy place, having obtained eternal redemption. (13) For if the blood of bulls and of goats, and the ashes of a heifer sprinkling the unclean, makes holy to the purifying of the flesh: (14) How much more shall the blood of Christ, who offered himself without blemish to God through the eternal Spirit, cleanse your conscience from dead works to serve the living God? (15) And because of this he is the mediator of the new testament, so that by a death happening for the full payment for violations that were under the first testament, those who were called might receive the promise of eternal inheritance. (Hebrews 9:6-15)

The writer of Hebrews has repeatedly made the point that the temple ceremonies couldn't make a person perfect. We see more clearly in this passage what he means. Verse 9 speaks of the cleansing of the conscience, that the ceremonies couldn't do that. Verse 14 speaks of cleansing the conscience from "dead works." What are dead works? Hebrews 6:1 speaks of "repentance of dead works." Now although some would love to say that this refers to the dead words of the ceremonial part of Moses' Law which is abolished and done away with, but this conclusion makes little sense. Even Paul never equated the Law with a sin you need to repent of. What is clearly repented of in the Bible are sins. So this must be what the "dead works" refer to: "repentance of dead works" is the same as "repentance for sins [or sinful deeds]."

So what normal sacrifices couldn't do, Jesus' "sacrifice" is supposed to accomplish: to free a person from the power of sin. Again, I ask you to just think about this. Did you know that "born again" christians and everyone else in the world has something in common? We all sin! There is no righteous person in the world that only does good and never sins (Ecclesiastes 7:20)! That was true in the "old covenant" and it's the same now, whether you are a christian or not. Even christians admit this. So what exactly have the christians been freed from? How are they any more free than a Jewish rabbi intent on living according to the law of the one true God given through Moses? How is this christian more free than any Jew or Gentile who observes God's law for that particular individual?

The fact is that this cleansing or freedom, this picture of Jesus offering his blood in some higher temple, all of it is totally invisible and seemingly non-existent. I've been in enough churches of "saved" christians that is just as full of gossip and backbiting and political intrigue to know this. "But we are saved by faith" you may hear them cry. But with no backing from God's law, the foundation of all and any scripture, then they are just shouting in the wind with claims worth nothing.

verses 16-28

(16) For wherever [there's] a testament, it is necessary for the death of the one who makes the testament to be carried out. (17) For a testament is in force because of dead [men] seeing that it has no strength at all while the one who made the testament lives. (18) So neither was the first [testament] dedicated without blood. (19) For when Moses spoke every commandment to all the people according to the law, taking the blood of calves and of goats, with water and scarlet wool and hyssop, he sprinkled both the book and all the people, (20) saying, This [is] the blood of the testament which God has commanded you. (21) And he sprinkled with blood both the tabernacle, and all the vessels of the service. (22) And almost all things are purified by blood according to the law, and forgiveness doesn't happen without blood-shed.

(23) [It was] therefore necessary for the copies of things in the heavens to be purified with these; but the heavenly things themselves with better sacrifices than these. (24) For the Christ didn't enter into handmade holy places, symbols of the true; but rather into heaven itself, now to appear in the presence of God for us, (25) but not so that he should offer himself frequently, as the high priest enters into the holy place every year with blood of others, (26) since he would have had to suffer frequently from the foundation of the world. But now - at one time - in the end of the ages, he has appeared for [the] nullification of sin by his sacrifice. (27) And as it is reserved for mankind to die once, but after this, judgment, (28) in such manner the Christ, being offered once to bear the sins of many, shall appear a second time without sin for salvation to those who have persisted waiting for him. (Hebrews 9:16-28)

Ok. This is kinda lengthy so I'll break it down and we'll test the line of reasoning of the Hellenist author of Hebrews.

(16) For wherever [there's] a testament, it is necessary for the death of the one who makes the testament to be carried out. (17) For a testament is in force because of dead [men] seeing that it has no strength at all while the one who made the testament lives. (18) So neither was the first [testament] dedicated without blood. (verses 16-18)

Now I've got to re-iterate something I've said many times before. Sola-scriptura christians, which makes up the vast majority of Protestant christianity, only accept the written text of their Bible as having divine authority. Many of them are not even 100% sure on who actually wrote Hebrews so that adds to the fact that whoever the author was did not start or help maintain any traditional interpretation of what he actually meant when he wrote these words. Reading the christian commentaries of the past centuries, such as Calvin, Wesley, John Gill, Matthew Henry, and consulting the Latin Vulgate, I do see some consensus and some disagreement about what actually is being spoken of in these verses. I'm not going to get into the debate of the true meaning, whatever it is. I'll just deal with the face value of what is said.

The Hellenist starts off a false comparison. He starts off using the example of a "testament." The context points to this "testament" being what we understand as "the last will and testament" of a person. That means that before a person dies, they arrange their affairs and estate and write out or declare what they want to happen to their possessions after they die. This declaration or document is called a "last will and testament." And when that person dies, what they have declared or what they have written takes effect and their possessions are divided amongst those they have chosen. And as the writer says, the person make in the will or testament, the "testator," has to die for it to take effect.

Now the Hellenist then tries to equate a biblical covenant with a testament. I've already said what a testament is. But what is a covenant? It is an agreement between two people involving shared promises. For example, the Creator makes a covenant with Noah in Genesis 9. Note that neither party in the covenant, neither Noah nor God, had to die for it to take effect. The same point is true with regards to the divine covenants of Abraham, Moses and Israel, and Phinehas. This is a fundamental and important difference between a testament and a covenant. In a testament, a will, the person making the testament must die for it to take effect. In a covenant, no one dies. They are essentially two different things.

[ASIDE: There are some christians that have said that the author of Hebrews isn't talking about a testament, but rather a covenant. Thus, for them verses 16-17 would state "For wherever [there's] a covenant, it is necessary for the death of the 'covenant-victim' to be carried out. For a covenant is in force because of the dead seeing that it has no strength at all while the 'covenant-victim' lives."

There are reasons why this rendering is strange and still is invalid. Firstly, as far as I know, there is no other place in any Greek text where the Greek word translated 'covenant-victim' is understood like that. Normally it just means the person who makes the will, as opposed to some sacrificial offering.

This seems to be an attempt to make the author of Hebrews make sense when he obviously doesn't.

Secondly, the text and the surrounding context points more to a will. The previous verse refers to an inheritance, and the natural flow of what comes next (in verses 16-18) seems to be the way a person gets an inheritance in the Greek sense of things, i.e., by means of a will or a testament.

Thirdly, even if the text could be twisted into this "covenant-victim" picture, the Hebrew Bible doesn't agree that an animal offering or animal sacrifice is needed. There are two divine covenants that were not confirmed with a sacrifice: the covenant of Noah which classically starts from Genesis 9 and not the previous chapter; and the covenant of Phinehas in Numbers 25 (no divine covenant in the Hebrew Bible is ever confirmed with human blood.) So that would make the logic false in Hebrews 9:17 if we are talking about a covenant-victim. A covenant-victim is not needed for a covenant to take effect.(ASIDE FINISHED)]

So the fact that blood is shed to institute the Mosaic covenant means nothing with regards to the Hellenist's logic since it is neither the testator (the one who makes a testament) or one of the parties of a covenant.

A christian may say tell me to wait, and put forward the idea that the similarity between a covenant and a testament is that something has to die. But did you know that a chicken had to die for me to eat and enjoy my roast chicken meal? Animals die daily for so many humans to enjoy meals, to enjoy hunting, even to do some other stuff with the body parts of an animal. Something has to die, right? So can my roast chicken mean be equated to a divine covenant? No! Why? Because the similarity is too superficial and there are not enough fundamental similarities to make the comparison valid or to equate one with the other. The same is true when trying to equate a testament with a covenant.

Let me just add the opposite problem. The Mosaic covenant may have been instituted with blood - literal blood - but you don't need blood to put a will into effect, only a death. In fact, it wasn't just any blood that was used to institute the Mosaic covenant: it was the blood of a ritually clean animal that was slaughtered in a special ritual to both obtain its blood and to give a satisfactory offering to God. None of these elements are part of what is needed for a will to come into effect. So there really isn't enough similarity to equate a covenant, especially a covenant with God, with a testament.

(19) For when Moses spoke every commandment to all the people according to the law, taking the blood of calves and of goats, with water and scarlet wool and hyssop, he sprinkled both the book and all the people, (20) saying, This [is] the blood of the testament which God has commanded you. (21) And he sprinkled with blood both the tabernacle, and all the vessels of the service. (Hebrews 9:19-21 quoting Exodus 24:8)

The writer of Hebrews quotes Exodus 24:8 but it doesn't really help because the supposedly infallible holy spirit inspired writer of Hebrews makes an error: he adds to the words of the Hebrew Scripture! I ask you to read Exodus 24:1-8. Once you've read it, take a look at Hebrews 9:20. Pay careful attention to what was sprinkled and who it was sprinkled on.

Exodus 24:1-8 - blood is sprinkled on the people
Hebrews 9:20 - blood, **water, scarlet wool and hyssop** is sprinkled on the people **and the book**.

Moses didn't even use half the stuff that the Hellenist author of Hebrews claims he did, and he only sprinkled the people not the book. To quote the relevant verse that applies to the Hellenist's misdeed:

Every word of God is refined. It is a shield for all who take refuge in it. Don't add to his word lest he rebuke you and you are found to be a liar. (Proverbs 30:5-6)

I guess that makes the writer of Hebrews a liar!

... and forgiveness doesn't happen without blood-shed. (Hebrews 9:22b)

This verse is also translated more popularly as "without the shedding of blood, there is no remission/forgiveness."

This is one of the most fundamental errors of the Hellenist writer of Hebrews which christianity readily absorbed as a foundational position in their doctrine of sin, atonement and forgiveness. Let me show you how the Hebrew Scriptures contradict this notion at its core. But I ask you to be clear as to what the claim of the Hellenist is: if you have no blood, if someone or some animal doesn't die with blood loss, that means you have no forgiveness from God, i.e., God will not forgive you! Does the Hebrew Bible really state this or show this? A great many Jewish articles and books refute this sort of thinking. But I'll emphasize a few scriptures here.

Leviticus 5:11-13 has a sin offering commanded by God Himself that has no blood being given for atonement and forgiveness. Take note that the plain reading of these verses state nothing about blood being needed. Thus it is not true that there is no forgiveness without bloodshed.

[ASIDE: There are those who, because they accept the new testament first before the Hebrew Scriptures, will read their bloody notions and pre-conclusions into texts like Leviticus 5:11-13, ideas that are not there. My approach is to read the bible in the right direction, from the beginning to the end, and not backwards. So the plain text of Leviticus 5:11-13 comes first.

If someone afterwards says that blood is needed for atonement, then that person is obviously wrong.

Also, there are some christians who attempt to quote the writings of the Jews, such as the Talmud, to make it seem as if ancient Jews accepted their bloody notions and pre-conclusions. Again, remember that it is their beliefs in the new testament that come first and everything else must bow to that. This is evident in the commentaries of John Gill, Albert Barnes, John Lightfoot and Michael Brown. I recommend that you find sources like articles by Rabbis Blumenthal and Moshe Schulman. At the writing of this work, these can be found at http://judaismresources.net, www.jewsforjudaism.org, and www.judaismsanswer.com. I'm sure there are other sources, but I'm just referring to these. (ASIDE FINISHED)]

Numbers 14:1-25 has the Almighty pardoning (or forgiving) the people's sin without blood. Some will say, "but the people were still punished." And I would agree. But guess what! They were still forgiven, according to the word of Deity Himself (Numbers 14:20), and not only that but forgiven without blood!

In 2 Chronicles 7:13-14 (compare with King Solomon's prayer in 1 Kings 8), it is clear that prayer without blood brings forgiveness.

In Psalms 32:5, confession to God, without blood, brought David forgiveness.

Ezekiel 18 is clear that a total forgiveness, a forgiveness where past sins are forgotten, comes when a person starts living a righteous lifestyle and forsaking wicked ways.

Proverbs 16:6 says that deeds of kindness and truth bring atonement.

Isaiah 43:22-25 has God wiping out Israel's sins without sacrifice!

Even if one of these passages proves the point that forgiveness is possible without blood, then the writer of Hebrews is wrong. If two or three of these passages or the others in the Jewish Bible show that forgiveness is possible without bloodshed, then it is even more clear that the Hellenist author of Hebrews has got it wrong, dead wrong! In fact, reading through the Hebrew Bible, it becomes plain that the Hellenist betrays his pagan thinking, focusing on blood as opposed to what the Hebrew Bible focuses on, repentance and acknowledgement of sins.

There is no place in the Hebrew Bible that says that only blood can be used to gain forgiveness for sins from God. The one verse the christians can use is Leviticus 17:11 which says nothing about blood being the only means of forgiveness. It only says, in context, that blood should not be eaten because it is used on the altar to gain atonement and for that reason blood should not be eaten. It doesn't say that blood alone gives forgiveness.

One important note before I end this section on the need for bloodshed for forgiveness. The author of Hebrews and those christians who follow him have greatly oversimplified what the Law of Moses says about the use of blood and how it is used in the sacrificial system. The law of Moses isn't saying "any blood will do." You can't just cut your finger, shed some blood, and thus get forgiveness. And it is not that any death will do either. You can't slaughter a pig and expect forgiveness.

According to this Law, you can only give what the Law tells you to in order to get forgiveness. In no place of God's Law does it say that human death or human blood is an acceptable sacrifice. In fact, since God only says that certain animals could be sacrificed and only in a certain place, the Temple, and only using certain rituals, no other sort of sacrifice is allowed. That means that human sacrifice is not allowed. It is a special stipulation of God's Law that no one is allowed to add to it (Deuteronomy 4:2; 13:1 [or 12:32 in christian versions]). So by looking closely at whether the Hellenist's logic is correct, we see that Jesus' death was an illegal sacrifice.

I think it becomes clear that the Hellenist has done more harm than good with this sort of reasoning. It's blatantly false to say that only blood gives forgiveness from sins.

(23) [It was] therefore necessary for the copies of things in the heavens to be purified with these; but the heavenly things themselves with better sacrifices than these. (24) For the Christ didn't enter into handmade holy places, symbols of the true; but rather into heaven itself, now to appear in the presence of God for us, (25) but not so that he should offer himself frequently, as the high priest enters into the holy place every year with blood of others, (26) since he would have had to suffer frequently from the foundation of the world. But now - at one time - in the end of the ages, he has appeared for [the] nullification of sin by his sacrifice. (27) And as it is reserved for mankind to die once, but after this, judgment, (28) in such manner the Christ, being offered once to bear the sins of many, shall appear a second time without sin for salvation to those who have persisted waiting for him. (verses 23-28)

With the foundation of logic used by the Hellenist author of Hebrews seen to be "weak and unprofitable," this further point of the Hellenist can be seen to be baseless, empty of any fact and filled with pure imagination. As shown before, according to the law of the Lord, Jesus' death is not an acceptable means of getting forgiveness or atonement. In fact, it is illegal according to God's law.

It has also been shown that Jesus has no claim to a proper priesthood. It could be added here that as well as Jesus having no rights to any priesthood - Melkhizedek or Levite - the supposed Melkhizedek priesthood is not linked with any temple or tabernacle. A Melkhizedek priest had no rights to enter the tabernacle or temple, which was only open to a high priest who was descended biologically from Levi and Aaron through the father. There is no explicit statement in the Hebrew Bible that there is some heavenly temple and the verses the Hellenist brings forward can never be used as a clear proof.

There is something else, something amazingly obvious, that needs to be highlighted. It may not be important to "christians," those who claim to follow Jesus, but it should be important to those who take seriously the claim of christians that they follow Jesus. Jesus, in the record of his life on earth in the new testament, never claimed or made a clear statement that he was a priest of any kind, neither that of Aaron, Levi or Melkhizedek! What makes this point even more significant is another fact: none of the disciples of the earthly living Jesus ever made the clear and explicit claim that he was a priest of any sort in the writings of the new testament! And this is true even after his death. It is only the anonymous writer of the book of Hebrews that makes this claim, apparently without any recorded backing from Jesus or his disciples.

It should seem strange to those who take christians seriously when those christians claim to follow Jesus that they would accept a doctrine he himself didn't teach, neither did his disciples.

I know what some may say, that Jesus apparently referred to Psalm 110:1 as a messianic verse in Matthew 22:42-45 and his apostles used that same single verse in Acts 2:34. But with the new testament's habit of using verses out of context, it doesn't mean that Jesus himself meant that the whole chapter was messianic as well. For examples of taking verses out of context, see Matthew 2:6 when it relates to Micah 5, taking into account one verse but making little sense of the following verses about the Assyrian coming and the raising of seven shepherds; or John 15:25 where Jesus uses the verse from Psalm 69 which supposedly says, "They hated me without cause," yet this supposedly sinless man, Jesus, ignores the following verses which states that the person who the Psalm refers to commits sins and is foolish at times. There are many more examples, but I'll leave it there.

The point is that for the writers of the new testament, referring to one verse in an "old testament" chapter doesn't seem to imply that the whole passage is accepted in the same fashion. Therefore, Jesus quoting one verse or his disciples quoting that same verse, doesn't tell us a thing about what they thought about the whole psalm.

Seeing all this, Jesus couldn't save anybody by dying, no matter how righteous he was supposed to be. His death was no sacrifice! He had no heavenly temple to go to! He was part of no priesthood! He didn't even claim to be a priest! He had nothing and therefore he did nothing to save anyone from the sins.

Chapter 10

verses 3-4

(1) For the law - having a shadow of good things to come, and not [being] the very image of the things - can never make those who approach it perfect with those sacrifices which they offered year by year repeatedly. (2) For then wouldn't they have ceased to be offered? because the worshippers once they were made pure should have had no more conscience of sins. (3) But in those [sacrifices there is] a reminder of sins every year. (4) For it is impossible for the blood of bulls and of goats to take away sins. (Hebrews 10:1-4)

The claim is that it is impossible for the blood of bulls and goats to take away sins, or to atone for sins. In the eyes the Hellenist author of Hebrews, the only purpose of sacrifices was for people to have a constant reminder of their sins every single year.

For people who care about what God Himself has to say on the subject, as opposed to some unknown commentator such as the author of Hebrews (it makes no difference if Paul himself wrote this, he would still only be a commentator), I would implore you to please read the relevant parts of the Law of Moses and the passages amongst the books of the prophets, in particular Leviticus 1-9 and Ezekiel 45. One concerns the past and the other is about the future. A sample (but by no means exhaustive one) of the relevant passages follows.

Past: Leviticus 1:4; 4:20,26,31,35; 5:6,10,13,16,18; 6:7.
Future: Ezekiel 45:13-20 (please take note of the KJV's handling of a certain Hebrew word. In Leviticus, it always translates the word as "to atone" or "to make atonement for", but in Ezekiel 45 it is changed to "reconciliation")

All of these verses and passages have a certain thing in common: their plain contextual meaning is that the blood of bulls and goats make atonement for and thus removes sin. That's what God said!

So if the Almighty Authority says that blood sacrifices do atone for sin, i.e., takes away sins, cleanses from sin, then that fact alone kicks away the foundation from the Hellenist's logic and argumentation! If more than that is needed, then it would be because someone has put the words of the writer of Hebrews - words which are known to come from a man's mind (whether supposedly spirit-driven or not) - above the plain words that were taken straight from God's mouth and written down. We have direct revelation in God's law and from his prophets against someone trying to prove his point!

For someone to still choose to force the plain words of God in the Law of Moses to bow to the logic of the writer of Hebrews proves one important thing: the seeds of idolatry is in the mind of such a person, and the new testament helps those seeds to blossom and grow. A central aspect of idolatry is to put something else above the authority of God. To make God's plain word in the Law of Moses bow to the author of Hebrews is to make the Hellenist superior to God and his Laws. Nothing good can come of it.

verses 5-7

(4) For it is not possible that the blood of bulls and of goats should take away sins. (5) Because of this, when he came into the world, he said, You didn't want sacrifice and offering, but you have prepared a body for me: (6) You have had no pleasure in burnt offerings and sacrifices for sin. (7) Then I said, Look, I come (in the volume of the book it is written of me,) to do your will, O God. (8) Previously he said, "Sacrifice and offering and burnt offerings and offering for sin you didn't want, neither had pleasure in them;" which are offered according to the law. (9) Then he said, "Look, I come to do your will, O God." He takes away the first, that he may establish the second. (Hebrews 10:4-9 quoting Psalms 40:6-8)

The Hellenist author of Hebrews seems to quote Psalms 40:6-8 to say that the covenant containing sacrifices is abolished and Jesus' covenant begins.

But again we start with problems. [How many times have I said that?] two things contradict the validity of the author's interpretation.

1) The real Hebrew text and context, and
2) The author's over-reliance of the LXX, an ancient Greek translation of the Hebrew Bible.

Point 1 - The real Hebrew text and context

The real meaning of Psalm 40:6-8 can be seen by reading the whole of the Psalm which says nothing about messiah or a new covenant. The writer of Hebrews tries to put the Psalm in the mouth of Jesus but we hit upon a snag in that the writer of the Psalm says that he has committed iniquities (Psalm 40:12). Did christianity's perfect high priest commit sin like a common man? And if they say that the latter part of Psalm 40 doesn't apply - even though Psalm 40 carries no break and the person who the Psalm is talking about remains the same - then that proves a continual self-refuting aspect of the whole new testament, especially the writings of Paul: the abundance of quotes taken out of context.

But rather than re-create the wheel, I'll summarize here. All Psalm 40:6-8 means is that obedience is better than sacrifice. The Lord prefers the hearkening to his word/law than the slaughtering of animals (Jeremiah 7:22,23; Exodus 19:5,6; Deuteronomy 10:12,13; Proverbs 21:3). The writer of the Psalm is saying that as opposed to giving sacrifices "I have the scroll of the law with me and within me, to do your will," i.e., obedience (vs 8-9, verse 9 conveniently omitted by the author of Hebrews). This continued keeping of the Law of Moses in Psalm 40 contradicts any notion of its being done away with.

Point 2 - The author's over-reliance on the LXX

If you read a normal translation of Psalm 40:6 or if you can read a copy of the Hebrew, you'll see these words:

זֶ_בַ_ח וּמִ_נְ_חָ_ה לֹא־חָ_פַ_צְ_תָּ אָזְ_נַ_יִ_ם כָּ_רִ_יתָ לִ֑.י

TRANSLATION: Slaughtering and offerings you didn't desire,
My ears you bore through for me [or, you opened/exposed my ears
for me].

The Hebrew word translated "bore through" or "exposed," the Hebrew verb כרה, k-r-h, which more "literally" means to dig a hole, gives the meaning of ears that were closed being opened up to hear and thus listen to and obey Deity; or it can be something similar to a servant who wants to serve his master forever having his ear bored through on a doorpost (Exodus 21:5-6), and thus it means an eternal servitude to Deity. Either way it's clear that the verse talks about ears being opened up in some manner.

Now compare this to the version of the Septuagint/LXX that the writer of Hebrews chooses to use. I'll translate it straight away as the Greek doesn't matter too much. [It should be noted that that there are different versions of the LXX, some of which give a much better rendering of the Hebrew.]

*Sacrifice and offering you didn't want, **but a body you have prepared for me**.*

Now this is totally different to what we saw before in the Hebrew. There's a big difference between having listening ears or having ears pierced, and having a whole body framed and formed for a purpose.

I'm not gonna say a lot about this for now. I'll try to strip this down to the basic when it comes to using the LXX as proof of anything. This argument also includes the use of translations in other languages.

1) The LXX is a translation, an ancient one too. It is well known that the quality of translation varies throughout the LXX versions that we have. Some bits are reflect the Hebrew quite well, and other parts either seems like a loose translation, like a paraphrase, or is generally quite an atrocious attempt at translation.

2) There's no such thing as a perfect translation. No language can wholly and completely capture the meaning of the Hebrew language. Even today, normal translation between modern languages like Chinese, English, and German aren't perfect. You can convey a general sense when translating between the languages but not exactly. Plus, although the original Hebrew Scriptures are acknowledged to be from God through through his prophets, which were copied with great care and sanctity, a translation is the attempt of a man to first understand the scriptures in his own mind and then convey his understanding in the other language. That's why translations are always like commentaries as opposed to exact representations of the original language as if it were a perfect clone in another language. In fact, they are not just "like" commentaries; in effect, they are commentaries. So to rely on a translation is to put oneself in a weakened position, especially when compared to someone who holds a copy of the original.

3) No one really knows the source of the LXX translation of the prophets and the writings, the latter sections of Hebrew Bible after the Torah, the Law. By that, I mean that it is known that the pre-christian-period Jews translated the five books of Moses into Greek. But after that, the whole translation process and history of the texts and versions gets obscure. Some people guess or assume that other Jews (the religious mindset of such Jews is unknown) must have done such translations, although which sect or exactly who, nobody really admitted it. And then its history is again obscured and what is known is dirty and sullied, eroding a person's trust in such a piece of work. The text of the Jewish Bible, as said before, was revered as coming straight from God, and thus strictly preserved and copied. Everything was done to make sure that not even a letter was moved out of place, which is why there is such great uniformity between Hebrew texts throughout history. No such reverence was given to the Septuagint translation which was soon rejected by the Jews and preserved by christians who didn't even treat their early writings with such reverence. Even the translation of the books of Moses was either changed or new versions were made by others with doubts about what changes were made. Different version of the other books of the Hebrew Bible were made and then mixed together with varying quality in translation, and so on and so on. So it is difficult to put as much trust in the LXX or those who rely on its strange translations.

But let's get back to the main point with all this in mind. Knowing the context of Psalm 40, it is obvious that the one who wrote that Psalm did not give across the meaning that the Hellenist author of Hebrew did. The Hellenist even uses a shady translation of the Hebrew Bible to put across his point, a version that doesn't even accurately reflect the Hebrew of Psalms. The writer of the Psalm gives no explicit mention of a first covenant ending so that a new one could begin, but speaks of obedience being more important that simply giving sacrifices.

The Hellenist author of Hebrews not only takes a text out of context but distorts its meaning into something entirely strange and new, and therefore loses all credibility, making an essentially invalid point.

verses 15-18

The author of Hebrew quotes Jeremiah 31:33-34 again to make a certain point.

(11) And every priest stands daily ministering and offering often the same sacrifices, which can never take away sins. (12) But this man [Jesus], after he had offered one sacrifice for sins for ever, sat down on the right hand of God. (13) From that time expecting till his enemies be made his footstool. (14) For by one offering he has perfected for ever those that are sanctified. (15) The Holy Ghost also is a witness to us: for after that he had said before, (16) "This [is] the covenant that I will make with them after those days, says the Lord, I will put my laws into their hearts, and in their minds will I write them; (17) And their sins and iniquities will I remember no more." (18) Now where remission of these [is, there is] no more offering for sin. (Hebrews 10:11-18)

So this seems to be the author's point: with the law in a person's heart, and sins forgiven, then after that there is no longer any sacrifices for sin. There is no more need for any more sin sacrifices. Verses 15-18 confirms this point. Earlier on in the passage it is said that Jesus' death perfects those who are sanctified.

But with this point, the Hellenist seals his own error. In the new covenant, according to his understanding, people keep the law and don't sin, and thus they need no more sacrifices. And yet even today christians are still saying they are wretched sinners, not only still struggling with their "sin nature," but also committing sins. What is also laughable is that hardly any of them actually know the law of the Lord, much less keep it!

Thus, since all this was supposed to happen when Jeremiah's new covenant is put into force, and it hasn't happened yet even now, 2000 years later, then I guess that tells us if "the death of the testator" put into effect anything at all!!!

My challenge to you, reader, is to find a good Jewish resource (and I don't mean the christian "messianic Jews") and ask if there will be a time when no one will make any mistakes whatsoever, especially in the messianic age. They should say, in agreement with Ezekiel, that the Third Temple age won't start off with world perfection and thus, to begin with, sin sacrifices will be still in use. But if sin sacrifices are ever gone, and humanity is perfected, there will still be thanksgiving sacrifices, but sin offerings will simply not be used.

There is a big difference between a law still existing but not being used, and the claim that it was useless, a practice that never did what it was supposed to do, and thus done away with and abolished.

At least the Jews have that much respect for their divinely given law, whereas christians pay it lip service and then call it defective and weak.

verses 35-39

(35) So don't throw away your confidence, which has great reward. (36) For you have need of endurance so that, after you have done the will of God, you might receive the promise. (37) For yet a little while, and the coming one will come, and will not delay. (38) Now the just shall live by faith: but if any man draw back, my soul shall have no pleasure in him. (39) But we are not of them who draw back to destruction; but of them that believe to the preservation of soul. (Hebrews 10:35-39 quoting from Habakkuk 2:3-4)

The writer of Hebrews quotes Habakkuk 2:3-4 to say that his followers should keep their faith and not turn back or backslide. Again, if his words are compared with the Hebrew of Habakkuk or a traditional translation, you would see that the Hellenist depends on a mistranslation. The text of Habakkuk 2:3-4 has been altered both in structure and in wording with even the "blessed" LXX not agreeing with him.

First, let's deal with the mistranslation of the Hebrew.

כִּי עוֹד חָזוֹן לַמּוֹעֵד, וְיָפֵחַ לַקֵּץ וְלֹא יְכַזֵּב; אִם־יִתְמַהְמָהּ,
חַכֵּה־לוֹ־ כִּי־בֹא יָבֹא לֹא יְאַחֵר; הִנֵּה עֻפְּלָה לֹא־יָשְׁרָה
נַפְשׁוֹ בּוֹ וְצַדִּיק בֶּאֱמוּנָתוֹ יִחְיֶה

TRANSLATION: Because [the] vision [is] yet for an appointed time,
and He shall speak about the end, and it shall not fail. If it tarries,
wait for it, because when it comes, it shall come. It shall not delay.
Look, an obstinate one, his soul is not upright in him and a righteous
one in his 'emunah shall live.(Habakkuk 2:3-4)

[I've stated before that 'emunah refers to faithfulness and steadiness as opposed to "faith"]

It is easy to see what the writer of Hebrews has done. Habakkuk is referring to the fulfilment of the vision mentioned in verse 3. That fulfilment will come and not tarry. All the normal translations agree with that interpretation and say "it (not "he", as many christians translations of Hebrews has it) will not tarry."

The Hellenist chooses to go with his own agenda. He then proceeds by chopping verse 4 in half and re-arranging the verse as he wants. He mistranslates the first half of the verse, which he moves to the end; it should speak of an obstinate, insolent, arrogant or stubborn person who is not upright, whereas the Hellenist author of Hebrews thinks it is talking about someone who draws back or who shrinks/slips back - two totally different subjects!

Habakkuk is speaking of the judgment that shall fall on the Chaldeans (Babylonians) and their arrogant king (read the whole of Habakkuk, but an indicator can be seen in 1:6) and the protection that the Lord will give to the righteous. The Hellenist is talking of someone backsliding from their faith!?!

But, as I said before, even the ancient Greek translation of the Hebrew Scriptures, the LXX doesn't help the Hellenist. All the previous mentions I've given out Paul's quoting of Habakkuk come into play here.

LXX: διοτι ετι ορασις εις καιρον και ανατελει εις περας και ουκ εις κενον εαν υστερηση υπομεινον αυτον οτι ερχομενος ηξει και ου μη χρονιση; εαν υποστειληται ουκ ευδοκει η ψυχη μου εν αυτω ο δε δικαιος εκ πιστεως μου ζησεται

TRANSLATION: for [the] vision [is] yet for a season and it shall rise/shoot forth to the end and not for failure. If it/he come later, wait patiently for it/him, because what [or, he who] comes shall come and won't linger. If he should draw back, my soul has no pleasure in him, but the righteous shall live by my faith. (Habakkuk 2:3-4; translation from LXX)

At the very least, we see that the writer of Hebrews, the Hellenist, moves phrases as he wills. But something else can be seen: The last part is not what Paul or this Hellenist writer makes of it! Paul and the writer of Hebrews make it seem like a righteous person lives by his own faith. Even the Septuagint (LXX) contradicts this notion. The person speaking in the LXX appears to be the Almighty. So it is the Almighty saying that the righteous lives by his (the Almighty's) faith (see Habakkuk 2:2 according to the LXX), meaning his faithfulness to his promises and to his nation (which is a possible interpretation of the Hebrew version).

What Paul does in his epistles is that he misquotes the LXX!!! He omits the word "my" and he does this repeatedly! So he goes with neither the Hebrew version nor the Greek but by his own agenda!

Now of course, someone may say that there is another possible way of understanding the Greek version of Habakkuk 2:4, "the righteous shall live by my faith," but the fact that cannot be dislodged is that Paul repeatedly misses out a word when he quotes this verse, a word that changes the meaning of the phrase.

And the christian commentators who are the followers and disciples of Paul and the writer of Hebrews are no better! When it suits them, they follow the Hebrew version, and that is generally when that accepted Hebrew version agrees with Paul and their doctrine or when it is irrelevant. But if the Septuagint agrees with Paul and his doctrine, then, for them, it is the Septuagint that has the true meaning. But then when the Septuagint doesn't translate things as they want, as in the case of Habakkuk 2:4b, it is seen as corrupted and wrong.

It is important to understand that, for many christians, their standard of truth is not the Hebrew Scriptures, and it is not the ancient Greek translation, the LXX. It is the new testament, Paul, the Hellenist who wrote Hebrews, and their doctrine/tradition. Yes, I do mean most forms of christianity, be it Catholic or Protestant or any of the others. To them, only Paul had the real insight into scripture and what it means.

So when arguing with them, bear that in mind. The aim must be to help them see what the Jewish Bible says for itself, because presently all that is seen when they look at scripture is Paul's interpretation of Jesus. If it's not the literal meaning, it is the "spiritual" meaning (i.e., not what is based on the text but rather doctrine).

What is still plain is that the writer of Hebrews is only concerned with his agenda and not the expounding of scripture using methods to extract meaning already within it; he chooses to make scripture sing his tune rather than sign his tune in accordance with scripture!

Chapter 11 – Faith

Now faith is the substance of things hoped for and the evidence of things not seen ... (Hebrews 11:1)

Faith?!? Now don't get me wrong: the right sort of faith is important, i.e., not blind immature faith without facts, but a trust in the Deity of history revealed through revelation and human experience.

But for all that, the writer of Hebrews crafts a one-dimensionall view of the prominent characters of the Hebrew Bible. He say that "by faith, so and so does this and that" and "by faith so and so did something and something else". But it was never just faith that caused the accomplishments of this important figures, but rather action, obedience, and an active lifestyle of trust in the Creator, a life of doing!

"Faith" in Pauline writings is more like a mental or emotional conviction, a state of being persuaded to accept something. The proper understanding of the characters of the Jewish Bible is that of reliability, faithfulness, and obedience, things that are only known through action, not just what goes on in one's mind or heart. Abel didn't just believe. He acted and obeyed. [In fact, there is no mention of faith in his story] Enoch didn't simply believe, but rather he walked with God, meaning that he conducted his life and lifestyle in obedience to God.

In every case, it is obedience that is overtly mentioned in scripture as the definition of righteous as opposed to a mental conviction! It is obedience that makes a righteous person, not just faith!

No man in scripture was rewarded for simply believing. They were rewarded and accounted righteous because they lived by active obedience! Faith does play its part, but even as the apostle James said "faith without works is dead," and "by works/deed is a man justified" or a better way of putting that "a person is shown to be righteous by what they do, not just what they believe" (James 2:24,26).

So the Hellenist writer of Hebrews says "For by [faith] the elders obtained a good report" (KJV) or "faith is what the ancients were commended for." Well, James, me, and the Hebrew Scriptures disagree. The ancients were mainly commended for what they did, the righteous things they did, not what they believed!

Chapter 12

verses 18-24

(18) For you didn't come to the mountain that might be touched, and that burned with fire, and to blackness, and darkness, and tempest, (19) And the blast of a trumpet, and the voice of words; which they that heard begged that the word should not be spoken to them any more: (20) For they could not bear what was commanded, "And if [even] a beast touched the mountain, it would be stoned, or shot through with an arrow." (21) And so terrible was the sight, that Moses said, I am greatly afraid and trembling. (22) But rather you have come to mount Sion, and to the city of the living God, the heavenly Jerusalem, and to an innumerable company of angels, (23) To the general assembly and church of the firstborn, which are written in heaven, and to God the Judge of all, and to the spirits of just men made perfect, (24) And to Jesus the mediator of the new covenant, and to the blood of sprinkling, that speaks better things than that of Abel. (Hebrews 12:18-24)

The writer of Hebrews then continues his "hatchet-and-twist" job on the Jewish Bible. He makes a comparison between his "covenant" and that of Moses, making the Sinai covenant look like an emblem of nightmarish fear and dread whereas his "Jesus" covenant is full of encouragement and love.

Now concerning his "lovely" image of his "heavenly court," that is nothing but a figment of his imagination. At least Sinai was real, a real event experienced by the real eyes of people, rather than merely a nice thought as is the image presented by the Hellenist.

But let me just deal with his depiction of the Israelite people and Moses. The guy, the Hellenist, says that the place was so scary that the people begged to hear no more "because they could not bear what was commanded." And an example of what was commanded? "Don't touch the mountain" (Exodus 19:12,13). And if you read Exodus 19, you won't see anything about the people being afraid of that command or anything else in the chapter. In fact, Moses had to stop them from getting close to the mountain, to gaze at what was going on (Exodus 19:21). The time when the people show fear is after the Lord has given the Decalogue. And the relevant verses are quoted below:

(15) And they said to Moses: 'Let it be you that speaks with us, and we will hear; but don't let not God speak with us, or else we'll die.' (16) And Moses said to the people: 'Don't be afraid; because God has come to prove you, and in order that His fear may be before you, that you don't sin.' (17) And the people stood afar off; but Moses drew near unto the thick darkness where God was. (Exodus 20:15-17 (19-21 in christian versions)

Note that what frightened the people was not what the Lord said, i.e., the commandments, since all they want is for Moses to give it as opposed to the Lord Himself doing it. If they couldn't stand the commandments, then they would have asked Moses to stop everything completely, not to let them hear anything anymore.

But they ask for Moses to continue commanding them, giving them the commands of Deity. So it is not as the Hellenist author claims: the Israelites could bear the commands - it was the awesome surroundings of God's manifestation that caused them to draw back!

Now the writer of Hebrews puts this all in a negative light in order to make his imaginative image to look much better. But as Tovia

Singer would say: what is God's opinion? Moses tells us what God thought of Israel's reaction in Deuteronomy 5:19-26:

(19) And it came to pass, when you heard the voice out of the midst of the darkness, while the mountain burned with fire, that you came near to me, even all the heads of your tribes, and your elders; (20) and you said: 'Look, the LORD our God has shown us His glory and His greatness, and we have heard His voice out of the midst of the fire; we have seen this day that God does speak with man, and he can live. (21) Now therefore why should we die? for this great fire will consume us; if we hear the voice of the LORD our God anymore, then we shall die. (22) For who is there of all flesh, that has heard the voice of the living God speaking out of the midst of the fire, as we have, and lived? (23) [You] go near, and hear all that the LORD our God shall say; and you'll then speak to us all that the LORD our God will speak to you; and we will hear it and do it.' (24) And the LORD heard the voice of your words, when you spoke to me; and the LORD said to me: 'I have heard the voice of the words of this people, which they have spoken to you; they have well said all that they have spoken. (25) Oh that they had such a heart as this always, to fear Me, and keep all My commandments, that it might be well with them, and with their children for ever!

So what is God's opinion? He commends them and wishes they always had such reverence. But this isn't what the Hellenist put forward, is it? Again he twists things.

And the author of Hebrews makes it seem as though Moses too was afraid of the sight of the mountain (Hebrews 12:21) quoting Deuteronomy 9:19. But again, when read in context, it will be seen that Moses means not such thing! According to Deuteronomy 9:19, Moses' fear has nothing to do with what he was on the mountain but of the Lord's anger due to Israel's idolatry.

(16) And I looked, and, behold, you had sinned against the LORD your God; you had made for yourselves a molten calf; you had turned aside quickly out of the way which the LORD had

commanded you. (17) And I took hold of the two tables, and cast them out of my two hands, and broke them before your eyes. (18) And I fell down before the LORD, as at the first [time], forty days and forty nights; I did neither eat bread nor drink water; because of all your sin which ye sinned, in doing that which was evil in the sight of the LORD, to provoke Him. (19) For I was in dread of the anger and hot displeasure, wherewith the LORD was wroth against you to destroy you. But the LORD listened to me that time also.
(Deuteronomy 9:16-19)

So the meaning is distorted by the writer of Hebrews yet another time!

In fact, this guy not only sees it fit to twist the Hebrew Scriptures but he's also not afraid to add to the LXX, the Septuagint (that ancient translation of the Torah). Look at the following quote from the LXX compared to the Hellenist.

LXX: και εκφοβος ειμι δια την οργην και τον θυμον
TRANSLATION: ... and I am terrified because of the anger and the wrath ...
HELLENIST: εκφοβος ειμι και εντρομος
TRANSLATION: I am terrified and trembling ...

Do you see the added words, "and trembling?" That is called "adding for emphasis," emphasis that the writer of Hebrews chooses to add which isn't even part of the Septuagint! Imagine that! The plain word of scripture isn't good enough. Context doesn't help his point. So he just adds some words to get the desired effect on his readers.

If my respect for this guy could get any lower ...

verse 26

(25) See that you don't refuse him that speaks! For if those who refused him that spoke on earth didn't escape, much more we won't escape if we turn away from him that speaks from heaven: (26) Whose voice then shook the earth: but now he has promised, saying, Yet one more time I shake only not the earth, but also heaven. (27) And this "Yet once more" refers to the removing of those things that are shaken, as of things that are made, so that those things which cannot be shaken may remain. (28) Because of this we receive a kingdom which cannot be moved, let us have grace, by which we may serve God acceptably with reverence and godly fear ...
(Hebrews 12:25-28 quoting Haggai 2:6)

The Hellenist quotes Haggai 2:6 to say that the Lord will shake things up, in judgement, for those that turn away from him. What is shaken? The created things! What remains will be the stuff that can't be shaken.

And what is Haggai's real subject of discussion? The Lord's shaking the heaven and earth, namely the nations, in order for their riches to fill "this house/Temple." Which house? Let me just show you a sample of verses from the context including the verse in question.

(1) In the second year of king Darius, in the sixth month, on the first day of the month, the word of the Lord came through means of Haggai the prophet to Zerubbabel the son of Shealthiel, the governor of Judah, and to Joshua the son of Jehozadak, the high priest, saying, (2) Thus has said the Lord of hosts, saying, This people have said, The time is not yet come, the time for the Lord's house to be built.
(14) And the Lord stirred up the spirit of Zerubbabel the son of Shealthiel, the governor of Judah, and the spirit of Joshua the son of Jehozadak, the high priest, and the spirit of all the remnant of the people, and they came and did work on the house of the Lord of hosts, their God. (Haggai 1:1-2,14)
(3) Who is there yet left among you that has seen this house in its first glory? and how do you see it now? isn't it like nothing in your eyes?

(6) For thus has said the Lord of hosts, Still one thing - it is little - and I will cause to quake the heavens, and the earth, and the sea, and the dry land; (7) And I will cause to quake all the nations, and the precious things of all the nations shall come to here: and I will fill this house with glory, says the Lord of hosts. (8) Mine is the silver, and mine is the gold - a declaration of the Lord of hosts. (9) The glory of this latter house shall be greater than the former, said the Lord of hosts: and in this place will I give peace - a declaration of Lord of hosts. (Haggai 2:3,6-7)

So the topic of the context is the rebuilding of the temple in the days of Haggai, Zerubbabel and Joshua. So what does this have to do with the subject in Hebrews? Nothing! There is no point in christians saying that this refers to the influx of gentiles into the church or whatever christological interpretation they wish to put on it because that is not what Haggai is talking about.

Basically this is just another case of taking a verse out of context.

Conclusion

When I started this endeavour, this project, I had only a fraction of an idea about what Paul (and the writer of Hebrews) had done to the Jewish Bible. I had gone through his proofs, his quotations from the Jewish Bible, in Romans 3 for the idea that no man was good, and had found them to be sorely lacking as good evidence for his view. I had also been to Romans 10 and seen how he almost re-writes Deuteronomy 30 to make it seem as if it were talking about Jesus when the original passage did not at all. I had also seen some of what had been done in the book Hebrews, using the Jewish Bible to come up with contrary doctrines.

But going through all of his epistles, as well as Hebrews, I realise now that it was only the tip of the iceberg when it came to Paul's tearing to shreds of scripture. He is happy to cut verses apart and stick them together. His consistent practice is to take verses out of context to make up ideas that have nothing to do with the original text. To see this practice occur again and again and again …

Before I went into this study, I had misgivings about Paul based on a few instances of his treatment of the Jewish Bible. After the study, I had realised that Paul had twisted the Jewish Bible to such an extent that he broke himself off from it.

But that's my journey. I'll leave it for you to consider things for yourself.

###

Thanks for reading my book. I hope it was beneficial to you whether you agree or not. Please, if you get chance, leave some feedback at your favourite retailer. All the best!

Connect with me:

Twitter: http://www.twitter.com/hesedyahu

Check out my blog: Seven Laws Blog UK

Or the blog I contribute to: Leaving Jesus

Appendix: Scriptures from the Jewish Bible that Paul cites

Habakkuk 2:4 (Romans 1:17)

Psalm 62:12 or Proverbs 24:12 (Romans 2:6)

Isaiah 52:5 or Ezekiel 36:22 (Romans 2:24)

Psalm 51:4 (Romans 3:4)

Psalm 14:1-3 or Psalm 53:1-3 (Romans 3:10-12)

Psalm 5:9 (Romans 3:13a)

Psalm 140:3 (Romans 3:13b)

Psalm 10:7 (Romans 3:14)

Isaiah 59:7 (Romans 3:15-17)

Psalm 36:1 (Romans 3:18)

Genesis 15:6 (Romans 4:3)

Psalm 32:1-2 (Romans 4:7-8)

Genesis 17:5 (Romans 4:17)

Genesis 15:5 (Romans 4:18)

Genesis 15:6 (Romans 4:22)

Genesis 21:12 (Romans 9:7)

Genesis 25:23 (Romans 9:12)

Malachi 1:2b-3a (Romans 9:13)

Exodus 33:19 (Romans 9:15)

Exodus 9:16 (Romans 9:17)

Hoshea 2:23 (Romans 9:25)

Hoshea 1:10 (Romans 9:26)

Isaiah 10:22-23 (Romans 9:27-28)

Isaiah 1:9 (Romans 9:29)

Isaiah 8:14 (Romans 9:33)

Isaiah 28:16 (Romans 9:33)

Leviticus 18:5 (Romans 10:5)
Deuteronomy 30:12-14 (Romans 10:6-8)
Isaiah 28:16 (Romans 10:11)
Joel 2:32 (Romans 10:13)
Isaiah 52:7 (Romans 10:15)
Isaiah 53:1 (Romans 10:16)
Psalm 19:4 (Romans 10:18)
Deuteronomy 32:21 (Romans 10:19)
Isaiah 65:1a and 2a (Romans 10:20-21)
1 Kings 19:10 or 19:14 (Romans 11:3)
1 Kings 19:18 (Romans 11:4)
Isaiah 29:10 (Romans 11:8)
Deuteronomy 29:4 (Romans 11:8)
Psalm 69:22-23 (Romans 11:9-10)
Isaiah 59:20-21a (Romans 11:26-27)
Isaiah 45:23 (Romans 14:11)
Psalm 69:10 (Romans 15:3)
2 Samuel 22:50 or Psalm 18:48 (Romans 15:9)
Deuteronomy 32:43 (Romans 15:10)
Psalm 117:1 (Romans 15:11)
Isaiah 11:10 (Romans 15:12)
Isaiah 52:15 (Romans 15:21)

Isaiah 29:14 (1 Corinthians 1:19)
Jeremiah 9:24 (1 Corinthians 1:31)
Isaiah 64:4 (1 Corinthians 2:9)
Isaiah 40:13 (1 Corinthians 2:16)
Job 5:13 (1 Corinthians 3:19)
Psalm 94:11 (1 Corinthians 3:20)
Genesis 2:24 (1 Corinthians 6:16)
Isaiah 28:11-12 (1 Corinthians 14:21)
Hoshea 13:14 (1 Corinthians 15:55)

Psalm 116:10 (2 Corinthians 4:13)
Isaiah 49:8 (2 Corinthians 6:2)
Leviticus 26:12 (2 Corinthians 6:13)
Isaiah 52:11-12 (2 Corinthians 6:17)
Exodus 16:18 (2 Corinthians 8:15)
Psalm 112:9 (2 Corinthians 9:9)
Jeremiah 9:24 (2 Corinthians 10:17)
Deuteronomy 19:15 (2 Corinthians 13:1)

Genesis 15:6 (Galatians 3:6)
Genesis 12:3 (Galatians 3:8)
Deuteronomy 27:26 (Galatians 3:10)
Habakkuk 2:4 (Galatians 3:11)
Leviticus 18:5 (Galatians 3:12)
Deuteronomy 21:13 (Galatians 3:13)
Isaiah 54:1 (Galatians 4:27)
Genesis 21:10 (Galatians 4:30)

Psalm 68:8 (Ephesians 4:8)

Psalm 2:7 (Hebrews 1:5a)
2 Samuel 7:14 (Hebrews 1:5b)
Psalm 104:4 (Hebrews 1:7)
Psalm 45:6-7 (Hebrews 1:8-9)
Psalm 102:25-27 (Hebrews 1:10-12)
Psalm 110:1 (Hebrews 1:13)
Psalm 8:4-6 (Hebrews 2:6b-8a)
Psalm 22:22 (Hebrews 2:12)
Isaiah 8:17b-18a (Hebrews 2:13)
Psalm 95:7-11 (Hebrews 3:7-11)
Genesis 2:2 (Hebrews 4:4)

Psalm 95:11 (Hebrews 4:7)

Psalm 2:7 (Hebrews 5:5)

Psalm 110:4 (Hebrews 5:5)

Psalm 110:4 (Hebrews 7:17)

Exodus 25:40 (Hebrews 8:5)

Jeremiah 31:31-34 (Hebrews 8:8-12)

Exodus 24:8 (Hebrews 9:20)

Psalm 40:6-8 (Hebrews 10:5-9)

Jeremiah 31:33-34 (Hebrews 10:16-17)

Habakkuk 2:3-4 (Hebrews 10:37-38)

Deuteronomy 9:19 (Hebrews 12:21)

Haggai 2:6 (Hebrews 12:26)

Made in the USA
Las Vegas, NV
17 November 2023

81036620R00217